ARISE, SHINE

FOR YOUR TIME HAS COME

365
DAILY INSPIRATIONS

compiled from the teachings of
Michele Longo O'Donnell
by Lee Lanning

VOLUME ONE

La Vida Press
Boerne, Texas

Library of Congress Cataloging
in Publication Data

ISBN 0-9814649-4-7   softcover

Published in 2011 by
La Vida Press
107 Scenic Loop Road
Boerne, Texas 78006
830-755-8767

Other publications by
Michele Longo O'Donnell

Of Monkeys and Dragons: Freedom From the Tyranny of Disease
The God That We've Created: The Basic Cause of All Disease
When the Wolf is at the Door: The Simplicity of Healing
Only Receive: No Barriers, No Boundaries

To Peg and Ray:
To the hundreds of thousands of
"Pegs and Rays" out there who also
never heard these truths.

INTRODUCTION

This is a compilation of several years of radio shows all rolled together in a daily devotional format. You will notice certain topics will run for several days, but each page can stand alone. Take your time reading it each day. Close your eyes and think about what you have read. Then, in so far as you are able, sit still without words or even thoughts of truth, and allow the Holy Spirit of eternal Life that lives within each one of us to begin to surface with its thoughts. By this you will receive directly from Divine Wisdom whatever you need for healing and direction in your life. These pages are doorways to communication and relationship with God and the abundance of goodness that is prepared for each one of us.

My good friend and faithful follower of Living Beyond Disease, Lee Lanning, has offered this to you as her gift and labor of love to encourage you on your way. My eternal gratitude to her for this work.

As always, a special thanks to Phil and Melissa Raymond for their tireless editing and book formatting.

Personally, I probably like this more than any other work we have done here at Living Beyond Disease. It is clear, concise, and teaches the application of the truths we have all come to love and cherish.

My encouragement and love to each one of you as you press on to the experience of living his fullness.

Michele

DAY 1

We were intended to live in a state of peace and harmony.

I do believe that we can live beyond dis-ease. I believe that there is no such thing as a disease that cannot be healed, or a situation that cannot be cured. I don't care how long the person has experienced what they are experiencing, I don't care how entrenched it is. It's for everyone.

There is a principle to healing. It isn't just chance, or a magic prayer. This principle is as simple as if you were driving down a one-way street, going the wrong way-- the odds are you are going to be hit--then someone finally clues you in that you're going the wrong way, you turn your car around and start going with the flow of life. Then you find you're living beyond disease. You're living beyond dis-ease in your family, dis-ease of your marriage, dis-ease of your finances, dis-ease of your career, dis-ease of your mind, your thoughts, your emotions. Dis-ease is anytime your life is out of order, out of balance, out of harmony, out of control, and it's going in a direction that's causing you pain or discomfort.

We don't have to put up with what we're putting up with. There is a way to live whole and complete, as we were intended. It was intended that we come here to this earth and live in a state of peace and harmony and love.

"Wisdom's ways are ways of pleasantness, and all her paths are peace." Proverbs 3:17

DAY 2

I was created to live in order, balance, harmony and wholeness.

We are raising consciousness above the experience of dis-ease. Einstein said no problem can be solved by the same consciousness that created it. We believe the mass consciousness of humanity without even questioning it. We subject ourselves to this thought process and think it's right. That fear-based philosophy is enough to choke down the flow of Life. The flow of Divine Life is dependent on our trust and surrender to it.

We get herded along right to our destruction. We're not stopping, we're not saying, "I was created to live beyond disease. I was created to live in a state of health, in order, balance, harmony and wholeness." Stand up and say, "NO!" Claim a higher sense of being, take hold of it, demand an existence of wholeness.

Health is not the absence of disease, health is regaining a sense of wholeness, an internal sense of harmony, peace and balance, a sense of order, a sense of self-control. It's living beyond that feeling of being vulnerable to anything that comes along, a potential victim. We've got to challenge these things we've been told.

When you live in a certain conscious understanding, you will see the fruit of it in your life--the manifestation of whatever consciousness you're living in. You cannot establish health while you are talking about all the symptoms, the names of diseases, the diagnosis, the prognosis. Health is feeling Life, living Life, the "you" inside the body, that "eternal you" that doesn't change.

"God has made with me an everlasting covenant, ordered in all things, and sure."　　　　2Samuel 23:5

DAY 3

I see Life from a different perspective, the way it was meant to be.

People have risen up and healed, and learned to live beyond whatever prognosis they were facing. When my daughter was born prematurely, mentally retarded and with so many problems, I will tell you what I did. I prayed for 18 months. I have never in my life been that focused or that devoted and consecrated to anything. I spent day and night reading the Bible again and again, and doing whatever I thought it was telling me to do. I never had a television set, a radio, a telephone, I never went anywhere, except to get groceries. I literally immersed myself in praying over my two children and reading this book that suddenly began to make sense to me. I was praying constantly for help, for something in my life to turn around. I never prayed for her to be healed, because it never occurred to me that God could do such a thing.

Something began to happen during those 18 months of intense focus. I began to see life from a different perspective than I had my first 25 years. I began to see life the way it was meant to be. I began to pick up a change in my thought, or my consciousness, toward this child who was so sick. I realized that when I was praying for her I was actually seeing her, feeling her, as a normal whole child. I surrendered to this child's Creator. The mind that formed her began to move into my mind, where I saw her. I saw beyond what everyone saw, I began to feel it, somebody with Life surging through her. It wasn't something I deliberately set out to do, it was happening to me, and I let it happen.

"God sees not as man sees, for man looks on the outward appearance, but God looks on the heart."

1Samuel 16:7

DAY 4

*It's time to let the light in,
it's time to see differently.*

Your experience changes in direct proportion to the way that you're seeing things, and what you're believing. We're so used to seeing the world as a solid entity, therefore we see the cause and effect as being solid. If something solid caused this problem, how can a change in my perception or a change in my understanding, or a change in my expectation, actually change the circumstances? It does. We experience something because we are educated into believing in it, we live in that mindset.

It's like when they believed the world was flat, then someone got a vision, and now the whole world has been lifted to a new understanding. We no longer fear we're going to fall off the end of the world. We all share the same change in consciousness.

This is a whole new way of seeing life, a whole new expectation of life. This is not meant for one person or a handful of people, not for the chosen few. Everybody is the chosen, and everyone was intended to live in this higher understanding. It's time to burst open the doors, open the shades and shutters, it's time to let the light in. It's time to look at something different, or, look at the same thing and see it differently.

You may be ready for a change in understanding, ready for something new, different from the mass consciousness that is leading us right now.

"If thine eye be single, thy whole body shall be full of light."   Matthew 6:22

DAY 5

We trust the life force to produce its own wholeness, health, balance, order, harmony, peace.

Holistic treatment is treating the whole person. We take into consideration the whole system, the person's lifestyle, problems or confusions they may be having to deal with, things that are not necessarily visibly seen. By the time you see it, you've already externalized something that was going on long before you actually saw it.

Life is an energy force. Life does not originate within the body, but is, in fact, a force and energy that flows through the body. As a matter of fact, it's a force and energy that forms the body. When it flows through the body, wherever that energy might be obstructed, that's called a negative energy field, an area of disease. Whether you see something or not, whether you feel something or not, that is the beginning of dis-ease. The dis-ease began long before the physical symptom appeared, and it began as an interruption in the flow of energy.

This Life energy is not something of our own creating. It is something that is self-created, self-sufficient, self-governed. It knows no obstruction, it knows no boundaries. It is the most powerful force ever known to man. It is the force that creates and forms everything that is-- we call that God. We trust it to produce its own wholeness, health, balance, order, harmony, peace. If we remove the barriers within the mind, in the arena of belief, which are obstructing the flow of energy, that flow of life will produce the healing we are looking for.

"There is a river, the streams whereof shall make glad the city of God."   Psalm 46:4

DAY 6
Get a big dose of Life!

In my mind I see a rushing, gushing river, crystal-clear, so you can look down at the bottom of the river and see all the little fish and little pebbles and stones at the bottom, crystal-clear. As long as that river is rushing and flowing, it remains pure and clear and whole.

But there are areas along the sides where the water becomes trapped, particularly when it's not flowing rapidly, when it's kind of sluggish and has been allowed to slow down in its flow. These areas that are trapped are like lagoons, like marshes, and that's where all the moss and all the little creatures and mosquitoes breed, and that's where all the slime is built up and that's where disease is, so to speak.

If you can get a big dose of Life, get that river to flow again, then you can flush out these marshes and these lagoons and these trapped areas, and you can allow for the free flow of this crystal pure, clear river to go into these areas and flush out, clean, purge, and make them crystal clear and beautiful and whole again.

Have confidence in Life. Have confidence that Life is its own energy, its own force, able to manifest all of its characteristics and attributes as a viable physical existence. Have confidence in Life as a viable existence in which we live and move and have our being. Healing happens when we go from the old thought of believing what we see, to believing in Life, the unseen energy that is the Spirit of God.

"Everything will live where the river comes...but the marshes shall not be healed."　　　　　Ezekiel 47:9,11

DAY 7

Life is an eternal, free flowing, never ending, perfect manifestation of God.

Life is an ongoing expression of divinity. Life energy forms what is formed and animates it and is the origin or source of its life. Life originates outside the body, not from within the body. Life is the dominating force, the body is subservient to Life. The focus is on looking at and for Life, and looking to increase the flow of Life. That, in and of itself, has within it the characteristics and properties available to open up the system.

If the channels of Life are flowing, if there is harmony and balance and order and peace, and if there is no obstruction to this flow, then our immune system is working in the manner in which it was made and created to work. It goes to work for us without us even realizing what's going on. We don't have to direct it to do that, it does it on its own. That's part of the characteristics of this Life that flows through us. Life is an eternal, free flowing, never ending, perfect manifestation of God.

This Life energy forms that which is formed out from its own being and hence we have nature, we have plants, we have trees, we have grass, we have rolling mountains, we have all the beauty that is set before us. We have the stars above us and the sun and the moon and planets. We have all the little creatures and bugs and creepy crawly things, we have fish in the water, birds in the air, we have all the animals that roam about the earth, and we have ourselves, as well.

"God saw every thing that he had made, and behold, it was very good."   Genesis 1:31

DAY 8
Always look beyond the form to the Life.

The more we study Life, the origin of Life, the characteristics of Life, the attributes of Life, how Life appears, the more we walk with Life, the more we look at it, the more we see it everywhere. Learn to see the Life of people, not just the people, learn to see Life, not just nature, not just what Life produces, but learn to see Life beyond the form. Always look beyond the form.

If your life is a direct result of being formed by Divine Life, then you start out with a clean slate. You start out with perfection, you start out with order, harmony, balance, stability. *Only if something is introduced in the thought process or the belief system that would choke that down,* would you experience an interruption in that flow.

We're not talking about an individual person who thinks an individual disease and then that disease jumps on them. We're talking about the whole consciousness of man as one thought process, one belief, one understanding. Thought is a bit like the atmospheric levels above the earth--there are very low atmospheric levels of thought that are fear-based, and there are very high and lofty atmospheric thoughts that are divinely based, based on Life, based on wholeness and the expectation of health, the expectation of goodness.

When we live in that atmospheric thought, we can expect that as our life experience, but when we as a whole people live in a thought of fear and dread and the expectancy of disorder and disease, then that's what we can expect to experience.

"Open thou my eyes that I may behold wondrous things out of thy law."   Psalm 119:18

DAY 9

*Put your faith more in what's not seen
than what is seen.*

By redefining health, we are reestablishing the sense of wholeness and reestablishing the sense of harmony, balance and order. That is the natural way to be. The unnatural is to live in a sense of fear and dread, even though that's what we've been educated to believe. We tend to believe that because it appears as a physical entity, it must have a physical origin, instead of dealing with it on a thought level. We need to go back to the expectation and the thought of the individual and what they have accepted as reality.

There needs to be something within that says no, this isn't right. this isn't the way it's supposed to be. I'm not supposed to be putting up with this. There has to be a way out, and I will find it. I'm not going to keep on going this way, I'm going to find a better way.

There is a higher truth than what we have been buying into that makes us no longer victims. Surrender to the very essence of that higher power, the character, the attributes, the principle, the absolutes of that higher power, as it pours out from within our own being, brings us to a life of wholeness and order.

We're going to have to be personally responsible, we're going to have to do a lot of praying, we have to believe that when we pray there is a response. You're going to have to put your faith more in what's not seen than what is seen. Look beyond what our eyes see.

"We walk by faith, not by sight."   2Corinthians 5:7

DAY 10

The normal state of existence is a sense of wholeness.

When we talk about being personally responsible for our health, we're not talking about needing to know the in's and out's of the body. We're not talking about needing to know where to go to get that kind of help. We're not talking about having to have all the answers.

We're talking about, first of all, realizing that the normal state of existence is the sense of wholeness. Why? Because we come forth from the image of God, and the characteristics of the Source of our existence are wholeness, order, harmony, balance, peace. That is our inheritance. That is the substance of our true being. That is who we really are.

We wear a body. I wear a body of wholeness and health, a body that's strong, because I insist on staying in that sense of wholeness. When thoughts come that produce a sense of fear and dread, I substitute it with another image, an image of wholeness. Right where that image was put in my mind, I'm going to send that image out, and I'm going to put another image there.

We used to have a saying, "You can't stop the birds from flying over your head, but you don't need to let them build a nest in your hair." You don't have to buy into it simply because everyone else has bought into it. The whole world looks different when you come from a sense of wholeness, rather than from the vantage point of being a victim.

"God created man in his own image."   Genesis 1:27

DAY 11
I was created to live in a state of health.

After a man and his five year old daughter heard a dire prognosis from the doctor, the man said to his daughter, "Honey, did you hear what that man said about you?" She said, "Yes, daddy." He asked, "What did you think of it?" She answered, "It was pretty scary." He said, "Yeah, it really was. Now what are we going to do about this? Are we going to accept this?" She said, "No."

"No, we're not. This is what we're going to do. Every time that I ask you a question, like, how are you Amanda? You're going to answer, I am whole. I am complete. I am perfect. I am healthy. Because God made me that way."

He asked her that question 500 times a day for two years, and 500 times a day she responded with, I am whole, I am complete, I am perfect, I am healthy, because God made me that way. Today, many years later, she is still healthy.

What happened? They reprogrammed their thought, reprogrammed their belief based on a higher truth. They chose not to see what the evidence showed or what man proclaimed, but that God made them a certain way, and that was the way they were going to be.

Any one of us can do that, can say, I was created to live beyond this concept called disease. I was created to live in a state of health.

"We are his workmanship."   Ephesians 2:10

DAY 12

What we live out in our physical experience is what we have taken into our thought and belief.

We are a spirit being. We are not our body. We wear our body. We are a spirit being, and as such, we are created from the blueprint of God. The blueprint from which we come is order, harmony, balance, a sense of control, a sense of peace, a sense of wholeness. That's what we are. It's uninterrupted, it's unchallenged.

We wear a body depending on our image. We wear our lives, so to speak, depending upon the images that we hold in thought. We are our thoughts, we wear our beliefs--we live in our beliefs. If we change our beliefs, if we can challenge them, then we can live a different life.

Health is feeling Life, not in your body, but feeling the *you* inside the body, that eternal *you* that doesn't change. What we live out in our physical experience, or the expression called our body, is what we have taken in, in our thought and our belief.

There is a spiritual law higher than physical law. It says, you are not what you have been told you are. You are not even a body. You are something far greater than that, far more eternal, far more intact than a physical body that is vulnerable or susceptible to whatever comes along. This higher truth makes us no longer a victim. We can stop believing in the physical law, reach out to a higher principle, surrender to that higher power, and its very essence pours forth from within our own being. We find our lives in order, balance and harmony.

"As he thinks in his heart, so is he."   Proverbs 23:7

DAY 13

Take on a sense of Life as it surges and flows through you.

There are people who rise up and say "no", who stop and take control. They say, "I was created to live above this. I was created to be in control. I will pray. I will not continue down this road." They went from "I am a victim, I am suffering, I can't help myself", to "What I need is strength, what I need is truth, something sub-stantial to hold on to while I crawl out of this thought process." When this happens, physical symptoms begin to go away. They are resolved in proportion to this person taking on more and more of a sense of being in control of their life.

These people took hold of higher spiritual laws and said, "If I was really created in the image and likeness of God, then why am I living like this? If God is Love, why am I putting up with this? Why am I accepting something less than what I could be accepting?" They challenged their belief system. They said, I've got to stop and choose a better way. Their consciousness began to rise, and as that began to change, they began to take on a sense of being in control of their life. They let go of the vulnerability of being the victim, and took on a sense of wholeness and sense of life, as it surges and flows through them.

This is how healing happens!

"Out of his belly shall flow rivers of living water."
John 7:38

DAY 14
Can I see Life in a different way?

"Do you mean to say that I can take personal responsibility, that I can walk away from this experience? That I'm not locked into it? That though it appears as a physical something, it does not have a physical origin? That I can surrender to my higher power, or God, and can draw on that grace and strength?"

Yes. What you're drawing on is the truth that you were made in the image of God. He said that. It says in Genesis 1, "I'm going to make man in my image and likeness." Ecclesiastes 3:14 says, "Whatsoever God does will be forever: nothing can be added to it, nor anything taken from it." Disease can't be added to it, health can't be taken from it. Harmony, peace, order, wholeness and strength cannot be taken from it. But can we give it away? Yes, we give it away by fear, dread, educated images in our mind. The power of suggestion is very great.

By correcting that belief system, by being willing to lift ourselves out of that social consciousness of the expectancy of disease, by learning to see life in a different way, we can change our thinking. This is not mind over matter, this is based on absolute principles that are true, unchangeable. We only need to be made aware of them, to grab hold and see our way clear. This is living deliberately.

"I am fearfully and wonderfully made: marvelous are thy works."   Psalm 139:14

DAY 15
This day is a manifestation of the Presence of God.

Living deliberately is saying, I am not subjected to the external circumstances of what I see, of what I have been led to believe, what the mass consciousness believes or how it feels. I am not going to decide how I feel based on what my body tells me. I'm not going to decide how I feel based on what day of the week it is, what the weather is like, who's mad at me and who isn't, if somebody loves me or doesn't, if my kids are healthy or not, if my mother and father are ok, if my neighbors are still angry, or if they are happy, if I have enough money in the bank. I am not going to live according to external circumstances.

I am going to live deliberately out of this realization: today I wake up and this day is a manifestation of all of the attributes and characteristics of the Presence of God. Today is good because "This is the day that the Lord hath made." (Psalm 118:24)

Today my body is strong and healthy and whole and complete. Because I feel it that way? No, it makes no difference what I feel on my body. What makes the difference is who made my body, and that it was made in perfection and in wholeness and in order and in beauty. Today I'm going to choose how I'm going to feel and what my body is going to feel.

Today I feel love all around me. I am created in love, everyone else is created in love. I am the recipient of God's love, and I am going to live out from that, and I'm going to love.

"This is the day which the Lord has made; we will rejoice and be glad in it."   Psalm 118:24

DAY 16
What does the mind of God know about this?

Today I am not going to be concerned about my finances. I'm not going to go to work so that I can get a paycheck, because I am sustained by the Presence and Love of the God that made me, that put me on this earth, and said, "Take no thought for your life." (Matthew 6:25) Take no thought for your life, I'll take care of you.

The job that I have is not so I can get a paycheck and live, but because I have the opportunity to love and to give and to be creative and to express the wonderful attributes of the God that I possess. It's an avenue for me to give. I am really employed by God, who created me, and I'm going to be as intelligent and as productive as He is, and at the end of that day, I'll feel wonderful about what I have done and given. The paycheck is incidental because God will take care of me.

That's living deliberately. That's choosing to reprogram your thinking into a higher consciousness, a consciousness of truth, a consciousness where the mind of God reigns and rules. In the human consciousness, it's normal to feel separate from your good, separate from God, separate from the wonderful feeling that the world all around you is also created by the same wonderful Divine energy.

We can choose to see differently. Just turn away and calmly and quietly say, in our mind, "What does the mind of God know about this that's unchangeable, eternal, and absolute?"

"Therefore take no thought, saying, what shall we eat? or what shall we drink? or wherewithal shall we be clothed?"   Matthew 6:31

DAY 17
To live deliberately is to live by truth.

Living deliberately is living by choice, how I choose to feel. Living randomly is living by emotions, living by how I feel. For example, you are driving and somebody runs you off the road. The first instant, you have a choice. You can have a knee-jerk reaction and emotion immediately arises. If you entertain that emotion, it has its physical effects. That's living randomly. Living randomly is living by circumstances, feeling a certain way depending on the circumstances. If the circumstances are good, that works, but if circumstances go sour, that doesn't work, and lends itself to dis-ease.

Living by choice, if someone runs you off the road, you get yourself back onto the road, and choose not to allow your emotions to run rampant. You choose to let go of it, you choose to have a little compassion and mercy, you choose to wish the person well, or you choose to be grateful there wasn't an accident, but you're not reacting in anger or remaining in fear. That's living deliberately.

To live deliberately is to live by truth. Rather than living by what we see, we recognize a world around us that we live in, move in, walk and talk and laugh and love in, the world of the unseen, the spiritual kingdom. This world that's around us actually formed and created us, the earth, the universe, and everything in the physical realm. The way that you can do this living by truth is by getting in touch with your spiritual being.

"You shall know the truth, and the truth shall make you free."   John 8:32

DAY 18
What does the mind of God know about this?

We can decide to let go of a particular emotion or drama, we can re-choose the way we see it, we can walk away, so to speak, or turn away from the human consciousness, and how we ever got to thinking this way and feeling this way. We are not going to sit and analyze how that happened. Analysis is paralysis. We're not going to do that. We're not going to look at how we ever got to feeling this way, and blame our mothers, fathers,whoever.

What we're going to do instead is turn away from it. We're going to calmly and quietly say, in our mind, "What does the Mind of God know about this that's unchangeable, eternal and absolute?" Then we're going to wait. Suddenly, or gradually, we're going to recognize that we are beginning to see it differently, perhaps more clearly, certainly in a more elevated manner. We're beginning to judge it differently than the judg- ments that we had previously put on the circumstance or situation. In time, if we continue to turn away from the human consciousness and all that we have been programmed and educated to see, to believe, to judge, to know, then we take on the Mind of God.

I willingly surrender what I think I've been knowing, and the conclusions that I've drawn and all the suffering that it has brought into my experience, and I take on a higher knowing, a higher consciousness.

"He is in one mind, and who can turn him?"   Job 23:13

DAY 19

Healings come because we choose to see something beyond what we have been programmed to believe.

Healings come because we choose to see something beyond what we have been programmed to believe-- even beyond what our very own eyes see or our very own body feels.

There was a little boy who went to his doctor because he had warts all over his hands, ugly, unsightly warts. Nobody wanted to hold his hand on the playground, or touch him--he began to feel like he had leprosy. He hated those warts. They tried everything, went from doctor to doctor, but nothing made the warts go away.

Finally he went to a doctor who had him put his hand on a piece of paper and gave him a pencil and told him to outline his hand and his fingers on this piece of paper. He did that, and of course there were lumps and bumps all in between the fingers from these warts. The doctor said, take this home, take the pencil, and use the eraser, and erase all those lumps and bumps and make nice, clean, smooth lines until you have an absolutely perfect, smooth outline on this piece of paper, then bring it back to me in two weeks. He did that and when he came back his warts were all gone.

What happened was a belief based on education was replaced with a stronger belief, a belief more to be desired, a belief of greater significance. This is elevating the consciousness to a higher consciousness.

"Do ye look on things after the outward appearance? Think again."   2Corinthians 10:7

DAY 20

We really are the wholeness and fullness of the God that made us.

Living randomly is giving away the peace and harmony of our lives, the wholeness and completeness of our lives, to circumstances as they appear. We're bounced around like ping-pong balls, living in a state of confusion. Behind the confusion we really are the wholeness and fullness of the God that made us. He said so: "Of his fullness have we all received." And, "He is the true light that lights every man that comes into the world." (John 1:16, 9)

We need to look at what we are buying into and see the contrast between what we're experiencing and believing, compared to what we now know is true. Then we want to choose again, to choose a higher consciousness that will superimpose itself over the lesser, where our experience can be more whole, more complete, and we can be happier and healthier.

Instead of letting disease be such an engraved image in our heads, so we expect and are alarmed at disease, we must learn to look at Life. Learn to look at the beauty of Life, not the forms. If we take the time, we will see even the wonders of our own body--not looking at the body but beyond the physical form and getting in touch with the Life, the attributes of the Life that formed everything and animates everything that it has created.

"Two blind men followed Jesus, crying, Have mercy on us. Jesus said unto them, Believe ye that I am able to do this? They said, Yea, Lord. Then he touched their eyes, saying, according to your faith, be it unto you. And their eyes were opened."   Matthew 9:27-30

DAY 21

We can make a leap to seeing ourselves as we were created.

Your true spiritual being is that part of you that always has lived, lives now, and always will live, that part that never changes, that part that is perfect, whole and complete as it stands. This kingdom of spiritual consciousness has rules and principles, just like the physical world does. The problem is we don't see it so clearly, it's not so obviously visible.

We are instructed to "Look not at the things that are seen but at the things which are not seen." (2Corinthians 4:18) We are told that we are to "Call those things which be not as though they were." (Romans 4:17) We are told to look beyond the visible into the invisible and there we will find not only the Source of our life, but the stability of our life.

Whatever is in the spiritual kingdom, or spiritual consciousness, is eternal--the rules, the principles, the laws, the characteristics, the attributes. Everything in the physical world is changeable, it is not eternal, and it is subservient to the spiritual world and all of its laws. The law of the visible world is called the law of chance and probability.

We are not going to accept whatever comes. We can make a leap from seeing ourselves victimized by disease, by chance and probability, to seeing ourselves as we were created. We can choose to see beyond the visible, into the spiritual law, the law of Life. We have a choice.

"I will make thee an eternal excellency."   Isaiah 60:15

DAY 22

All the works of his hands are perfect.

We can live by the law of Life. The law of Life is living by spiritual principle, living by the laws and characteristics of a world that we live and move and walk and talk in, although we don't see it. But if we start looking for it, we will see it all around. If we continue to press in, to discipline our minds, if we have that "seeing" as a desire in our hearts, the day will come when we will see that so clearly that it will take precedence over the visible, with very little effort. Right now, though, there is a lot of effort, a lot of self-discipline, a lot of self-control, a lot of perseverance, a lot of praying. There is a lot of praying for a lot of grace, so that we can remain consistent, so when we start to falter, grace can kick in and lift and carry us past that little faltering step.

People who choose to live by the law of Life see the perfect, see the all, see the complete, the unchangeable. They take hold of a higher principle. "It is he that has made us and not we ourselves." (Psalm 100:3) "All the works of his hands are perfect." (Deuteronomy 32:4)

Ecclesiastes 3:14 says, "Whatever God does, it shall be forever: nothing can be added to it, nor anything taken from it." The law of chance may try to take away the harmony, balance, order, perfection and wholeness that is intrinsically ours by inheritance, but God said, I've made them in my image and likeness. While we may not see with our eyes the whole, perfect and complete, we can know in our hearts that it is the true and permanent state of being.

"We are the clay, and thou our potter; we all are the work of thy hand."   Isaiah 64:8

DAY 23

Feel the Life that is beyond the form.

How do we tap into a higher spiritual consciousness? This consciousness is whole, complete, perfect, beautiful. It is what forms everything that is formed in the physical world. Out from this unseen consciousness, everything that we see has formed. The Life of that form is this spiritual Life. That's the origin of all that is living.

Instead of looking at the form, as you desire to become more cognizant of the world beyond form, beyond the physical, you begin to no longer see the form. You begin to see the Life that is beyond the form. Instead of looking at a tree only, you begin to feel the Life of the tree. It's the same Life that animates you. That is your Life. You don't just look at a bird now, you begin to feel the Life of that bird. You feel his song.

Until we get to that place where we are more and more cognizant of Life, we cannot enjoy wholeness and health, because we are still seeing the form and all of the physical laws of the world of the seen. We're still giving it all our power. We're surrendering to that.

What allows us to look beyond the physical? Humility. Not information, not affirmation, not a defiant attitude, but being in the silence of your own soul. When we learn to see beyond, to feel the Life that pulsates through our form, we begin to take on the characteristics of that Life. What you see, what you surrender to, is what you will experience.

"God gives grace unto the humble. Submit yourselves therefore to God." James 4:6-7

DAY 24
In a state of humility, we release.

You cannot put new wine in old wineskins. You can't put something in a space already filled with something else. In a state of humility, we release, we let go of all of our opinionated beliefs, judgments, educated under-standings, our experiences, that which we have been told, even that which we have seen. I take the whole package and come before the Source and origin of Life. I get very, very still and quiet and I deliberately release and let go of everything the human mind contains. I just make a decision and I release it.

I realize an emptiness. I realize I've created a vacuum. I realize I have completely surrendered. By that I am saying the same words that Jesus said, "I can of my own self do nothing." (John 5:30) As I hear, then I can do. You cannot hear when your mind is already full of what you already think is true, of all your judgments, all your opinions, all your decisions, all your experiences, all your fears, all your accumulation of the human layers of beliefs and understandings. There's no space.

This atmosphere of spiritual consciousness that's all around us speaks to us constantly, day and night, speak-ing words of truth that will free us and take us into higher levels of understanding. It speaks to us individu-ally and collectively. It speaks to us right where we can understand, and what we need to hear. It is constantly imparting truth and awareness and a higher sense of Life and wholeness.

"Neither do men put new wine into old bottles: else the bottles break, and the wine runs out, and the bottles perish: but they put new wine into new bottles, and both are preserved." Matthew 9:17

DAY 25

*Everything already is in a state of
wholeness and completion.*

God knows no vacuum. Truth knows no vacuum. It is
constantly and continually speaking of itself, constantly
unfolding itself. If we present to it an empty vacuum in
the quiet and silence of our own souls, it will be filled.
When it is, you'll know it. You will know because your
entire perspective on life changes in an instant. You may
see the same thing, but you'll know something different. What your eyes see no longer has any effect, bringing fear into your heart.

Isaiah 25:7 says there is a veil, a covering, cast over
the face of all the people of all the nations. When that
veil or covering is removed, there will be no more
sorrow, disease, death, sadness, or distortion of understanding. Behind the veil, it already is. There's nothing
to be done. Everything already is in a state of wholeness
and completion. There's nothing to be changed, nothing
to be healed, nothing to be fixed. It already is.

When we go in a state of humility and request the
truth that will make us free, and we let go of everything
that we have accumulated, offering an empty vessel,
then a truth comes--that is a removing of a veil. We see
that which has always been and has never changed.

James 1:17 says "He is the father of lights, with
whom is no variableness neither shadow of turning."
That means there is no change. What he has made is
absolute. What is left to do is recognize the veil is
removed by a higher understanding which comes
through quietness, surrender and humility.

*"The veil is done away in Christ, but even unto this
day...the veil is upon their heart. Nevertheless, when
they shall turn to the Lord, the veil shall be
taken away."*   2Corinthians 3:14-16

DAY 26
Surrender to the mind that knows the truth.

We make a decision to trust. Trust does not come simply because you want to trust, you wish you could trust. What you don't realize is, you've been trusting all along, but you've been trusting that which has brought you deeper and deeper into bondage. You've been trusting by not taking hold of something else to trust.

With God, with Truth, with the spiritual consciousness, you make a decision to trust its Presence, to trust its continuing desire to unfold itself. You trust that if you go into this state of quietness and surrender, unloading all the baggage you've carried all your life, and just go empty, a vacuum, if you surrender your soul and trust, truth will come.

Does it come the first time you do that? Sometimes. Does it sometimes take weeks, months? Sometimes. What difference does it make how long it takes? What you need is the truth. I can of my own self do nothing, but what I hear, that's what makes the change. That's why the healings come. The benefit far outweighs any minor sacrifice or self discipline that is necessary in order to get there.

Healings happen when a higher spiritual truth comes to bear upon a lesser so-called physical law of mortal man. I pray for grace and ask that a Mind far greater than my own superimpose itself over my own. I surrender to the Mind that knows the truth, who is Truth, the Source and origin of all truth, from whose Mind creation came.

"I can of my own self do nothing. As I hear I judge...I seek not my own will." John 5:30

DAY 27

Never own your affliction.

Never own a problem. Never possess it. Do not personalize it. Why? Because it's not yours. Don't let your identity get wrapped up in the problem. Don't let it become who you are. See it as an intrusion into your life, rather than identifying with it as part of your life. Deal with it but don't own it. Don't deny it, but don't take it into your consciousness, either. Inside, you feel whole and intact.

To focus on the problem is to give it power in your mind and to subconsciously cling to it, never allowing yourself the possibility of release. There is a difference between dealing with what you have to deal with, and building a shrine to it. It is critical that we not give permission for this thing to be part of our lives.

You've been born in the image and likeness of God. (Genesis 1:27) You've been created in perfection, because all the works of his hands are perfect. (Deuteronomy 32:4) Nothing that is made by God can be changed, nothing can be added to it, or anything taken from it. (Ecclesiastes 3:14) Being born of God, your genetics and DNA consequently would be the characteristics and nature of this Divine Life and Eternal Life.

We cannot own dis-ease and own being the image of God. God is not an entity of confusion. If we own affliction, we are buying into the mortal human path, discarding our divine origin and source. When affliction comes knocking on our door, that's the time for us to say yes or no, the time to realize, *I am of Divine Source and I cannot and will not accept this as a reality, I will not allow it into my experience.*

"The king's daughter is all glorious within."
Psalm 45:13

DAY 28

Do not allow your situation to mesmerize you.

No matter how fierce the symptoms, no matter what the picture, no matter how long you have suffered, keep your eyes, your heart and your hope on the path of LIFE before you. Though you may have to deal with it on some level, never become mesmerized by it. Never stare at it long enough for it to become a part of the deep-down-inside, real you.

Let Life rule your heart, not death, not images of disease, not trouble. Let thoughts of Life fill your mind. Look at Life all day. Let gratitude fill your heart instead of fear. Don't speak of the problem. Crowd problems right out of your experience until all that is left is Life and wholeness.

Enjoy your days, enjoy every little detail of the wonders of nature and the newness of life all around you. LET Love and Life fill your heart, live each day being grateful for each day.

Pray. Acknowledge that your life is in the hands of the one who created you, not at the mercy of chance or circumstances. You can surrender to God, but never surrender to trouble or disease. Surrender to the Spirit of Love and Life, surrender to the goodness of God, who is only good. Fill your heart, mind, and vision with goodness and beauty. To surrender is to enjoy the Life that is ours, regardless of the outcome.

Wisdom guides us through these situations, however the impulses of Wisdom can only be heard where fear has been set aside and an internal quietness and a degree of calmness has been insisted upon.

"Thou will keep him in perfect peace whose mind is stayed on thee: because he trusts in thee." Isaiah 26:3

DAY 29
Look beyond what your eyes see.

No matter the state a person seems to be in, no matter what they are doing or believing or experiencing on the outside, there is a whole, complete, perfect being down deep inside. What we see on the outside is not what we need to deal with. We need to connect with the person who lives within that picture, beyond that veil. That person is divine and intact. That person is whole and complete, regardless of the apparent circumstances. Connecting with that whole, complete Being within strengthens that being and empowers it, drawing it out into expression.

Look beyond what your eyes see. Look beyond what is evident, what is apparent, what is obvious. Look beyond what you're feeling in your body. Look beyond the sadness that you're feeling in your heart, the confusion that you're feeling in your mind, the limitation that you're seeing in your life, the lack that you seem to be experiencing in your life. When you look beyond what your eyes see, what do you see?

Anything that appears as a tangible substance cannot be dealt with on that level only, because the underlying source of the problem is thought. Everything physical, everything seen in the world, started out as a thought, and then a word. Words are thoughts externalized. Whatever we're thinking we eventually speak. If we don't say it out loud, at least we're forming the words in our minds. Thoughts and words are the power behind the scenes.

"Judge not according to appearance, but judge righteous judgment."   John 7:24

DAY 30

Keep the river flowing.

God is Life. Life is like a rushing river that flows through eternity. We are in that river, whether we are in the body or not in the body. It makes no difference to the Life of the river. As we are in It, It flows through us. As long as we allow It to flow, we enjoy the many benefits and wonderful effects of the Presence of the Life. It is the energy and strength of our very existence.

Sometimes, through ignorance or willfulness, we "choke-off" the flow of the Life. It is still flowing around us, we are still in It, but we are unable to perceive Its Presence or to feel the wonders of all Its attributes and goodness. When we "choke it", we suffer. It may take the form of physical suffering, or it may take the form of any disturbance in life.

Eyes that focus on the beauty of Life will surely see only the goodness of Life, and that then will be their inheritance. But if we look through the eyes of hate, jealousy, judgment, even self-condemnation, we will find the darkness that we feel in our own hearts. This makes us suffer. This literally blocks the flow of Life-energy, causing a "choking down" of the flow, and a choking down of Life experiences.

"Waters issued out from under the threshold of the house...a man brought me through the waters; the waters were to the ankles...again he brought me through the waters, the waters were to the knees...again he brought me through, the waters were to the loins...then it was a river that I could not pass over: for the waters were risen, waters to swim in...Everything that lives, which moves, whither the river shall come, shall live...for they shall be healed, and every thing shall live whither the river comes."

Ezekiel 47:1-9

DAY 31
Realize Divine Life as the Source of all Life.

Learn about Life. It is far more than the opposite of death. Learn to trust it more than you trust in disease and death. Learn to trust in Its continuing Presence and absolute goodness, and Its ability to keep all things intact--without your help.

Trust in Divine Life. Know Its unending Presence. Know Its utterly unchangeable nature, no matter what the human picture or human condition might be saying. Know Its impersonal, unconditional, constant Goodness.

Know that Divine Goodness isn't the least bit involved with your beliefs, or your fears, or your failures. It knows only Its own nature of pure, glorious, never beginning, never ending Life. That Life is always complete, always fulfilled, always in perfect order and harmony. Know that the entire world of form and physical substance is contained within this Life.

We have only to get our thoughts, our beliefs, and our fears out of the way, and this unseen, but oh, so real, Life, with all Its wonder, reveals Itself in every situation. We are faced with a choice, to look away from all our previous beliefs and convictions, with all their "matter-based" causes and effects, and reaping and sowing principles, to look away from the overwhelming personal responsiblities to know, to fix, to fear, and to look to Life. It takes a tremendous amount of discipline, watching every thought, staying focused on the "truth beyond the appearance." I began to see Life everywhere and in everyone, and the overwhelming evidence of disease and misery began to disappear.

"Your soul shall be bound in the bundle of life with thy God."   1Samuel 25:29

DAY 32
Look in the direction you wish to go.

It is our perceptions and attitudes that determine our experiences. We are living the life we imagined. We create from imagery. First something is seen in one's mind and then it becomes a reality.

Before one builds a building, or takes on a spouse, the imagining of it takes place. It may be an achievement, such as climbing a mountain, excelling in a sport or playing a musical instrument. We are told in every phase of life that to gain anything, one must first see it in one's mind. When creating, we are told to be specific. The more specific we are in our imagination concerning any particular goal, the more detailed will be our response.

We are told that we were in the Mind of God before ever the world was framed. He, too, first imagined us and all creation before it took form.

What do you suppose we have been filling our minds and imaginations with day after day? Concerns about disease, all the efforts toward avoidance of disease? We have been programmed to expect disease. How can we enjoy health while checking to find disease? How can we produce Life while staring at disease? We, thinking as a collective human mindset, carry about an unchallenged belief in our vulnerability to disease from the time we're born. We open ourselves up to disorder in our lives through allowing a constant flow of negativity to pass unchecked through our thoughts daily.

Look in the direction you wish to go!

"Through faith we understand that the worlds were framed by the word of God, so that things which are seen were not made of things which do appear."
Hebrews 11:3

DAY 33
Allow only those thoughts you wish to experience.

God formed each one of us by his own imaging. The Mind of God thought us, and we took the form that was imagined.

Consider our body as a city set on a hill. Our mind is the wall that surrounds the city. Our spirit, the real us that lives within our consciousness, is the gatekeeper. We decide what thoughts we will allow to enter through the gates. We don't have to entertain every thought that passes by. We wouldn't allow a thief into our home without a fight, but we allow thoughts into our "city" that are actually destructive. We decide, without even realizing it, for the good that comes into our life or for the negative.

We have to learn to listen to the thoughts that come to us. They come to give us an oppportunity for us to make a choice, for life or death. We must think about each thought as it comes and decide if it is worthy to be allowed into our city. Will it bless us or harm us? We can always reject a thought and replace it with another. we are the watchmen on the wall.

As we develop habits of thought and patterns of reponse, we will like ourselves better, we will be happier and healthier. We will feel more in control of our lives. This is Wisdom. Life must be well thought out and treated with respect. The beginning of Wisdom is the realization that there is a law of cause and effect, sowing and reaping. Every action has a consequence. Every thought has a consequence. While it may appear that problems have a physical origin, all true cause is behind the scenes, in the unseen world of thought.

"I have set before you life and death, blessing and cursing: therefore, choose life."   Deuteronomy 30:19

DAY 34

Live in that absolute, perfect, whole and complete Life that we call God.

There's a difference between living in what we see, and living beyond the visible, in that absolute perfect and whole and complete Life that we call God. This Life, this Being, is what formed you and is the very substance of your being.

This Being is Life and the fullness thereof. It is light, and in it is no darkness at all. It is eternal, it has always been, is now, and always will be. That means that you are eternal, the real you is now, always has been, and always will be, an intact being, an intact representation of this Life that animates you, that flows so freely through you, that cannot be interrupted, cannot be challenged, cannot be overcome.

One day I was driving down the road and the trees were bare. The very next day, every mountain laurel tree was full of blossoms. It's like they had some invisible connnection and they all blossomed at one time. They do have an invisible connection, and that invisible connection is the very substance of those trees, the Life, the energy, the intelligence, the order, the eternal, immutable, unchangeable, absolute truth of that Life. This energy is the very substance and intelligence and order and wisdom that has kept creation intact and will continue to do so. When we learn to see the Life beyond the form, to feel that Life, we will see everything in our environment healed, and ourselves healed, too.

"Thou will show me the path of life: in thy presence there is fullness of joy."　　　　　　　　Psalm 16:11

DAY 35
See beyond the facts, and get hold of the truth.

There is truth, and there are facts. The world and the five physical senses and all the laws and attributes and characteristics of that are called facts. It's a fact that you can't see without putting those glasses on, it's a fact that somebody you love is suffering, it's a fact that you don't seem to have the finances to meet your needs, it's a fact that your kids are in trouble. Everything we see out there are facts, and we can live according to those facts or we can live with purpose.

The purpose that we have come for, been sent here for, is to see beyond facts, to get hold of the truth, the absolute truth that never changes, and to insist on seeing it. We were sent to heal. We have been sent as a light to walk through this maze of darkness and to bring the light of the truth.

Look out beyond yourself. and see a world full of the pulsation of this Life, this Divine Life, this eternal, unchangeable order, perfect order. In the quietness of your own soul, when you see someone suffering, you can choose to bring healing to that situation. Or you can agree with the fact, the physical manifestation. If you do that, you have become part of the problem and not a healer of the problem.

Every moment, look beyond the fact, and grab hold of a truth. You've been lied to long enough, the world's been lied to by their own beliefs and their own fears and their own imagery long enough. It's time to burst that door wide open and let the light shine in the darkness of our minds.

"Let us cast off the works of darkness and let us put on the armor of light."   Romans 13:12

DAY 36
See what God sees, feel what God feels,
know what God knows.

Every day and every circumstance is an opportunity
for us to correct the visible and to insist on the Life
that's behind the veil, or beyond the visible, to see the
absolute intactness, the wholeness and completeness.
We would then see what God sees, feel what God feels,
know what God knows. That is our inheritance, that is
our possession. It is with this Mind that we have come,
but it has been clouded over by a lot of confusion, a lot
of facts that bear no resemblance to the truth.

It's a river of Life that's been clogged up with tons of
boulders of confusion and mis-education. We're going to
clear those boulders out. You know how you clear them
out? You don't try to move the boulders, you increase
the flow of the Life of the river, by filling yourself with
the knowledge of the truth. Let that truth push the
boulders aside. Let that truth flow around and over
those boulders.

We don't deal with every little fragment of confused
thought that's in our heads, that is futile, and makes us
so self-absorbed that we can't see out to a world of
wholeness and completeness. What we do is look at the
Life beyond the veil, look at the true Life that forms
everything, inhabits everything, animates everything,
and is the Life of all that is.

That Life is pure good. It can never produce evil or
harm. It is the abundance of every good thing, beyond
your wildest imagination, beyond your deepest desires.
Take time to have a relationship with that Life.

"I am their inheritance...I am their possession."
                                            Ezekiel 44:28

DAY 37

Let Life have its way.

Divine Life is the fulfillment of everything you've ever thought, desired, needed, prayed for, wanted, agonized over, run everywhere to get--it's right where you are right now. You will find it when you stop running, when you stop searching everywhere, when you stop talking about the problem, when you stop rehearsing the problem to everyone who will listen, when you look away from the things that seem to be causing so much pain and hardship and conflict and confusion in your life.

Look at the Life that never changes. Get filled with the realization of its goodness. Decide to put aside time to go out in nature, go for a walk, sit on the porch and close your eyes and breathe in the air and smell the buds that are blooming, listen to the birds, get filled with Life.

Turn off the radio, turn off the TV, turn off the confusion in your life. If you can just hold on to your seat for a moment in that aloneness, you find yourself filled with something that you have run all over everywhere all your life looking for, and it's been right here, right now, with you, and it is the very Life of you.

It is the very Life of you wanting to have a relationship with you, wanting to be with you, wanting to speak of its truths, of its wholeness, of its goodness, of the joy it would bring to your life, and the peace and the wholeness and the completeness that you would experience, if you would just let it have its way, if you would set aside your own will and your own predetermined way.

"Acquaint now thyself with him and be at peace: thereby good shall come unto thee."   Job 22:21

DAY 38

We find ourselves in the midst of Life, enveloping us, embracing us.

The true Life of us is never diseased, knows nothing about disorder, darkness, confusion. As we are willing to take a moment to be still and let that Life come forward, we find ourselves in the midst of it, enveloping us, embracing us. The more we do this, the more this river of Life becomes huge instead of just a little trickle. It becomes a rushing, gushing river, and it moves aside all the obstacles in the way of happiness and wholeness and health and order.

Leaving the material picture and going into the unchangeable truth of existence is like visiting a foreign country. We can read all about it, listen to people talk about it, but until we go ourselves and enter into the experience of it and feel the feeling of that country and be a part of it, we really don't know it at all.

When entering spiritual consciousness, the more we go there, the longer time we spend there each time, the more we learn the ways, the wisdoms of that place, the more we will find how easy it is to enter in, how accessible it is, how near it is. It is as near as the breath we breathe. It is as accessible as the thoughts we think. We learn to covet our time in that place, we learn to protect the time we've set aside to go into that place. We find that we want to go there more and more, and we find that we can stay longer and longer. After a while, we find that we can live right here with everybody else and still hold the realization of that which is beyond the physical always in our heart, in our mind, in our thoughts.

"He brought me forth into a large place; he delivered me because he delighted in me."   Psalm 18:19

DAY 39
"If anyone be in Christ, he is a new creature."

"If anyone be in Christ, he is a new creature." (2Corinthians 5:17) To be in Christ means realizing you are in, enveloped by, spiritual life or consciousness. You are not the same creature that you envisioned yourself to be before realizing the One Divine Life that is your Life. The old is a vision of the physical life only, with all the laws and all the restrictions, all the barriers, all the limitations and all the lack and all the disorder of that physical life.

The new is the spiritual life with its identity being eternal and whole and complete and perfect and lacking nothing, no limitation to happiness, no limitation to joy, no limitation to love, no limitation to supply of anything we need, no limitation of health, no limitation of strength. To be a new spiritual being, I mean new to my mind only, because really eternally I've always been that. Now I realize that I'm complete and I'm whole, and I don't have anything to get rid of.

How do we get from one to the other? Do we try to take the old and bring it into the new? Or take the new and bring it into the old to fix the old? If you're praying for a healing, you're trying to take the new understanding and bring it into the old belief, to fix that belief. This doesn't make a new creature out of you, doesn't bring you into a life that is unchangeable joy, which is available right now. There is no need to pray for something, but rather there is something we need to identify with and realize. What if we stopped praying for a healing and just left the old behind?

"Old things are passed away; behold, all things are become new. And all things are of God."
2 Corinthians 5:17-18

DAY 40
I am pure light. I am the goodness of God.

You came as a light bursting into this world of darkness and confusion and you got caught up in it for a while, forgot that you were the light, forgot you had within your own soul all the truths and understandings of who and what you really are and who and what everyone else really is. Leave it all behind and say, I am pure light. I am the pure goodness of God. I am Life, wholeness, completeness, fulfillment. I can lack nothing. There are no limitations, there are no restrictions, there is nothing to fear, there is nothing that needs to be changed. I have never been anything but this spiritual identity. I leave all the old imagery, old belief. I choose to see myself and know myself as this complete identity.

It's a bit like the fairytales where people wake up and find out, "My goodness, I wasn't some poor waif out selling flowers on the street, I've always been this princess. I've always been this wonder of wonders. Now I know who I really am."

Maybe right now you still feel like a tourist in this country, and you don't know how long you'll be able to hold on to the understanding of it. You don't have to hold on to anything, it's holding on to you! As you spend time there, looking at the characteristics of that Life of you, feeling it, being with it, as you stay focused on it, you let go of all that you have seen and believed about the old life.

It is your choice. You don't have to do anything to make it happen, you only have to hold on to the choice you make. This is the way to freedom. The way to live in the majesty and splendor of who we really are.

"For God, who commanded the light to shine in the darkness, hath shined in our hearts." 2Corinthians 4:6

DAY 41

*Spirit contains within it everything
that could ever be needed.*

The realm of Spirit contains within it everything that could ever be needed by any person at any time. It makes no difference what type of need, whether it's a physical need, a financial need, employment, relationship, the need for Wisdom or intelligence. No matter what the need is, this Life that is all around and about us, this spiritual existence, contains the abundance, exceedingly abundantly above all that we could ask or think, (Ephesians 3:20), which readily flows out as we allow it expression. We don't have to earn it, we don't have to go anywhere to get it, it is readily available.

It's like the air. We don't see air, but we can't live without it, and we all agree that it's all around and about us. We agree that we walk and talk and live and laugh and love in this atmosphere called air. We don't question it, we just accept it. We don't have to earn it, we don't have to go through some religious ritual to gain it. If you need air, then, without even thinking about it, you inhale.

If you were very cold and you were standing in the shade of a tall building, you would have no problem knowing that if you stepped out from the shade into the brilliant light of the sun, you would be warmed. It is that simple for us to enter the spiritual world. There is no place to go, no person to see, no ritual to do, it is as near as the air that you breathe, and freely flows into your system as you take that inhaling breath.

"They seek the Lord, feel after him and find him, thought he be not far from every one of us."

Acts 17:27

DAY 42

Spiritual consciousness readily corrects anything unlike itself.

Spiritual consciousness is way beyond those facts that you have accumulated all through your life, even the facts that you feel, even the facts that you may see. Spirituality says, *I am the purest of all Life. I am love flowing through all things. I am completeness and wholeness and harmony and balance and peace. I cannot be interrupted. There can be no obstacle in my path. I am not moved by the human mentality. I am not moved by the human belief, the human fears, and all their laws of cause and effect. My cause and effect is my own being, the wholesomeness, the goodness, the completeness, the infinity, and the absolute unchangeableness of my nature. I am all around and about you. I flow through you. I am the energy that gives you life. I am the intelligence and the wisdom and the order of every cell in your being.*

If you would tap into, or tune into this, if you would find the simple means of getting in contact with this realm or atmosphere of existence all around and about us called our spirituality, then you would find it very readily corrects anything unlike itself.

We need to know what is seen in the world of the spiritual kingdom, what God sees, what is in the heart of God, what is in the Mind of God, this unchangeable vision that he knows, sees and is. As soon as we have that answer, and it becomes our vision, we have our healing. God only sees what he has made, and he's made everything perfect.

"All the works of his hands are perfect."
Deuteronomy 32:4

DAY 43

The answer is within our own being.

I see Life as flowing through the body exactly like the Life that flows through the trees, the same Life that animates and is the intelligence and Wisdom and order of the purple martins that come at the same time every year, of the robins that are always the first birds that come. They all seem to know what to do, don't they? They all seem to know exactly what to do to protect their species, to make their nests and to come back to the same place every year. How do they know all that?

There is an intelligence, there is a Wisdom, there is a Divine Order that flows through them. There is nothing within them to block or obstruct the very free flow of this Life, so it just flows very calmly, freely, happily, through all that it has formed and is its own expression.

Life expresses its own self as creation, all these different things that we look at in wonder, that we admire in beauty and in majesty--all but our own bodies. We see ourselves as a completely different entity, and all the rules change when it comes to the human. We think we're supposed to know what to do, we have to have our own intelligence, our own wisdom, our own knowledge, we have to know what to do, when to do, how to do it. We have to know the future so that we know how to make the right choices. We have to know what to do for the children that are born to us. We have to know things we don't know. We might want to rethink this. Everybody is looking for answers, and the answer is within their own being, in the silence and stillness of their own souls.

"You are the temple of God and the spirit of God dwells in you."   1Corinthians 3:16

DAY 44

We are creators.
We create by what is in our hearts and our minds.

We have been made in the image and likeness of God, and in that image and likeness we are also creators. God creates by what he knows, what he holds in his heart and in his mind, and he brings that forth by his word. We too have this ability to create by what is in our hearts and what is in our minds and we bring it forth by our word. We have been doing that since day one. Whatever is in our mind and in our heart, we find that we are experiencing that.

The unfortunate thing is there is a lot of stuff in our mind and heart that is not in the mind and heart of God. We experience it because we have this attribute of creativity. And what's going on in our mind, we're speaking out of our mouth. When we do that, we are creating our own events and our own circumstances. Mostly we're doing it in the negative, and we're reaping what we have sown, we're getting back what we've put out. There are certain laws of this physical world that we live in, and we are getting back every one of those laws.

The best way to extricate yourself from this is to see what God sees, know what is true about your spirituality. Know what you want, what you really, really want, then stop speaking words and allowing thoughts to remain in your mind and allowing feelings to remain in your heart, that would continue to propagate what you don't want. Let's start redirecting that creative energy of our being.

"In the beginning was the Word, and the Word was with God, and the Word was God... All things were made by him."   John 1:1,3

DAY 45

The best way to starve your problems
out of existence is to not speak of them.

Look beyond the facts to the truth, to the source and origin of all truth, the absolute source and origin of Life. By looking into the heart and mind of God, by letting the realization of the attributes and characteristics of that Life fill our minds and fill our words, we actually begin to have a change of consciousness and begin to re-create what we desire. Don't examine the facts, instead look to the Source and origin of the Life that is intended to flow through all of its creation. Let all the wonderful attributes and characteristics of that Life freely flow and bring forth out of its own being, healing.

If Life was allowed to have its unencumbered free expression, we would be living in a state of harmony and peace and wholeness and order and happiness and fulfillment beyond anything we have ever imagined.

To every one of these "facts" that come up, apply the truth of your true spiritual being. Deal with it on a spiritual level, seeing the truth. Don't speak of it, for what we speak, we are actually solidifying, giving it life, giving it energy, giving it form, giving it permission to rule over our life.

The Hebrew word for "fasting" means to cover one's mouth. As Jesus said, it is not what we put in our mouths that defiles us, but what comes out. (Matthew 15:11) We can enter a time of fasting, a time when you don't speak, you don't rehearse your problems to any-body. The best way to starve them out of existence is to not speak of them. You'll hear the thoughts coming in like a tidal wave, and it's hard to keep quiet, but this is true fasting.

"Life and death are in the power of the tongue."
Proverbs 18:21

DAY 46

Let us not speak of the things
we don't want to experience.

Many men and women in the Bible went away by themselves. Moses went 40 years in the wilderness, Elijah went three years, Jesus went three years, Paul went three years, Jacob left his family and went to work for Laban for 14 years. These people went into what they called a wilderness experience. The wilderness experience is any prolonged time of quietness, of silence, whether you do it for an hour, two hours, three days, weeks, whatever your circumstances allow.

You may already be in a wilderness experience, in a tight place, between a rock and a hard place, as they say. This is the time to silence all the fears, all the anxieties, all the horror, that's pressing in on you, bringing all these "facts", the world events or human circumstances that want your undivided attention. You can call on the grace of God to cover your mouth. These thoughts want their own life, want you to express it and speak it, give it more life, but you don't want to give it more life.

"Life and death are in the power of the tongue," (Proverbs 18:21) not in medicine, not in surgery, not in religion, but in the tongue. Let us not speak of the things that we do not want to experience. What we hold in our consciousness as being true is what we are going to speak. If we have notions of life that don't come from truth, and we keep speaking out from these fears and misconceptions, we will keep propagating the same problems over and over.

"One that keepeth his mouth keepeth his life."
Proverbs 13:3

DAY 47
Abundant goodness supplies all our needs.

I knew a woman who had very little income. She lived alone in a very small home on a property that had been in the family for generations. She owed her doctor a lot of money, thousands of dollars, for a hysterectomy years before. She paid him five dollars a month, every month, year after year.

She talked to me about her limitation of financial supply and I pointed out to her that if it looks like you only have what comes in from the government check once a month, or a paycheck or an investment, and in your mind that is the source of your supply, *you limit yourself.* You limit your concept of what you have, what you expect, to that amount.

I said, if you could just break the shackles of that mindset and realize that the Source and origin of all financial supply, and supply of everything, comes from God, or comes from this river of Life, this force and energy of Life that flows through all of creation. It is whole and complete and abundant and is filled with every wonderful thing that we could ever need. It knows nothing about withholding, it is not in its nature to withhold. Its nature is love, is giving. It's up to us to put ourselves in the position of receiving from that constant giving.

She prayed driving home that she would no longer look to the physical evidence of what came in as her supply, that she would look to this Divine Source. When she got home, she had a Christmas card in the mail from the doctor's office saying, "Because you have been so faithful, I want to absolve you of the remainder of the debt as my Christmas gift to you."

"You open your hand and satisfy the desire of every living thing,"   Psalm 145:16

DAY 48
The true Source and origin of our existence is Divine Life.

We think that the life of us comes from our body, from within us. Actually the true Source and origin of our existence is Divine Life...we have never had a beginning, we will never have an end. The true life of us that flows through us, that is the substance of us, that animates us, that sent us to the earth with a purpose, is the Source of our life. As it flows freely through us, the evidence of its Presence is the wholeness and the strength and the vitality and the peace and the energy and the happiness that we live in, that we experience.

If we turn our attention away from our body when we look for health and wholeness, and instead look to this spirituality, this Life that flows through us, we find there--not in our body--the Source of our Life. The evidence of it appears on the body and in every other aspect of our life. When we look to that as the Source of our life, then it blesses every other aspect of our life, appearing as wholeness and abundance. This is how we live above and beyond dis-ease.

We will never get out from the stranglehold of the experience of suffering or lack or limitation in our life until we stop looking at and believing that the Source of our life is in physical forms. Who opens the channels for this flow to come to you? This abundant, Divine good-ness that we live in, that is the supply of all our needs.

"I will open you the windows of heaven, and pour you out a blessing, that there shall not be room enough to receive it."   Malachi 3:10

DAY 49

Stop talking, stop thinking.

What we speak that comes from the abundance of the heart is what releases the power to free us. The evidence of what we are holding deep in our heart is what we are experiencing in our life. Are we still holding on to old thoughts? To that which is not the absolute truth? How do we know what that is?

I am often led by the Wisdom of God to cover my mouth, to stop talking, stop thinking, stop reasoning, stop analyzing. Analysis is paralysis. We always have an idea of what's causing our problem, but if that were the truth, we would be free of the problem.

It's a heart issue. We must have our heart, our consciousness, purged from whatever nonsense might be going on there, or memories, or resentments, or confusions, or beliefs. We cannot figure it out, nor are we supposed to figure it out. We become very self-absorbed, very self-centered, when we try to figure it out for ourselves. Stop thinking that you are the one that is supposed to know.

Can you imagine a tree thinking that it is personally responsible to know when it's supposed to bloom? Can you imagine the salmon thinking that they're going to have to figure out what time of the year it is so they can start swimmming upstream? No. There is an intelligence, a Divine intelligence and an order and a Wisdom that never changes, that is always flowing through all of creation, that instructs and keeps everything in order. The same thing flows through us.

Let Life flow and just enjoy it. Let Life bring deep into your heart what you need to know. The truth comes in the silence of our own soul.

"The word is very nigh unto thee, in thy mouth, and in thy heart, that thou may do it." Deuteronomy 30:14

DAY 50

We have to make a choice.

There seem to be two types of people. One, when they are faced with something they do not want in their life, there is something inside that they allow to rise up --which incidently is inside everybody--that says, "This ought not to be. I will not accept this. I will not allow this to consume my life or the life of someone I love." The other says, "I can't believe this has come." They go and tell all their friends, rehearsing the tragedy. They go to all kinds of people who have all kinds of options, all the human ways and means of extrication from their problem, and that becomes part of the drama.

Truly, our Creator is the only real Source of extrication from any problem. The truth can be applied against a lie--a lie is anything that contradicts the absolute truth. What truth can you hold on to no matter what? The absolute truth of who you are, your true origin, what you are, and the unchangeable nature of your true identity, your true spirituality. That truth is enough to withstand any and every attack against it, but we must apply that truth.

Those who do this stand fast, and don't falter. They are the ones that experience the reality of who they are. They actually walk in that wholeness, that completeness, that perfection and that health. They get to experience the reality of who they are, and they rise up above, like Jonathan Livingston Seagull. They rise up above the flock, up above mass consciousness and world belief, up above being dazzled by the wisdom of men.

We have to make the choice.

"Choose this day whom you will serve."

Joshua 24:15

DAY 51

Thoughts are contagious.

Thoughts are contagious. Just because someone else believes something to be a certain way, or has gotten into the drama of the way they see things, or the way that they have experienced things, or what they believe to be true, you must be very aware and very cognizant of how contagious those thoughts can be, and will be, to you. Even if the words are not spoken, it is amazing the thoughts that are perceived from one mind to another. You can feel a person's fear. You can feel world fear, the whole mass consciousness of world fear, by just a word that's spoken. There are words that make the hair on the back of everybody's neck bristle, because we have played into a belief about what those words mean. We have given them power.

We do not have to go the way that everyone is going. We don't have to believe it because it's said, we don't have to believe it because we see it. We don't have to believe it because someone else believes it, we don't have to believe it because there is all kinds of physical evidence. We can still say, I personally am going for a higher Wisdom. I personally am going to throw up all these walls to protect me, and I'm going to insulate myself from your words, from your beliefs, from that tragic look in your eyes, from all your expectation that accompanies it. I'm going to pull myself away from your words and thoughts and all the options that accompany what you believe, and I am going to go to a higher Wisdom.

"Let no one deceive himself...the wisdom of this world is foolishness with God."
1Corinthians 3:18-19

DAY 52

Life is not our own.

There is only one Life, and that is the Life of God, a Divine Life, a Life of love, peace, wholeness, harmony, the absolute eternal unchangeable Life that we call God. From that Life everything that is formed is formed and is given Life as a manifestation of that Life. Never was it intended that that Life would form something, separate itself from it, and leave it to its own devices, to suffer in pain until it finally finds a way to climb back into the presence of that Life. The truth is we have never been separated from that Life. That is always the Life that flows through us and animates us. Our true being, our true reality, is a manifestation of that Life. We honor that Life by knowing it and standing steadfast regardless.

That Life is not our own. We do not own that Life, we do not own this body, we do not own this mind. We do not own anything. We are not personal creators of anything, not even our children that came from our own bodies. They also were formed by this Life, and this Life that flows will be responsible for them, if we will allow that.

What choices do we make because we know that we are not personal owners of that Life? When things come against us, we have choices to make, and what we experience will be based on our choices.

Really you have no option when it comes to making a choice for Life. There is only one choice, and it's the way of Wisdom.

"Ye are not your own."   1Corinthians 6:19

DAY 53

Life has its own way that will produce Life and goodness.

What is the way of Wisdom? First of all, we do not jump and react to the circumstances. We do not take an action through a reaction. The course that we choose to take must be deliberate. It cannot be a reaction to fear. Nor can it be a reaction to options...if you are still mulling over your options, then you have not heard the Voice of Wisdom. When you hear the Voice of Wisdom, all the other options fade off into the sunset instantly.

Along with that Wisdom that comes from down deep within your own soul, comes the confidence and the peace and the assurance that you have been told and directed to go a certain way or to believe a certain truth or whatever comes up.

Stop cold in your tracks and stop considering man's options. Pull back, pull your spirit back, be by yourself. Pray for Wisdom, pray for the heart and Mind of God. Don't move to the left nor to the right until you have experienced the Mind of God in this matter. That's Wisdom.

Father, what do you know right now about me and about this situation? What do you know, what do you feel, what do you think, and what must I know, feel, and think?

It makes no difference what it is, any human situation. That's the beauty of recognizing, realizing and holding to this realization that our life is not our own. There is one Life and it is its own existence. It has its own purpose, its own way that will produce Life and goodness.

"God gives wisdom: out of his mouth come knowledge and understanding."   Proverbs 2:6

DAY 54

"Call unto me."

How do I know I'm going to hear the Wisdom of God? Because it says, "Call unto me and I will answer you, and show you great and mighty things, which you know not." (Jeremiah 33:3)

Start with little things, little situations, as you go through your day. *What about this, Father? What should I do about this? What's the mind of God about this situation? How can I view this situation and line up with the way you see it?*

If we do this with little things along the way, we're going to find that answers start coming, and they come faster, and we become more confident and assured of these answers. There will never be a doubt in your mind when you hear it, because with those words, or with that understanding, comes the peace and the confidence, and you will know.

One block to hearing clearly is fear. What I do is I take my fear as though it were heavy baggage on my back and I actually, physically, see myself taking that bag off my back and laying it down and walking away from it. I ask for the strength, for the courage, to let the fear go, at least long enough to be able to hear clearly. When I ask that, I always get it, because I'm being honest. I make a choice to lay this fear down, but I pray for the strength and the courage to do so. Sometimes I'm able to do it forever. Other times only long enough to hear clearly, but once I've heard, the fear takes a serious backseat, because in the driver's seat now is the Wisdom and the Mind of God, and I know I'm on the right track to having this situation completely resolved.

"For God has not given us the spirit of fear, but of power, and of love, and of a sound mind."

2Timothy 1:7

DAY 55

The goodness we seek is as near as the breath we breathe.

Do you already have in mind the answer you want? I've been guilty of this, I think I know what I want, I think I know what's best for me, then I am convinced this is what God wants for me. When I ask God what is in his mind, I can't see anything but what I already believe he's going to say, or what I want him to say.

The reason we do that is we don't really trust the goodness of God. We don't really trust that if we let go, and if we acknowledge that Life is not our own, and say, "Let me see your Wisdom, your mind, your heart in this matter," we're going to find something wonderful.

We're going to find a peace that we haven't had before. We're going to quit manipulating and we're going to allow the Wisdom of God to take that place and space in our heart and in our mind. We're going to find that it's true that "Eye hath not seen nor ear heard, neither has entered into the heart of man" the magnanimous abundance of all that God has prepared for us, right here, right now, in this Life, in this experience. (1Corinthians 2:9) The only thing keeping us from experiencing it, from seeing it, from hearing it, from knowing it, is getting ourselves out of the way and trusting in the goodness of God.

The Anglo-Saxon word for God is good. This goodness fills all space. we walk in it, we talk in it, when we take a breath we're breathing it in. We laugh in it, we love in it, sometimes we cry in it, and sometimes we have a lot of fear in it, but if we would open our heart, we would find that the goodness that we seek is as near to us as the breath we breathe.

"Trust in God with all your heart and lean not unto your own understanding."   Proverbs 3:5

DAY 56
Everything begins with thought.

Wisdom fixes everything that needs to be fixed. If you will seek Wisdom, you will find everything else is added to you. That's a promise, and that's an experience, not only of my own life, but of the lives of people I've counseled, people I've prayed with and people I have watched for years, every single time.

Even if we deny this truth, it will not deny itself. It will be faithful because it cannot deny itself. Even in our unbelief and in our fear and in our denial, even if we cannot make ourselves believe it, it still will be faithful to us. That gives me a lot of peace, and a lot of confidence, and enables me to turn away from trusting in my own wisdom, and makes me turn away from trusting in the wisdom of man.

We understand and we know that the truth will make us free and extricate us from whatever situation we're believing that we are experiencing. But how does it work? How does knowing the truth, speaking the truth, affirming the truth, actually change the physical human circumstances?

Everything begins with thought. Everything. Not necessarily your own thought, but thoughts are contagious, and we live in this atmosphere of mass consciousness filled with human thoughts. It's impossible to walk through any given day and not think thoughts that, while we think they are our own thoughts, they are in fact just world thoughts that have been floating around in the air, and we picked them up. Before we know it, this thought has made a nest in our mind, it's laid a few eggs, and when those eggs start hatching, we start having experiences that we're not interested in having.

"Surely as I have thought, so shall it come to pass."
Isaiah 14:24

DAY 57

The first choice is to go for Wisdom.

When we know and believe that everything begins in the thought realm, we take a truth that comes from the mind of Wisdom, not something that we just reached up and grabbed ourselves, not something that we think if we say it over and over again, because it worked last week or last year, that this is what we're going to use this time. No. For every single situation we must go brand-new to the heart and mind of God for the Wisdom of God, for this higher Wisdom. Whatever comes up is going to be new and fresh. That's good, because with each situation, new truths become real to our hearts and souls, and we take greater steps and leaps forward in the understanding of our true identity and who we really are.

How does this work? If we take on a truth, a voice of Wisdom, it actually crowds out the negative thought that is unlike it. When this word of Wisdom or this truth comes up in our hearts and our minds and we say it and we speak it, again and again, and let it roll around in our hearts and in our minds, day and night, what it's doing is drowning out the thought, whether we are consciously aware of it or not. It's crowding out the thought that first was allowed to exist, in order for this experience to be happening.

When something appears in the physical realm, the first choice is to go for Wisdom, go for the Mind and the heart of God. When Wisdom comes, it may direct you to a certain place, person, or thing--that's okay, because first you waited and you heard. Your confidence is in God, in the truth, in your absolute intact wholeness that can never really be challenged or be interrupted.

"Your ears shall hear a word behind thee saying, this is the way, walk ye in it."   Isaiah 30:21

DAY 58
Defer to the Mind of God.

We will never find the answers we're looking for if we insist on living only in the five physical senses, by what we see, by what we feel, by what we hear, by what we believe to be true, by what we're told. We must reach out for a mind and a consciousness that is beyond what we have been living in. Once again I quote Einstein, "No consciousness that created the problem can ever solve the problem."

Deferring to the Mind of God is deferring to the intelligence and the Wisdom and the understanding that is so much higher than the human intelligence and wisdom and understanding.

I heard from a minister who had attended one of my workshops. He attended hoping he would be healed of years of struggle with severe depression. He wrote, "Michele told us that she never healed anyone and could not heal anyone, but she did tell us that God is greater than any disease, and that the image of God is in us."

He went on to say that he had identified the root of his difficulty as unresolved guilt. He asked, "Why can I not believe in the Mercy and forgiveness of God as adequate to relieve me from the necessity to punish myself?" Michele's answer was, "The mind that creates a problem cannot change itself to accept anything that will heal it. Defer to the Mind of God."

On the way home, he did it. He said, "I realize that my mind has created this convoluted thought process, and I can't find my way out of it using my own mind. I'll defer to a higher Mind than my own." His depression was lifted in an instant and he felt a tremendous joy flooding his mind. The healing has remained.

"Except the Lord build the house, they labor in vain that build it."   Psalm 127:1

DAY 59

The Eternal Mind of God looks right through the human condition and sees what it knows is true.

Unbeknownst to us, we develop a mindset about something. We have no idea that we've developed that mindset, because it seems to be such a part of our own personality, our own thought process. It comes from things we hear, things we're told, things that come from experiences we have, thoughts that come from experiences that others have had, things we read about, talk about. Then along the way, we reap what we sow. From a convoluted thought process comes something, and we start living in the misery of whatever that negative thing is.

Don't go back to try to figure out how you started thinking something, or what thought process led you to believe something. Analysis is paralysis. It makes us self absorbed, self centered, self indulgent, as we go around and around in our self-made quicksand.

We were created to love, to give, to be the deliverance and care and help for a world of confusion. We were created as Light, in Light, sent to a world of darkness to be the light of understanding. How can we fulfill that if we are delving back into our own "issues"? Don't spend one second trying to figure it out, just defer to a higher Mind.

Defer to the Eternal Mind of Wisdom, the Mind that knows all things, understands all things, that is never fooled into believing something different than what it knows is true, that never looks upon the human condition and gets into a state of confusion. The Eternal Mind of God looks right on through the human condition and sees what it always knows is true.

"God sees not as man sees."　　　　　　1Samuel 16:7

DAY 60

Let go of our own thoughts.

We have been formed from the Mind of God. It is the Life of God that gives us Life, that animates us, that gives us breath. It is the intention and purpose of God, the will of God, that we have come here. God has a purpose for us to be here, an intention, something for us to fulfill. Not one of us really knows why we're here, we're not supposed to know.

We're supposed to, instead, surrender to this higher Mind, this only Life, this Eternal Life that flows through us. We're supposed to surrender to the will, the purpose, the intention, of this Mind and let it move through us and form thoughts in our minds to direct us, so that at the end of the course we have fulfilled what is our purpose and intention, why we were sent here.

If we think we know our purpose without deferring to a higher Mind, then we will live in and experience whatever we thought we knew, and we will short-change ourselves. We will limit our existence and our experience.

I defer to the Mind that created me. I defer to the Life that flows through me. I defer to a higher Wisdom, a higher understanding, a higher knowing. I defer to a higher purpose and intention.

Then we wait. A moment, or longer than that, it takes as long as it takes until we really do let go of our own thoughts. As soon as you let go, in come tons of thoughts. Each person is going to hear exactly what they need in order to extricate themselves out from whatever limitation of existence they have found themselves in.

"Ye shall seek me, and find me, when ye shall search for me with all your heart."   Jeremiah 29:13

DAY 61
God is only good, and very, very near.

Stop and defer to the Mind of God, who always knows how he made you to be. That will come barreling through with no effort, and you will find yourself, for the first time in your life, relaxed, happy, joyful, and attracting everything to you that you've always wanted, without the fear of it hurting you.

Stop and ask, what should I pray? Then trust that only the right answer will come, only Wisdom. Only that which will heal could come from the heart of goodness. Knowing that God is only good, and very, very near us, gives us confidence and peace. Now we can trust enough to let go of all our own thoughts.

It is always us who blocks what we want, never a God who is reluctant, or for some reason is holding out. There is no such God. Divine Love cannot hold out. We have been created to live a Life of abundant joy and peace and wholeness, not when we've earned it, not when we're ready for it--we were ready from the moment we were born.

Do you believe God wants something different for you than what you want? Do you believe that if you defer to the Mind of God it will be more years of lack and pain and sorrow? The fact that in your heart and soul you ache for something, doesn't come from your own heart and soul, but is God speaking to you, God declaring to you what his purpose is for your life. His purpose is for you to be happy, to be whole, to be safe and secure, to feel wonderful about yourself. Agree with the mind of God and the heart and purpose of God for you.

"Be ye transformed by the renewing of your mind, that ye may prove what is that good, acceptable, perfect, will of God."   Romans 12:2

DAY 62

We are spirit beings.

If we awaken in consciousness to the realization that we are Spirit beings, awaken to our true spirituality, that we are much more than just a vulnerable body victimized by anything that might by chance come along, that is, if we can open our hearts and minds to the Mind of God, then we will see that there are certain characteristics, attributes, laws, principles, Wisdoms of this Mind of God. When we line up with these, understand them, practice them, make them our own, we correct the old thought patterns, the old actions and reactions. When we make a deliberate effort to live deliberately, according to these principles, then we find we are moving out of the atmosphere of thought, and out of the realm of experience, of disorder, confusion, and darkness in any aspect of our lives.

What stops us from deferring to the Mind of God? We do not believe that the will of God is translated in our heart as our desire. The old thought of God says we need to suffer, but we can't defer to that God if he rains misery in our life. We don't know the goodness of God, we don't know his Voice when it comes, but we can learn. We are going to live a Life beyond dis-ease, the Life that was given to us to live, a Life of goodness and wholeness and completeness and happiness.

We must make room for that Life, room in our mind and in our heart. With joy expect it to come. Don't be afraid to believe that. Expect the goodness of God to fill the space you have made for him. And make space in your life for this good thing to come that God himself will bring. Don't go out looking for it, sit back and let it come to you, because it surely will, it always does.

"Cast not away your confidence, which has great recompense of reward."   Hebrews 10:35

DAY 63

Life takes over effortlessly.

To go from sickness to health, or to live in a state of health, is not a miracle to God. The normal way we should be experiencing life is in health and in wholeness. There is a Divine Life, God, that created us, that formed us. We were actually formed from the Mind and thought of God. That energy, or Life of God, and all the characteristics and attributes of God, flow through us. That is our substance and is what animates us. That is what gave us Life and is our Life. It's not so much that God lives in us, as *God is the whole of us, the all and only of us.*

This Life that flows through us would express its own nature, which is wholeness and health and balance and harmony and peace, if it was allowed to freely flow. We inadvertantly set up barriers to the experience of wholeness, which blocks this flow through us. We have thought patterns that have been imposed upon all of mankind, that block the flow of this Life. We need to give more power to Life rather than to disease and death, so Life would take over effortlessly.

The experience that we live out in our life is in direct proportion to how we see God. If we tune in to the thoughts of God, the way God perceives Life, we are amazed to see how completely different it is from the way we perceive life and what we say is real. If we tune into that and get a picture of what he sees, what he knows, it changes our human circumstances instantly.

Father, when you look us, what do you see? Let me see what you see. What do you know that I don't know, that if I knew, I wouldn't see this problem?

"O send out thy light and thy truth;
let them lead me."　　　　　　　　　　　Psalm 43:3

DAY 64

Trust your body.

One man, when he deferred to the Mind of God, heard, *I have put everything in your body, I have created everything to heal itself, to maintain wholeness, to sustain the Life within. Trust it. It is my intelligence, my Wisdom, my working, my Life, my understanding. I did it, it is the nature of all the workings in your body, therefore it has an eternal quality.*

He felt an instant trust come over him, his thoughts, his mind. And he began to love his body, trust his body. He began to realize that it was not his enemy, it was not something to fear. It was not something that could break down and not get repaired. It actually had the eternal qualities of its Creator and he could trust it. Things don't change at the drop of a hat, don't change to meet human circumstances , don't change to meet what humans believe.

The body loves us when we trust it. It loves Life. It's happy, it's whole, it feels strong, it feels balanced, and it feels invigorated, when we are living in a state of trust, peace, and love. When we love our body, we are loving the God that made it. When we trust our body, we trust the God that sustains and maintains it. And the way we trust our body is by knowing and trusting the God that made it in his image and likeness.

A lack of trust in God comes from an idea of a God that hurts and harms, one you can annoy, as if he were a human with a short fuse, that can be irritated or wake up on the wrong side of the bed. No. God is a principle, the principle of goodness, of Life, of eternal harmony. Unless we understand the nature of God, we cannot trust our body.

"One who puts his trust in me shall possess the land."
                                                              Isaiah 57:13

DAY 65

*An intelligence far beyond human intelligence
works in every cell of the body.*

God is a principle. Out from that intelligent, well
ordered, unchanging, principle of Life and Love and
Harmony, all of creation is formed. That's why you see
the seasons change at the same time every year, you
see the tide going in and out at the same time, you see
the sun come up and you see the sun go down, and the
moon come up and the moon go down, you see certain
patterns of stars in the sky every month, exactly the
same as they were every year before in this particular
month. You see everything in nature moving in a Divine
Order, an uninterrupted order.

If you see Life that way, and if you see the order and
the unchangeable nature that's all around us, then it will
help you to understand the unchangeable nature of God.
If you see the beauty and the harmony, and if you feel
the love of creation and nature all around, that will help
you realize that this was formed from that type of a
being, or that type of a character or nature.

If you study the body, you will see an intelligence so
far beyond human intelligence working in every cell of
the body. And you will see how every individual part of
the body defers to the good of the whole.

Romans 1:20 says, "The invisible things of him from
the creation of the world are clearly seen, being understood by the things that are made." You look at all that
has been made and created, and you look at the nature
of it, and the details of it, and the workings of it, and
the consistency of it, and that enables you to better
understand the being that brought it forth, the mind
that brought it all forth.

"I set them in order before your eyes."

Psalm 50:21

DAY 66
Our true nature is the true nature of God.

The nature of God is to give and give and give. It knows no such words as "lack" or "limitation" or "withholding good." It's impossible. Matthew 5:45 says that the rain falls on the just and on the unjust alike. We don't earn the rain to fall, any more than a plant earns the rain to fall on it. Food is poured out for the good of the whole, the unjust or the just, it makes no difference. God is not giving or withhholding depending on our behavior or our nature or knowledge.

On our side of the fence, if we are living selfishly, unto our self, if we are not giving of our self for the good of the whole, then what happens is the Life of God, the Eternal Life that flows through our being and sustains and maintains Life from within, is blocked. It gets *to* us but can't get *through* us, because we're all choked down with our own self-centeredness and self-absorption, and our own fears. We're afraid to give, we're afraid to love, we're afraid to pour out from our own being. We're not fulfilling our true nature, because our true nature is the true nature of God, and that is a giving, loving, constant pouring out.

God is an ongoing giving being, giving Life, giving abundance, giving substance, giving goodness, which is translated on the human scene as everything we could possibly want. Life can't withhold. It's our belief systems that choke down the poured out abundance that's being given to us always.

"Let him give, not grudgingly, or of necessity, for God loves a cheerful giver."　　　　　　　2Corinthians 9:7

DAY 67

When you give, you've opened up your whole existence so Life can be poured in.

The body is constantly giving of itself for the good of the whole. By doing so, it is an open receptacle to receive more of the fresh substance of Life. That's the same as it should be in our existence as humans. As we give, as we love, as we trust, then more and more and more is poured in. But if we're fearful, if we're afraid of our own bodies, afraid to trust our bodies, then we don't know the God behind the scenes that created and formed us in his image, so how can we trust what it brought forth?

If we learn to trust our bodies, we will be more relaxed, not so fearful. We won't be so concerned when something seems to come upon our body. We will know, even though we don't know all the intricate workings, that whatever we're experiencing, the rest of the body is doing everything it was created to do to bring us back into harmony and balance.

Air is all around us. We live in the air, we walk and talk and laugh and love in the air. We need that air to survive. But we have to inhale in order to take that air in, so that it can give us Life. In order to inhale, we have to first exhale. We have to give out in order to be able to take in.

People are afraid to give. They're taught that to give is to lose something, so you have less. That's not true. When you give something, you've opened yourself up to get everything. When you give something, you can only gain, because you've opened up your whole existence so Life can be poured in, you have made space for more to appear.

"Freely you have received, freely give."
Matthew 10:8

DAY 68
We create through thoughts and words.

We're told that we're formed by the word of God. God, being Divine Eternal Life, had a thought and spoke a word and we were formed. The worlds were framed, it says in Hebrews 11:3, by the word of God. All creatures that appear, came from a word, a thought.

We are created in the image of God. That means that we have within our souls all the attributes and characteristics of whatever God is. What does that embrace? It embraces goodness. That means your soul has been created and is the substance of goodness. It embraces wholeness, completeness, harmony, balance, order, perfection, infinity, immutability, compassion, mercy, kindness, gentleness, power, creativity.

Creativity is part of our inheritance, our possession, our substance and our soul. How do we create? We create the exact same way that the Source and origin of our life creates, through thoughts and through words.

Everything physical, a tree, a bird, a plant, a human, the intricate details and workings of our body, and even the good that comes forth in our life and in our relationships, our purpose and direction, a career that we love, something that brings a tremendous amount of satisfaction into our life, and joy, all this, tangible or intangible, comes from thought. Once we understand this we will be far more cognizant when considering the thoughts that we allow. Once we consider the thoughts we allow, it's much easier to understand not only what seemed to cause a problem, but how we can change the course of any given situation. It is as simple as correcting our thought, substituting a true thought for one that is not true. Then sit back and watch the change.

"Out of the abundance of the heart, the mouth speaks."   Matthew 12:34

DAY 69
Let the Divine Mind come bursting through.

If you can understand and embrace these principles, you will find that you can correct physical evidence of discord, disease, confusion, darkness, chaos, disorder. You can see the evidence change into harmony and beauty and order and perfection. Unchangeable absolute infinity can come forth right in the place where lack and limitation seem to dominate, right in the space where pain and sorrow and suffering seem to dominate a life. You will be able to see something new, something beautiful, coming forth. This is not for the chosen few. These principles are for everyone to know and understand.

Humility is the key. You must have the humility to stand back, to let go of what you believe, or just let go of the whole scenario of the human consciousness and all of its analytical avenues of thought, and just calmly, gently, in the quietness and serenity and peace of your own soul say, "Father, what is Wisdom here? Show me what I don't see." Let the Divine Mind come bursting through.

You will know because your heart will be quieted--all the fear, all the anxiety, all the electrifying energy, will be silenced. Soon you will begin to perceive something different and something new. When that happens, you are in a position of healing whatever that situation is, because you have just been given the truth. An understanding, a wisdom, a perception, an insight, a vision, a moment of clarity. You smile, you nod your head, you are agreeing with the Eternal Mind of God. You are allowing this to correct and alter the human situation.

"He performs the thing that is appointed for me."
                                        Job 23:14

DAY 70

*Down in every soul is the unchangeable nature
of goodness out from the Life that created it.*

There is a world beyond what is seen, and we live in
it. It's a world of total acceptance and total love and
total wholeness. We are experiencing less than what is
being offered to us by this world that formed and created us and breathed its very Life into us.

God cannot create something unlike himself, nothing
can create something unlike itself. Each seed reproduces
after its own kind. (Genesis 1:24) Everything God has
made has all the qualities and characteristics of his own
self. Down in every soul is the unchangeable nature of
the purity and goodness, out from the Life that formed
and created it, and it can never be changed or altered.

We have been hypnotized by the mass human consciousness. We've been led to believe that suffering,
sadness, lack, limitation, misery, are a part of life. They
are not. Life is God. God is not the author of any of
that. It's a bunch of educated beliefs we've accumulated as humans through the centuries.

The external appearance is no more than a person's
own belief of who they are. We act out what we think
we are. Just because we don't know our true divinity,
our true nature, our true life, just because we don't
know the purity and the wholeness and the perfection
of all the characteristics of our true nature, and the
nature of our neighbors, does not mean that it's not
there. Learn to look beyond what is visibly seen to the
heart of each person. By connecting with that we have
healed them. It's that simple.

*"Whatsoever God does, it shall be forever: nothing can
be put to it, nor any thing taken from it."*
Ecclesiastes 3:14

DAY 71

How do I get out of this?

Johnny was such a rebellious kid in school, and the teacher kept saying, "Johnny, I want you to sit down. If you don't sit down, I'm going to take you to the principal." Finally Johnny sat down and she said, "I am so glad that you finally obeyed." He said, "Inside I'm still standing up!"

We may put up with what we have to put up with, but we're not going to accept it inside.Something inside says NO. We may not know what to do about what hit us, we may be groping around in the dark, and we certainly have to deal with what we're dealt, but that doesn't mean that we're accepting it. We may not be able to stop what it's doing at this moment to our body or to our finances or to our marriage or to our children, but we don't let this dominate our heart and soul. It's not right, and we don't have to buy into it. Rise up and say, "NO, not in this lifetime, not to me!"

Continue walking down the path of Life with hope and with joy in spite of the things that come against you. Don't give your attention and power to those--Life is not like that. Continue to hold fast to the truth that you were made by a perfect God in his image and likeness.

We've inherited the right to hear God speak to us and share with us directions that we should take. Go to God and say, "How do I get out of this?" This is difficult to do when the dragons are breathing down your neck. It's easier on a day to day basis to say, "This is a relationship that I must cultivate." Talk, listen, share your heart.

"Teach me thy way, and lead me in a plain path."
Psalm 27:11

DAY 72
The body knows what to do to bring itself into order, balance and harmony.

Our bodies flow in such balance and order, they have such incredible regenerative powers that no matter what, when something happens to us, the body sets everything in motion to restore a state of normalcy and balance and order. The body has a Divine Intelligence, and knows when and how and what to do to bring itself back into order, balance and harmony.

Why doesn't it happen all the time? We don't give it a chance. We start with the fear, with the expectation of getting worse, rather than resting, letting this pass, allowing the body to heal. Right away we go off for help, right away we introduce medications into our already fearful system, and now we have two strikes against our immune system, the fear and the toxic substances.

It is intended for our body to be in wholeness and in health, to regenerate and recuperate whenever it gets out of balance. But if we fill our minds and thoughts with fear, negativity, hurt, and worry, we are working against what the body was created to do, and would do, if we would allow it.

People who heal have a peace and confidence in their hearts. Not a false confidence based on false hope or gritting their teeth and just barreling through, but a confidence birthed in a deeper level of being, which includes our spirituality, our relationship with God, and the image we hold of who and what God is and what our relationship is to him. This deeper presence leads us and we feel safe. That safety superimposes itself over the fear.

"The thing which I greatly feared is come upon me."
Job 3:25

DAY 73

Teach me to hear your distinct voice.

It makes no difference what your background is, it makes no difference whether you are of Jewish descent, or Muslim or whether you are new age or Catholic, protestant, born again or not. If you ask, God will answer. He is the same Creator of all flesh.

You ask, you hear, you feel led, you obey. Confidence and peace is birthed from knowing you are doing what you have been led to do, a confidence greater than all the fears. Cling tight to the Source and origin of that word and that voice.

We humble ourselves, we declare that this life is not our own, we are not the source and origin of it, we are not the creators of it, we are not the owners of it, we are not the janitors of it. God is all of that. God will lead and guide if you ask and you faithfully wait until you've heard.

Simply ask: *God, teach me how to hear. Teach me how to hear you above and beyond all the other voices that I hear and particularly my own. Above my own fears, my own predisposed opinions, my own attitudes that get in the way, other people's opinions when I might think they know more than I know. Teach me to hear your distinct voice. And then, let me have the courage to follow it.*

The minute you hear it, there is no doubt. You know that you heard, and there's a peace beyond anything on this planet. When that comes, you are not shaken out of the path you felt led to. The courage comes with the hearing.

"Incline your ear, and come unto me: hear and your soul shall live."   Isaiah 55:3

DAY 74
When you have hope, doors open up everywhere.

It is incredibly necessary for one to have hope in order to be healed. There is a physiological, metabolic process that happens in hope. Endorphins are excreted throughout our system and they bring to life all the tiny cells, all the organs, all the systems. It actually brings hope to every cell in our body. There is intelligence in every cell in our body. It responds to the joy of hope, the expectation of goodness. When you have hope, doors open up everywhere. Resources happen that you never would have believed or imagined.

Hopelessness, or despair, on the other hand, is incredibly destructive. It shuts down the normal flow of the energy of life, shuts down the ability of the cells to take up the nutrients they need, shuts down the ability of the system to release toxins. It blinds us to perceiving what is set before us, causes us to make wrong decisions based on fear, causes us to be led by mass mentality.

I believe with my whole heart that if we turn to our Creator and acknowledge that we have come from that Source, we will always find our way out. I believe it when he says "I'll make the crooked way straight." I believe it when he says, "I'll take the valleys and bring them up and make them a plain for you to walk over." I believe it when he says, "I'll take those high mountains from you and I'll drop them down and make them a smooth path for you." (Isaiah 40:4) I believe it when he says, "I'll find streams in the desert." (Isaiah 43:19) And because I believe it, I get to see it again and again, not only in my life but others.

"Faith is the substance of things hoped for, the evidence of things not seen." Hebrews 11:1

DAY 75
What you hope for is already God's vision for you.

"Cast not away your confidence, which has great recompense of reward." (Hebrews 10:35) Confidence in what? Upon what do I found my hope? Our hope lies in the true nature of our spirituality. We cannot attain to health without getting in touch with our true identity, our true spiritual identity, our true spiritual origin, without some relationship and communication with that which not only made us but is the very substance of our being, that leads and guides and watches over us, that envelops us in its care and in its love.

Life doesn't even happen until your heart is filled with hope. Upon what can you base that hope? On the fact that what you are searching for already is, in the Mind of God. What you hope to attain is already and has always been God's vision of you and for you. Everything that is created was created to experience goodness. We have been brought forth in the image and likeness of goodness. Our hope is in our Creator who leads us and guides us in his love.

The enemy is not what's happening in your life, it's not disease, it's hopelessness and despair. Take despair and kick it out the window, and turn to the origin and Source of your existence. Be willing to look at your own heart and weed out what's dogging you, what you've given power to.

Choose not to look at the things that have come against you. Choose to look at God, who is the origin and Source of our existence, who is our hope, who is good, and who will lead us out of every situation. With joy and gladness go back to the Source of your being.

"Whatsoever things you desire, when you pray, believe that you receive them." Mark 11:24

DAY 76

Experience God as Love.

Our Creator calls himself Love and Goodness, is full of
Mercy and kindness, quick to forgive, quick to heal,
quick to lead and guide us into all truth and into joy and
happiness. If we have in our minds that God is something to fear and to dread, we always feel separate and
we feel that we are not worthy for any of that goodness
to come to us. If we don't believe we're worthy to get
it, then we don't look for it, and then we don't even
see it when it's right in front of us.

Go back to the Source and origin, from where we
have come, with a heart that says, *I would know you. I
would know what this is all about. I would understand
you. I would erase in my mind and in my heart, to the
best I can, everything I've ever heard, and I would
offer a completely blank chalkboard for you to write
upon it your nature. Who you are, what you are. What
can I expect from you? What do you expect from me?
What is our relationship? Where should it go? What is
my responsibility in this relationship? What is your
responsibility in this relationship? Why am I here, and
from where have I come?*

That's how I came to the understanding and the realization, not that God is Love because someone said so,
not that God is Love because it's written somewhere,
not even that God is Love because he said he was, but
because I began to experience God as Love. Once you
experience something, then nobody can tell you anything different. I finally saw that God is the Divine
energy of goodness all around us, the Divine energy of
Love.

*"We have known and believed the love that God has to
us. God is love."*   1John 4:16

DAY 77

Let us go on to perfection.

If there was a giant tree, let's call it the tree of Life, and one branch of it was broken or wounded or disfigured, does that change the basic root structure and the basic image of the tree? Does it change the Life of the tree? Absolutely not!

The Divine energy of Love brings forth the Life that we see all around us, including ourselves. As everything comes forth from that, you see that it fills all space and all place. You begin to look at things and see Life, instead of just seeing things. You see beyond the things into the Life that pulsates through it. You realize that's the same Life that pulsates through you and me and everyone else! It is the one Life that animates us, that is the substance of our being, that is good, that is whole, that is perfect, that is complete, that is eternal, that is immutable. It is not a changeable thing.

We want to line up with this, we want to gain access to the knowledge of this Life that flows through us. Once we get in touch with that, we're going to find out that it's an Eternal Life, and we're going to find out that it's whole and it's perfect.

Hebrews 6:1 says, "Let us go on to perfection, not laying again the same old foundation of doctrines." Jesus said that the Kingdom of God is within you, (Luke 17:24), so we ought to be able to experience that right now. We are able to go on to realize the true eternal perfection that has always been the Life of God that flows through us. That's the foundation upon which we can build the house of understanding.

"It is God that girds me with strength and makes my way perfect."   Psalm 18:32

DAY 78
What is the true substance of our being?

Why don't I dwell on the myriad of temporary relief offered by traditional and alternative healthcare? It does not make you whole or complete. It does not teach us the absolute truth of who and what we are, what we've been made from, what is the true substance of our being. Are we just flesh and bones and blood? Or are we this Life that flows through us? Does the state of that Life determine the condition of the flesh, bones and blood? It should and it does.

There is a Life within us and all around us that we walk and talk and live and love and laugh in, and that Life is God. If we learn to identify with that, it becomes the measure of our experience.

If something seems to attack my body or any facet of my life, I stop and I say, "What is this, God? How should I approach this? Is there something that I'm supposed to be doing?" I recognize that the Life is not my own. I didn't create it, I didn't send it here, I really didn't have anything to do with it. So I yield that Life to the owner, the progenitor of Life, whose purpose it was I was brought forth. The Wisdom that comes forth from that has always led me out of every mess that I've ever found myself in.

Many times I am led to do something of a temporary nature to bring relief. I feel thankful for it. I believe that's just God meeting my need wherever I can receive it at the moment. Still I am seeking the eternal, endless truth, and I continue in communication, desiring it, and listening, and letting it write its laws and its characteristics and its being upon my heart.

"Walk not after the flesh, but after the spirit."
Romans 8:1

DAY 79
Healing is the natural state of existence.

Keep in mind, no matter what we're experiencing, we are pressing toward the realization of a state of oneness with this Divine Life called God. And a realization that it is the only Life that is and it animates all that it has created.

What is the substance of our real being? What is the most critical thing for us to know and to understand concerning our spirituality that would not only heal us, but would cause us to live beyond the range of dis-ease and discord in any facet of our life?

In the Mind of God we've never left our first estate. God still sees us the way he made us, in the perfect, whole and complete expression of his being. Our healing is not a gift of God that he may or may not give. It is not a magic prayer. Praying does open up your heart and your soul and make you receptive to the understanding of the absolute truth that will heal you.

The absolute truth is that in the Mind of God you've never left your state of completeness and perfection, regardless of what the human circumstances are declaring. If you can just grab hold of those words, even though you don't see it, or feel it, then you are one major step into understanding why you can expect healing and why it's the natural state of existence. After you have understood God, after you've known the will of God, and after you have held to that with patience, you will receive the promise.

"Why is not the health of my people recovered? They know not me, saith the lord." Jeremiah 8:22, 9:3

DAY 80

We've all been sent by God.

Jonah was sent to Nineveh to tell the city to turn to God. He resists the calling and finds himself thrown into the sea and swallowed up by a whale. The belly of a whale is any dark, foreboding, frightening human experience, which you cannot find your way out of.

We've all been sent by God, and we all resist that. We set about living our own life, doing our own thing, pursuing our own goals, not questioning God as to why we're here, what we're supposed to be doing, what is his purpose, what is his intention for bringing us forth. We think our life is our own and we'll do it any way we please. We find ourselves in the darkest of human circumstances, and we can't find our way out of a paper bag. We cry out to God, as Jonah did. This is what he came to know: "They that observe lying vanities forsake their own mercy." (Jonah 2:8) What does that mean?

A lying vanity is something that is lying to our mind, denying us the visibility of the Divine Life. It means stop looking at the circumstances as having any power over us. Jonah was surrounded by the Love of God, the protection, the care, the Mercy, the goodness. There would always be a way out of the circumstances if he'd only stop looking at the circumstances and look at the God in which he lived and moved and had his being, and who lived in him.

Look away from the circumstances and know that what is true is that the Life that flows through me is the Eternal Life of God. That Life contains the Wisdom that I need, the understanding that I need, the grace that I need, the power that I need. It will direct me.

"In him we live and move and have our being."

Acts 17:28

DAY 81

See beyond the circumstances into the heart of Mercy.

When it looks like some bad thing is surrounding me, really it's God surrounding me. Really goodness is surrounding me, really Mercy is surrounding me, really Wisdom is surrounding me.

If you hold to that, that honors the truth. When you honor the truth, you strengthen it. When you strengthen it and you give all your energy to it, wham! You're out of the human circumstance and you didn't do a human thing to make it happen. You just knew something, you saw something that was not immediately visible to you. You had to look away from what you were staring at and look at the truth. You can't look in one direction and hope to see something in another direction. You've got to look in the direction that you wish to see.

Once Jonah did that, his heart filled with joy. He said, "I will sacrifice unto thee with the voice of thanksgiving." (Jonah 2:9) Was he still in the belly of the whale? Yes, he was. But he didn't even see that anymore. He was so filled with the knowledge of the truth. As soon as that happened, the whale spit him out onto dry land, and he was free. That's exactly how it happens to you and me.

We will be healed! We will find our way out of this situation. We will be delivered and freed from it. That's just the absolute truth. It is upon that basis that we can have confidence that we will be freed. Once we start seeing beyond the circumstances into the heart of Mercy, into the heart of love, and the absolute truth that never changes. It's upon that we build our confidence and our assurance.

"He sent his word, and healed them, and delivered them from their destructions."　　　　Psalm 107:20

DAY 82

I have a sure way out.

A preacher friend of mine in Alaska was driving home in a snowstorm and drifted off into a snowdrift. He was stuck, and the more he tried to get out, the deeper the wheels went into the snow. Night was coming, the temperature was plummeting well below zero, he didn't have enough fuel to keep the engine going to keep him warm, he didn't have blankets, he was simply not prepared for this kind of a disaster. There were no other cars on the road that would be able to help him. He saw himself in a situation that could potentially kill him, and he was becoming more and more afraid.

He prayed, and when he prayed, he heard, "Those that observe lying vanities forsake their own mercy." (Jonah 2:8) What that said to him was, if you keep looking at the circumstance, the circumstance gets bigger in your mind than God, but if you turn your mind and heart to the realization of the Omnipresence of God, realizing that God is always with you, God is good, God is here to lead you out, then you see God becoming bigger in your mind than the situation. Whatever has become the greatest focus of your mind, that which you're giving your energy and your thoughts and your expectation to, is what will finally dominate.

As soon as he heard that he remembered, "God is here with me! I'm not alone. I have Divine Wisdom, I have the goodness of God, I have the order that never is interrupted, I have a sure way out." He put his car in gear for the hundredth time, stepped on the accelerator and virtually catapulted out of that hole, right back on to the road and he drove home to safety.

"Thou has enlarged my steps under me so that my feet did not slip."   2Samuel 22:37

DAY 83

See God bigger than the problem.

We are striving to understand the Life that has been given to us freely by God, by our Creator, and that Life does not include misery, suffering, disease, disorder or confusion of any kind.

We have our promises: *I am your shepherd, I'll always lead and guide you into goodness, I'll always take care of you. If your foot stumbles, I'll pick you up. If you run into a mountain too high, I'll lower the mountain, if you run into a valley too low, I'll bring it up. If the way is too crooked, I'll straighten it out. I will find a way for you.*

But you have to acknowledge my Presence. You have to know I'm here, you have to know I can do it, you have to see me bigger than the problem, otherwise the problem will continue to dominate you.

We live out of our own perception. Our own perception becomes our reality. If we continue to stare at the problem, to mull it over, to rehearse it, to let the monologue go on in our mind day and night, it begins to be the greatest thing and the biggest insurmountable obstacle. We forget the hugeness, the vastness of the ever Presence, the Omnipotence, of our God.

If you'd look at the Omnipresence of your Creator, the perfect way that has been ordained for us, the self-governing aspect and characteristic of God, you would realize you are in safe hands. The more you look at that, the more you exalt that in your mind, then this is the thought that you are worshipping, giving all your energy to, the thought you're standing before.

"I have made and I will bear; even I will carry, and will deliver you."   Isaiah 46:4

DAY 84
The mind that is within you is the Mind of God.

What is truth? God is the truth. Goodness is the truth. God's government is the truth. God's ever Presence is the truth. God is the only power and that is the truth. God maintains and sustains that which he has created, and that is the truth. God is our life, and that is the truth. That means our life is eternal, that means our life is perfect, that means our life is complete, that means our life is harmonious, that means it's always in balance.

You can't believe these truths and believe in and give energy to fear and let it consume you. Be still and don't let all these fears function, but let the true Mind function. That mind that is within you is the Mind of God. It's the Christ mind. This is God breathing his Life into us, creating us in his image and likeness. Then you'll realize the Wisdom, the intelligence, the order, you'll find direction where you saw no direction, opportunity where you saw no opportunity, resources where you were unable to see any resources.

When Moses led the Israelites out of Egypt, they became trapped with their back to the Red Sea. They saw no way out. They gave all their energy, their fear, to that image. But what was Moses seeing? Moses was seeing the Omnipresence of God. He lifted his arms and said, "Fear ye not, stand still and watch the salvation of God" (Exodus 14:13)

He wasn't dwelling on how this was going to happen, he was dwelling on the person that makes it happen, on the characteristics of God, the unchangeable goodness, the unchangeable Presence, the unchangeable power, of the One who said I'll never leave you. The Red Sea parted, and they all went off onto dry land.

"We have the mind of Christ."　　　　1Corinthians 2:16

DAY 85

All is well.

In Second Kings, chapter 4 there is a story of a woman whose son died. She took off to find Elisha, the prophet, because in her mind, that was the closest thing to God that she knew. Now we know of the Omnipresence of God, we know God as a spirit, within, around and about us, and we don't have to go saddle up our horse to go find him somewhere. We only need to stop for a moment, be still, and we recognize and feel the Presence of God. We listen and we recognize the direction that we've been led to take.

But she jumped up and took off. Everywhere she went, people would hail her, "Hello, how are you?" And she would say, "All is well. Another would stop and say, "Hello, how are you," and she would say, "All is well." She never told them the devastating situation that she was involved in. She never rehearsed it, didn't dissect it, analyze it, didn't go from church to church asking everyone to pray, she didn't tell all her friends and relatives about it, she didn't keep giving it energy and power by rehearsing it, by lending her words and her fear and her spirit and her energy to that situation.

Instead, she kept her eyes absolutely focused on getting ahold of God, who gave her this life of her son. One thing she knew about God was that God was the giver of life, because she could not bear a life until God intervened. When she looked at her son, she knew, "God is the giver of this life." She might have had devastating, fearful thoughts, but she didn't let one of them come out of her mouth. To believe in the circumstance is to believe not in the truth of God. Elisha went back to the boy, prayed for him, and he received his life.

"With God all things are possible."   Matthew 19:26

DAY 86

Innocence was found in me.

The king sent Daniel to the lion's den. How is it that the next morning, when he went to check on him, Daniel was still whole and intact, the lions asleep next to him? Daniel said, "The God that has always been present, has always led my life, the God that I have served day and night, the God that I've come to know more than my life and my breath, he sent his angels and shut the mouths of the lions so they did me no harm, because innocence was found in me." (Daniel 6:22)

Innocence. Does that mean we never sin? No, it means in the eyes of God we are not guilty. The minute we surrender our life back to the Source and origin of all Life, we are not guilty. God sees you as he made you. He sees in you the whole and the complete, perfect, ordered, harmonious, balanced, pure, lovely creature, right out of the heart of his own love. Does that mean he's never seen you mess up? No, it's not that he didn't see it, he isn't paying any attention to it. He sees something greater. He sees his own Life. He sees what has never changed.

How does God bring forth the beauty, harmony and wholeness that he's created? He never takes his eyes off of what he's created. He's doing the same thing he's telling us to do, to see that which is not seen. God tells us not to give power to the visible. Don't look at this thing barreling down on you, don't look at devastation and how it can take your happiness away, don't look at the meanness of the next-door neighbor. Look at the God who never changes. Look at the invisible Presence that is the power of our life.

"Unto him that is able to present you faultless before the presence of his glory with exceeding joy, to the only wise God be glory and majesty."　　　　Jude 24

DAY 87

This is the way, walk ye in it.

We are directed, time and time again, "This is the way, walk ye in it." (Isaiah 30:21). This is the way to live above and beyond all these devastations that would come against you. This is the way to walk right out and walk on through the middle of them.

Don't take your eyes off me. Find out something about me, know it, hold to it, and that truth about me will deliver you.

If God tells us live that way, surely he is also doing the same thing when he looks at us. He sees what he's made. As long as he sees it and holds to it, then that's what will dominate. If you know that and you're willing to see it in one another, willing to see that perfect, whole, complete image of God in one another, and if you're willing to know that it's there within you--you may not see it, you many not be acting like it, your body may not look like it--but if you line up with the mind of God, then you can say, "God, at least I know that what you're seeing is perfect. That's what I choose to line up with."

He'll walk you right out of it.

"Woe to the rebellious children, saith the lord, that walk to go down into Egypt...and have not asked at my mouth. The trust in the shadow of Egypt shall be their confusion." Isaiah 30:1,3

"Woe to them that go down to Egypt for help; and stay on horses, and trust in chariots, because they are many; and in horsemen, because they are very strong; but they look not unto the Holy One of Israel, neither seek the Lord!

Turn ye unto him." Isaiah 31:1,6

DAY 88

I am of a Divine Source.

If affliction comes knocking on the door, I have a choice, right then, to realize, I am of a Divine Source, and because I am of a Divine Source, made in the image and likeness of God, I am not and should not and cannot and will not accept this as a reality. I will not accept it as something that I will allow into my experience.

Does that mean it won't come in anyway? Sometimes it does. Or you may have some struggling to do. But it is not your battle, not your struggle. It really is the struggle between truth and error, between light and darkness, between evil and good. It really is the struggle of, what is my true source? Is my true source Divine, or am I just a mere mortal?

In the Old Testament, remember, the children of Israel spent four hundred years in bondage to the Egyptians. then along came someone who said, "This is not the way God intended his chosen people to live. Why don't you follow me, follow what I'm saying, because God would have you live in a land of milk and honey, a land of promise, a land of joy and hope, goodness and gladness." They had forgotten in all those generations that life could be different, was intended to be different.

I liken this experience to us living in bondage again. Enough is enough, enough people have died, enough people have suffered. It's time for us to choose a different way. Can we? You bet we can. We're supposed to. We were meant to. We were created to and we shall. It's absolutely imperative that we go back to the drawing board, back to the blueprint, and find out the way it is supposed to be.

"It is he that has made us, and not we ourselves."
Psalm 100:3

DAY 89

Behind the scenes is what never changes about you.

See your body as a city, sitting high on a hill, with a wall around it for protection. All along that wall are truths, absolute truths about the purity, the wholeness and the completeness of that city as made in the image of God, coming from a Divine Source and origin. Every time something comes against the body, one of those truths needs to stand up and say, "No, you cannot enter."

You mean to tell me that physical afflictions will bow down to me by declaring who I am and where I've come from and why it doesn't have a right? I'm telling you exactly that! I'm telling you from years of having done it, for myself, my children, and hundreds and hundreds of patients, and seeing them walk in health.

We must begin to see our body as an intact, impregnable, unassailable entity, protected by the fact that it was made in the image of God, and cannot be challenged... no more than God can be challenged. Our Source is immutable, an absolute unchangeable being. That's what's behind the scenes, behind all the layers of human beliefs and experiences. Behind all that is what never changes about you. You can line up and start to identify with that and enjoy a life of wholeness, or you can keep identifying with this random human existence, waiting to see what's going to come next.

Your body was not created to be a host for disease. Your Divine Life is the "True Light that lights every one that comes into the world." (John 1:9)

"Ye were sometimes darkness, but now are ye light in the Lord: walk as children of light." Ephesians 5:8

DAY 90

Go back to the drawing board.

Do not allow your situation to cast a hypnotic spell upon you. Do not become so enchanted, so dazzled, by the temptation to believe that something can come against you, that you accept it as a reality and then build a shrine to it. To worship at that shrine is to tell more and more people about what's going on with you and what's happening. We don't realize how much we empower the very thing that has come to destroy us.

The people who are successful in walking away healed are those that zip their lip, that don't talk about it. They don't announce it here and there and everywhere. They're not trying to get sympathy, or a cast of thousands to pray for them. They go quietly back to the drawing board, asking, "Is this something I must accept? What is the way out? What must I do?" When they do that, and stay to themselves, the voice of Wisdom speaks, declaring one of these truths, declaring a way out... without fail, each and every time.

A healing is not only seeing the physical affliction gone, but also that sense of being vulnerable to disease, being a victim. We need to have a much higher expectation of life, so we can say, "I was not created to support this disease. I'm made in the image and likeness of God. The true life within me is eternal, unchangeable, and cannot be afflicted." We need to be elevated in our minds out of acceptance of disease as being the ordinary path of life, something that we have to put up with. It's time to come out from that.

"Return unto thy God...Take with you words, and turn to the Lord."   Hosea 14:1,2

DAY 91

What is the next step for me?

Seek the Wisdom of God: *What is the direction that my life should go now? I know I have been sent here for a purpose. I know my life is not really my own. What is the next step for me?*

We can find a tremendous sense of fulfillment and completion and joy in this experience called life if we know and follow the direction already set for us. That's when we're going to be the very happiest, when we find ourselves in that niche that was created for us, that we were sent to fill.

In the New Testament, Paul is cruising along on the road to Damascus and a brilliant Light comes before him and throws him off his horse and renders him immediately blind. He prays, not please heal my blindness, but "What would you have me do? What do I need to know? What is the direction that you want me to take?" He didn't pay attention to the blindness, he stayed focused on the direction God was leading him to go.

Seeking God's direction increases our confidence and assurance. It makes us think in terms of wholeness, of life, it takes us out of the quicksand of the present experience. It's saying to your problem, "You are NOT my creator and you have no power over me and I'm not going to waste any more time with you. I'm going on, I'm going on with the Life that I was intended to live." This increases the flow of the river of Life, the flow of Divine energy through you, lifts you to another level of hope, of health, of strength. It lifts you to the expectancy of good, the best medicine there is.

"In all thy ways acknowledge him and he shall direct thy paths."   Proverbs 3:6

DAY 92

In what does our confidence rest?

Why is confidence important? Because whatever we have confidence in is what we have imaged in our mind. It's what we have given our energy, our strength, our hope to. It's what we expect to see. Once you have determined, in your mind, something that you expect to see, something that your confidence is based on, then you will see that happen. You will see that appear in your experience. You may see it much to your dismay, because it may be that you are having confidence in something that you did not want to experience. In what does our confidence rest?

Confidence that we can walk away from a circumstance that seems to engulf us is the best and ultimate way to heal. A true healing should set you in a place where you never think of it again. A true healing should also heal the memory, the fear, the expectancy, the dread of ever having an affliction again. It's not just fixing the human condition, because then we live in fear, not having corrected the basic vulnerability, the basic concept of being a victim to whatever may come along. We have not corrected our mind.

My confidence is in the integrity and the wholeness and the intactness and the Divine Order that our bodies have been created in. My confidence is in the Creator of our bodies, the ever presence of that being of goodness that always makes a way when there seems to be no way. My confidence is in the ever Presence of the power of goodness over darkness. My confidence is in the Source and origin of all goodness, all abundance.

"I have set the Lord always before me: because he is at my right hand, I shall not be moved. Therefore my heart is glad, and my glory rejoices: my flesh also shall rest in hope." Psalm 16:8-9

DAY 93

Change the channel.

If you're watching a movie that you don't like, you can always walk out of the theater. Or if you're at home, you can change the channel, or turn the whole thing off. When you're watching a movie in your life that you don't like, how do you turn the channel? How do you walk away from what you don't want to see?

What we do is try to change what is on the screen and what is being shown in the actual circumstances and events of our lives. So, when we are seeing, on the screen of our life, poverty, then we are trying to get more money. When we are seeing aimlessness in direction, we are trying to find a purpose. When we see a lack of companionship, lack of love, lack of feeling a sense of belonging, we search out another person or a group of people. We are trying to correct it on the level of the screen.

What we need to do is go back to the projector and correct what is being put into the projector. Correct what we are allowing, the imagery, the thought, the expectation. What are we allowing to be put into our minds? What are we believing? What are we giving ourselves to? What are we yielding to? What do we have confidence in?

Without energy, without expectancy, without confidence being projected toward a situation, it has to fail. Because it's not what you see happening, it's what's going on in the unseen world that's making it happen. You cannot give your confidence to one thing, and expect to see something else happen.

There is a projector that is perfect, whole, complete, intact, eternal, that brings forth in its image: the Mind of God.

"I know the thoughts I think toward you, saith the Lord, thoughts of peace."   Jeremiah 29:11

DAY 94

Tune into a higher mind.

One of my favorite patients over the years is a boy who was only four years old, but had multiple physical problems. Chay's mom would take him to the park, scoot him around on his hot wheels. She would lift him up and say, "God made you to walk, and you will walk." Then she'd let go of him and just before he crumpled to the ground, because he couldn't support his weight, she'd catch him. She'd say, "Honey, God made you to be whole and healthy and you will be whole and healthy. God made you to see, and you will see. God made you to hear, and you will hear. God made you to live, and you will live."

What was she doing? She was *deferring to the Mind of God.* She was turning the channel on the program. "I don't like it anymore, I've seen enough of it, I've suffered enough in it. I'm going to tune into a higher Mind, the Eternal Mind of goodness."

This Mind has brought forth everything in the visible world after its own image, but we don't see everything like that. We have been bringing forth everything in our personal world after what we have allowed to come into the projector of our mind. It makes no difference how long you have been looking at the same channel, because there is another channel that has never changed. All you have to do is change the channel. This other picture has been going on for all eternity and it's going to continue going on, whether you choose to hang out at that channel or not. As you stay with it, as you defer to it, you find that the imagery which is appearing on the screen of your life begins to change.

"Out of heaven he made thee to hear his voice, that he might instruct thee."   Deuteronomy 4:36

DAY 95

Life has a rhythm.

Life is God. Life is whole, it's complete, it's beautiful, it's glorious, it's full of splendor, full of majesty, wondrous to behold, from its infinitesimal to its infinite characteristics, from the tiniest blade of grass, the tiniest molecule, the tiniest insect, all the way to the grand and glorious solar system. Life is a grand experience of beauty and order, an order that cannot be thrown into disorder or confusion or chaos. An order full of Light, that cannot have any darkness.

This Life has a beat, it has a rhythm, it has a flow. From that beat and that flow, come forth more of its own being. If we were to look beyond what our eyes see, and *feel* the Life beyond, we would begin to feel that rhythm of Life, always harmonious, always in balance, always in order.

Life is a being. It doesn't have a form, but it has a character and it has substance, and it has its own intrinsic attributes. Out from that being, that energy, that rhythm, that beauty, that order, come forth all these wonderful things, including us. The only way we can see it and feel it and become part of it, is to let go of the world image of what life is.

We think we have to live Life, we have to make things happen, we have to take hold of life, possess it as our own. Actually, it's the opposite. It's in quietness and confidence and calmness and assurance that we enter. Just stand still, and begin to feel the rhythm of Life. It's always going on, whether we choose to be a part of it or not. This rhythm of Life flows like a river. We can get into it or we can stay on the banks, trying to figure out how to make life work.

"My people have forsaken me, the fountain of living waters, and hewed them out cisterns that can hold no water."   Jeremiah 2:13

DAY 96
Leave the thoughts behind.

My worst enemy is a feeling of inability to meet the demands of all the needs that come to me. It's a sense of responsibility. I begin to look at myself: "Look what I have to do, how can I do this?" Of course the answer is, "Why are you looking at yourself? You know it can't come from you, it never was to come from you."

Cast aside self-reliance, or any kind of personal selfhood, thinking that something is supposed to come forth from you. Let go of your own self. Even though hundreds of voices seem to be coming and pulling, saying, "Please help." Stand still until you feel, once again, that rhythm of Life. As you feel it, you realize it is not you, and yet you're very much a part of it.

When I do that, I am able to flow back into my day through quietness and stillness, through separating myself from, not just people and circumstances and events, not just going away by myself--I do that--but leaving the thoughts behind. Leaving the imagery, leaving the thoughts of all that seems to be pressing in on me.

Whether it's disease pressing in on you, or loneliness pressing in on you, or poverty pressing in on you, it makes no difference what the image is. Stop trying to fix that, stop worrying about it, or thrashing about trying to fight against it, or trying to find somebody to fix it, or constantly letting it mull around in your head, producing anxiety and fear and doubt. Instead just separate yourself from it for a moment, and be still and wait, and allow yourself to feel that pulsation and that river of Life.

"Be not wise in thine own eyes."   Proverbs 3:7

DAY 97

As the river of Life flows, it heals.

I knew a young girl who had broken off an engage-
ment, and she was very sad and lonely. She loved to
play the trumpet, and every day I watched her walk
past where I lived, out in the country. She would walk a
mile down to the Guadalupe River, and she would sit on
the banks of the river and play her trumpet. She would
just sit and think and play her trumpet. At first I would
hear the saddest, mournful sounds coming from that
trumpet, because it was coming from her heart, what
she was feeling. As the weeks went by, I began to hear
little tunes from musicals coming out, and by the time
summer was over, she was playing all kinds of ragtime
and jazz on her trumpet. I could sense that Life had
come again, that she had gotten in touch with the
rhythm and the flow of Life.

What did she do? Did she go from place go place to
try to find somebody, because she lost that one? Or did
she go back into the destructive relationship so she
would not have to be alone? Did she lose herself in her
work, or school, just to drown out the aloneness? No,
she got closer and closer into the stillness and quietness
of her own soul, and she began to feel that rhythm of
Life flowing again. As it flowed, it healed. As it healed,
it restored. As it restored it began to bring hope, a new
image of Life. Before she knew it, the very thing that
she went into that experience feeling like she was
lacking, she got back in abundance. In the fall she met a
man that is now her husband, they have three wonderful children and she's a very happy lady.

*"The water that I give shall be in you a well of water
springing up into everlasting life."*　　　　John 4:14

DAY 98

Choose to be a part of Life.

In the quietness and silence of your soul, be still until you begin to feel the pulsation and rhythm of this Divine Life. It brings forth goodness, and it brings forth after its own nature, its own characteristics, its own attributes and its own being. This is a being! Life is a being, and we are all a part of it. If we choose to be a part of it, we will enjoy the experience of it.

We can experience this mortal existence in total arrhythmia, trying to force our own rhythm of life. That's like a heart that is beating aberrantly and independently of the way that it's supposed to be beating. There is a certain rhythm of electrical current that goes through the human heart and then the body experences rhythm, but when the heart starts beating erratically, the whole body suffers.

So it is with our life. If we are trying to establish our own rhythm and make things happen, we cannot bring forth anything whole or good. If we will let go of all that, we will find ourselves in quiet and in confidence, which shall be our strength. Our salvation is to sit still. Whenever these Bible figures got into trouble they went away by themselves, they poured their heart out to God, and then they sat still. They waited for this rhythm to start flowing.

If we are pushing against the problem, we are giving it attention, place and space. If we let go of all that and let the reality that Life is producing come forth in our experience, it actually corrects and changes it.

"In returning and rest shall ye be saved; in quietness and in confidence shall be your strength."

Isaiah 30:15

DAY 99

Goodness is going to reveal itself right where the problem seems to be.

How do we get into this rhythm of Life? Recognize it really is there. Look at the seasons that come and go, the weather patterns, the sun rising every morning and going down in the evening. Everything is exactly in a pattern, and in a rhythm. Go out into nature. Turn off the television, turn off everyone's voice, separate yourself. Sit in quietness and silence until you become part of that river of Life as it flows.

What are some of the things that block the flow? Not recognizing that it exists. Not having the courage to stop and insist that you get in touch with it. We're afraid that if we ever stop running, whatever's coming will completely overtake us. It's just the opposite. If we stop all that human activity, we find that the answer is right there speaking to us, a real part of our being.

I sit there, with all the pressure of my thoughts, and in just a few moments, it all dissipates and I start feeling calm again. I start feeling myself as part of that flow and that rhythm. I know I'm right where I need to be. As it continues to roll on through me, I feel peace.

How does that bring about change? Once you touch that, you can rest assured that your answer is coming. You have just gotten in touch with an internal Wisdom, with the Divine Source of all Life, all goodness, all order. That is going to reveal itself right where the problem seems to be, superimpose itself over the image and experience of whatever the problem seems to be. It doesn't depend on you, on your worthiness, on your ability. What it does depend on is that you let all that go, and you wait and let it have its way.

"It is the Lord: let him do what seems to him good."
1 Samuel 3:18

DAY 100
Stay 100% immersed in the Source of all LIfe.

A mother's three year old daughter had a malignant brain tumor. Upon hearing her options, she said to the doctor, "Before I submit my daughter to this, will it rid her of the problem?" They replied, "No, but it may prolong her life." She took that little girl home, and into the master bedroom with her. The husband ran the household, took care of the son, cooked all the meals.

The mother took her Bible, some Bible storybooks for her daughter, she took tapes of someone reading the Bible,which was constantly spoken into the room while they were resting. She read stories to her daughter. She had a guitar and they sang all their songs, they made up songs. They read, they listened, for months. She never left that room, never took a phone call. Her husband brought food to them.

She stayed 100% immersed in what she knew as the Source of all Life. She knew that God had created and formed that child. She knew that child belonged to him. She knew that ultimately he was the only responsible party in this whole scenario, and she was going to stay 100% focused on that realization and that thought. She made sure that her little girl heard that, day and night. At the end of four months, the tumor was gone, and it never came back.

These people did not fight against the image, they did not use all the human resources offered, they did not stay fearful. They chose to look in another direction. To look away from death and hopelessness, and to look into the rhythm and Source of all Life. They found there was nothing they needed to contribute. They let the rhythm flow, let it bring peace to their hearts.

"Fear ye not, stand still, and see the salvation of the Lord."   Exodus 14:13

DAY 101
Everything we need is already available.

Beyond the life of the body is the understanding that Life is Eternal. It had no beginning, it has no ending. As we are flowing with the pulsation or rhythm of this being, or this energy, or this force, or this dynamic space, as we are flowing with it in a nonresistant, deliberate mode, then we get to enjoy all the charcteristics of it, the fulfillment of it, the wholeness, health, abundance, love, safety, security, not to mention the eternal, infinite, never changing experience.

Life is a Being separate and apart from human definition or human effort. It's separate from all the religious do's and don'ts designed to bring us into a state of purity so we are acceptable to God. The truth is we are accepted by God because we're created by God, out from that energy, and in the very image and likeness of that. Just as your children are acceptable to you simply because they exist and breathe, and they are a part of you, so are we accepted by God. We don't have to earn that acceptance any more than your children need to earn it. We can never fall out from it, no more than your children can fall out from the love and acceptance you feel for them.

Human effort and striving have no place in this Kingdom of Love and Kingdom of Peace. It only requires us to know it, desire it, be still and accept it. Accept and receive are key words here. Everything we need at this moment is already available to us in abundance, exceedingly, abundantly above all that we can ask or think. (Ephesians 3:20) There are resources that we could never conceive of that would be made apparent to us if we would but receive.

"Every good gift and every perfect gift is from above."
James 1:17

DAY 102

See yourself completely intact in your created perfection and wholeness.

Affliction has no legitimate claim. We don't deserve it, we're not guilty, it's not sent as punishment, it's not even sent. It's not inherited--our true inheritance is God. We come from God.

God is all-powerful, but the rhythm of Life is where all that power is. If we step out from that, in our thought only, because we really cannot, but if in our thought we have given power to something other than God, we're saying there is another substance, another power, than the allness and goodness of God. It's up to us to turn away from that, jump back into the river and flow of Life and find there wholeness, completeness and health.

See yourself as an absolute entity not able to be touched by affliction, completely intact in your created perfection and wholeness. Make affliction, in your mind, separate and apart from you, an intrusion. It can only come in if you open the door and allow it in. The minute you decide you don't want it you just open that door back up and kick it back out again.

A woman tried this, playing a "knock, knock" game with pain. When pain came knocking, she said, "NO, you can't come in, you're not welcome, I'm slamming the door on you." Did it stay away? For twenty minutes, then it came back and she did it again. And again. Finally it stayed away for good, after years of intense pain.

Affliction is an intrusion and we don't have to accept it. Don't give it a cause, because as soon as you do, it allows it to come in, because you've given it legitimacy. Reprogram your expectation to receive goodness instead.

"He has made everything beautiful."   Ecclesiastes 3:11

DAY 103

Expect goodness.

When things are going well, someone may say, it's been going too good for too long. Meaning, I expect something bad to come crashing in on me. Our expectation has become one of sadness and suffering, instead of an expectaton of good. We don't feel worthy, we don't feel like we've earned it. The fact is, we haven't earned it, but it wasn't up for earning. It wasn't something we were supposed to labor for. It's not like we're going to get a prize because we did good and somebody else didn't.

The Divine Life is as available as the air we breathe. Tell me, have we earned the air that we breathe? No, that's silly. We don't earn the air we breathe, we just breathe it. That's exactly how this Divine Life is, with all of its goodness, and all of its abundance, and all of its completion, and all of its fulfillment and all of its perfection. We do not earn it, it's just there. It's just all around and about us. We live and we move and we walk and we talk and we laugh and we love in the midst of it. We can just take it in, receive it, as we would inhale air, take in that goodness, take in the expectancy of goodness. Live in a confident state that God is present, is good, and shares all of that goodness and Life, not only *with* you, but *through* you, and not only through you, but *as* you.

Reprogram your mind to expect and to receive goodness instead of expecting and receiving lack, limitation, sorrow, poverty, struggle. Do it with one problem after another after another, until you have come to expect goodness.

"The blessing of the Lord, it makes rich, and he adds no sorrow with it."   Proverbs 10:22

DAY 104
We need to know God.

God has resources that you don't know, and I don't know, and we don't need to know. We need to know God. That's it. Even though a physical appearance says that you cannot do something or that something cannot happen for you, or that goodness is not apparent to you, you are still in confidence and in trust, though you don't see it. That's what it means to "Take up your bed and walk." (Matthew 9:6) When Jesus said, "Take up your bed and walk," some of these people hadn't walked in 38 years. They looked at their legs, and their legs didn't look like they were going to hold them up. One of them was dead! Clearly Jesus saw something that no one else saw. He saw Life when everyone else saw death. He saw wholeness when everyone else saw crippled. He saw "can do" when everyone else saw "can't do." He saw God. He saw multitudes of resources beyond our imagination, education or experience. That's what we're called to do.

When things come threatening you, and they say there is no way out, what they should be saying is, I don't know a way out. God has resources that none of us know anything about. Let's defer to the Mind of God. Let's yield ourselves to what God knows about the situation. Let's defer to that which created you, the Source and origin of your very existence, that which holds you intact in its image and likeness, that which has promised you the Divine and Eternal Life. Why not? Why not go there and wait until the way opens up where there was no way? Until the door opens where you didn't know there was a door. Until foliage and greenery appears on the desert floor.

"Show me thy ways, O Lord. Teach me thy paths. Lead me in thy truth."   Psalm 25:4-5

DAY 105
There is One Life, and that Life is God.

The Life of the body does not come from the body, nor does it depend on the body. Life is eternal and continual. The body is going to have to line up with what I know and believe. *The body becomes subservient to Life, instead of Life becoming subservient to the condition of the body.*

We must have a thought process, an understanding of Life that refutes the worry and concern over our bodies, that refutes the fear of disease. God is the giver of Life. How could disorder and dis-ease overrule the purpose, intention and presence of God or Life? When we live above the fear of dis-ease, above the preoccupation with the health of our body, we actually start living. Fear is not Life. We fear getting what somebody else got, we fear our own environment, we fear blossoms and pollen. Stop.

I am created by this Supreme Being with wholeness and goodness and order and harmony and balance. Nothing that could come forth in my body would hurt something else in my body. Everything in the body was created to live in harmony with everything else in the human body, and to support everything else. The Creator that created a flower and created me made us to live in harmony with one another. A house divided can't stand. (Matthew 12:25) I quit accepting disharmony as a normal consequence of life. It is a denial of the allness of God. I challenge it with a higher truth, the God-given Wisdom and understanding that is a part of me. The main thought upon which all other understandings must be built, is that there is one Life, and that Life is God.

"All things were made by him; without him was not any thing made. In him was Life."   John 1:3

DAY 106
Look to God as the Source of Life.

The human belief is that each one of us has an individual life and that we are personally responsible for that life and that life comes from within our body. In fact, all that is made, all that we see in the visible world, is an expression of the invisible God, the Life of God--the Divine, Eternal, whole, complete, perfect, orderly, balanced, harmonious, healthy, abundant Life . From that energy, from that consciousness, from that realm, comes forth everything that we call the visible world. What I'm calling my life is not my life, it is THE LIFE. It does not start from within the body, it *formed* the body, it flows through the body, and it animates the body. It does not have its Source and origin from within the body.

Why is that important? If you think your life started with something inside your body, then you have to believe that your body dominates Life, that your body is the Source and origin of Life and therefore your body determines your experience of Life. Then, if your body decides to get sick, your life is going to be shut down. Then, your body determines whether you live or die, your body determines whether you're healthy or not healthy, whether you're crippled or you can walk, whether you're in pain or not in pain.

No. Life is God! God determines all of the characteristics and attributes of Life! As it forms and flows through creation, you can expect harmony, balance, order, perfection, wholeness, because you look to that as the Source of Life.

"Your body is the temple of the holy spirit which is in you, which ye have of God, and ye are not your own."
1Corinthians 6:19

DAY 107
The Life that flows through you is perfect.

Tell your body, the Life that flows through you is perfect, whole and complete, that's what animates you and what gives you substance. That's what gives you breath. That's what gives you motion. That's what gives all the organs their intelligence and their activity. That's what keeps everything in balance and in order and in harmony. The body is not the dictator of life. Life is the supreme thought with which the body must line up. *The body is subservient to Life, and Life is God.* It is impossible for one organ in your body to be in conflict with the rest, or for one cell to be different than all the others.

There is one Creator, one Life, one God. This thought heals conflict between peoples. Conflict says, these people are different, have different backgrounds, look different. But if you put them all together, you see the wholeness and completeness of this God Life that brought us all forth. If we believe our life came from within us, and our lives are different, how can we live in harmony? We have to change our concept to know that all come forth from the same Creator. There is this one Life with multitudes of expressions that make up the whole.

We see a diversity in people, just as within the human body, there is one Life, but we see a diversity of organs, all working together to bring forth a whole complete expression. That's how it is with God. There is One Life flowing through, one expression of goodness and harmony flowing through all, and all of us feel the effects of that. If you stick to that thought, things change, because you are holding a higher principle: One Life.

"All of you are children of the most high."

Psalm 82:6

DAY 108
God doesn't know lack or limitation.

There are spiritual laws, absolute laws of truth, that superimpose over the laws of the physical. When we know these spiritual laws, and insist on them appearing in our lives, we see healing. As these higher laws of truth apply, the world law, or the law of the five physical senses, is of no effect, it is rendered useless, it dissolves into its native nothingness.

On the human plane, there is a law of attraction: like attracts like. Whenever we have a need, that's a demand, and we are looking for a supply. On the human level, life is a continuation of needs with us racing around trying to meet these needs, trying to supply the demand. We believe that we are responsible to meet the needs and to supply all of the demands of this physical human life.

There is a higher law of supply and demand, but we must realize that our life is not our own. Our responsibility lies in knowing and holding in consciousness that there is one Life, not multitudes of lives. Out from that being of Life and Love comes forth the visible realm. Within that Life is the law of attraction. That means that God knows no vacuum. God doesn't know lack or limitation. Before a vacuum exists, the answer appears.

"Before they call I will answer, and while they are yet speaking, I will hear." (Isaiah 65:24) Before you even knew you had a problem, the answer was on its way, was there. It may not have been visible yet, but it was there. There is a completeness in this one Divine Life, and in this completeness there cannot be lack and limitation. You can expect that what you need will appear.

"Trust in the living God, who gives us richly all things to enjoy."   1Timothy 6:17

DAY 109
God is the fulfillment of your need.

A young girl moved to a community in Alaska with her family. As she became a grown woman, she was 6'1" tall, thin and attractive. She realized there were only a few people there her age, no eligible males, none taller than she was. She thought, there is no way that I can meet this demand, or need, for a mate. She went to the pastor who led the community and said, "I need to go to the lower forty eight states and go to college." The pastor said, "Do you feel like God is leading you to pursue some career?" She said, "No, I haven't felt that." The pastor said, "Then why would you go?" She said, "Because I want to be married and have children, and there's nobody here."

The pastor said, "That is not a reason for you to go. You don't go out seeking your own supply. If you have a need, God is the fulfillment of it. The Life that flows through you is complete. It does not know a vacuum, it does not know lack or limitation. Don't look around at what's not here, look to that Life as the Source and origin of all completeness, as the law of supply to every demand and every need that you could possibly ever have." He even said to her, "If needed, someone will fall out of the sky! But don't go looking."

Several months later, a group of men in survival skill training parachuted out of the sky, and one of them landed right in the middle of their camp. He was 6'6", 22 years old. They met, they married and had children, and that was years and years ago. They're still together and very happy.

"One can receive nothing except it be given him from heaven."　　　　　　　　　　　　　　　John 3:27

DAY 110
Relinquish a personal sense of responsibility.

How can you know what will bring you the greatest
satisfaction and the greatest sense of fulfillment? Yield
to the Life that actually creates and flows through you.
It is the Source and the supply and the substance of your
purpose for being here.

Pause, relinquish personal ownership of the decision,
reliquish personal ownership of a personal life, to a
Divine Life. Realize that this Life is always in a perpetual state of completion and fulfillment, is always the
law of supply to every demand. Relinquish a personal
sense of responsiblity to go and get and do yourself.
Pause and recognize that the answer must come from
that Divine Consciousness, then the right avenue will
appear, the right direction that will lead you into the
greatest sense of fulfillment. It may be something entirely different than the direction you're going now.

Let's look at relationship. If there are two people who
cannot get along, what they're doing is looking at themselves and each other as being responsible to bring forth
harmony and peace. They could each say, "I relinquish
my personal rights and personal ownership of this life,
and I recognize that the same life flows through me that
flows through the other person. It's all one Life. The
same Creator created both, and is the Life that animates us. Within that Divine Life is contained understanding, intimacy, harmony, peace, love, gentleness,
Mercy. The answer is already contained within the Life
that flows through us. Let the Divine Life bring forth
the right spirit, the right thought, the right attitude in
us."

*"The way of man is not in himself: it is not in man that
walks to direct his steps."*   Jeremiah 10:23

DAY 111

I am your Life.

Divine Life knows no vacuum. It will appear any place you give it space to be. Step back out of the way, and say, *Here is this body, formed in your image and likeness, formed from Divine Life, functioning and animated by the Life that flows through it. I do not have personal ownership of this Life, I do not have personal ownership of this body. I give the ownership and the responsiblity where it belongs, to the Divine Life.* This heals the most tenacious of conditions, sometimes immediately.

Be a doer of the word, not a hearer only. (James 1:23) Apply the things you're learning. Those that apply it are the ones that get the results. If you change your understanding, if you see a different picture, if you have a higher concept, if you have a better understanding of truth, of Source, or origin, of Life and existence, and what it really is, then you will find you can live above what others are believing and thinking and unfortunately suffering from. If you apply one sentence, one word, one understanding, from the Bible, from the Living Beyond Disease books, other books, then there is no reason not to walk out of, and be lifted above, whatever you're experiencing.

Divine Life knows itself. It knows its own wholeness, it knows its own completeness, it knows its own harmony, its own health. It would never let itself fall into disrepair. It does not know lack or limitation. Stop looking at your body and turn your mind and your gaze to this Divine Life and the Presence of it. Hear those words, "I am your life."

"He is thy life and the length of thy days."
                                        Deuteronomy 30:20

DAY 112

Let Life appear.

"When Christ, who is your life, shall appear..." (Colossians 3:4) Now let it appear. Let it appear by letting go of personal ownership of your life, your problem. There is one Life, that Life created all that is, therefore, the ownership and the responsiblity belong to that Life. Recognize the allness of it, and the wholeness of it.

Here is a prayer I prayed for my daughter: *You are her life. You are the activity and the animation of her life. You're the Source and origin of her life. You are all Life. The activity of this Divine Life is stronger, more powerful, more whole, more complete than anything that she could dream up and call life. You have more of a powerful influence over that which you've created than the world has. You are the law of attraction to her. You are the law of supply to her need for wholeness, for order, for balance, for purpose, for direction, for right thought, for right activity. You know no vacuum, no lack nor limitation. You are continually the activity of wholeness and completeness, always appearing in order, in harmony, in balance, in perfection, in purpose and direction, in joy and happiness and fulfillment.*

Christ, who is her life, did appear, and she appeared as him. That's what will happen to each and every one of us who apply these truths.

"Ye are of God, little children, and have overcome...because greater is that which is in you than that which is in the world."   1John 4:4

DAY 113

What if we perceived ourselves as the pulsating Light of Life?

We are accustomed to looking at an affliction and looking immediately for a physical causation. Right away we say, I was out in the sun too long, or I got my feet wet, or something flew into the environment, or my mother had this disease, so I knew I'd get it, or I ate too much of this kind of food, or I didn't eat enough of that kind of food. Now we are extricating ourselves from that process, and seeing thoughts, our mind, our expectations, our belief system, as more of the causation than the physical.

People who are healed rose up, something in their spirit, in their consciousness, in their thought, rose up, and they walked right out of the affliction. They saw things from a different vantage point--they were not a victim of life. They didn't live life in an atmosphere of chance and probability. They decided how their day was going, they chose.

Why don't you decide? Decide based on truth. Decide based on what you want to see. What if we really were the sum total of the Christ on earth, which we are? What if we all could shed the human body for a moment and perceive others and ourselves as this pulsating Light of Life, an eternal experience flowing through all of creation, flowing through all of eternity? Full of Wisdom, full of goodness, full of order, harmony, balance, peace, wholeness, and only the expectation of good.

That's the true definition of Eternal Life. That's what flows through creation and animates all of it. That is what gives the activity to everything that is, this Life that just flows.

"With thee is the fountain of life: in thy light shall we see light." Psalm 36:9

DAY 114

Get a Life!

Make up your mind every morning to see Life as it really is, everywhere. You don't want to miss it. That's the prayer I prayed every morning, *Don't let me miss Life. In every tiny little detail, let me see it. Don't let me go whizzing by in my busy schedule, answering phones, racing around in circles trying to get things done. Don't let me get so caught up that I miss the little expressions of Life that remind me of what Life really is. Don't let me miss that the Author and Source and origin of Life is right here with us, and is the activity of us, the purpose, the direction, the wholeness, the completeness and the health of us. It's the happiness of us and the goodness of us. It's the intelligence and the wisdom of us. It's every wonderful thing of us as it flows through us.*

I got an email that said, "Get a Life, a real Life. Not a manic pursuit of the next promotion, the bigger paycheck, the larger house. Do you think you'd care so very much about these things if you blew an aneurism one afternoon? Or found a lump in your breast? Get a Life in which you notice the smell of the salt water pushing itself on a breeze over seaside heights. A Life in which you stop and watch how a red-tailed hawk circles over the water. Or the way a baby scowls in concentration when she tries to pick up a cheerio with her thumb and finger. Get a Life in which you're not alone. Find people you love and who love you."

Get in touch with what Life really is. That, in and of itself, as it flows through us, becomes the passion for living.

"Awake thou that sleep and arise..."   Ephesians 5:14

DAY 115

Make a decision for Life.

Make a deliberate conscious decision for Life every moment of every day, thereby deciding and choosing what you are going to experience. What we put in is what we're going to be living. I know what I don't want to see and what I don't want to think about and what I don't want to get involved in. I can make that choice.

I saw, on a rural road, a huge nest of 30 ducklings, all huddled together. They were so tiny, I could have put 2 or 3 of them in the palm of my hand. The mother was on the side of the road, trying to get them to follow her voice across the road. It was the tenderest moment, I will remember it forever. There was Life! All of a sudden it appeared, and we got to be a part of it. We watched while a few of these little ducklings got brave and took off and the rest followed. Off they went into the high grass, and we could see them going up the hill following the mother.

There could not be anything out of order going on in my body or in my life that was not just corrected by the presence of the tenderness and goodness of that moment. That's how easy it is to get in touch with Life. It's not just the tenderness of a baby grasping your hand with their tiny hand, it's realizing that what you're seeing is God appearing as tenderness to you. That's God appearing.

Those ducklings with the mother duck said to me, "I'm your mother, and your father, I watch over you. I'm not going to let hurt or harm come to you. I will always lead you into green pastures, a better place, just follow my voice. I'll take you there." That moment spoke a volume of information to my heart and to my mind.

"The invisible things of God from the creation of the world are clearly seen." Romans 1:20

DAY 116

The energy of a moment is enough to heal anything.

I believe that the disease that appears on our bodies comes from the convoluted thought and experience and expression and expectation that we're calling life, which isn't life at all. All the confusion of that scenario finds its way to external manifestation on our bodies, confusing the Eternal, Divine harmony of our bodies, throwing them into chaos.

I believe that if we can touch the true Life, if we can find it appearing, here, there and everywhere, in a flower, in a friend's smile, when someone takes your hand, it's a moment of connecting, a moment of remembering that we are one. These precious moments are the true life appearing as a tender moment, as goodness, as a reminder that it's ever flowing all around and through us. Look behind the visible, and recognize that we were just visited by what Life really is.

To me that is so much easier to get in touch with than making long prayers, or finding myself in church listening to somebody, or thinking that I have to sit very, very still in some awkward position, trying to meditate. It's just not that hard. It doesn't take effort.

It's just saying, *Father, today open my eyes and let me see Life everywhere. Let me see you appearing in all the various ways you appear in my experience today, to show me that order is still stronger than disorder, that light still prevails over darkness, that true Life prevails over this plastic life that we think we're living. Remind me that if I am willing to pause and to recognize Life(God), the energy of that moment is enough to heal the most horrible scene.*

"Rejoice evermore. Pray without ceasing. In everything give thanks."   1Thessalonians 5:16-18

DAY 117
Go from goodness to goodness.

Our acceptance of dis-ease in any area of our life--allowing any interruption in the flow of goodness, harmony, abundance, happiness, peace-- is a direct reflection of our understanding of God. A long time ago, mankind took on the notion they were separate from their Creator, and we lost the expectancy of good.

All disorder in our lives comes from a thought process that allows and expects disorder. We are born into the human race, and that human race has already accepted certain things as being true--one of the things is the necessity for suffering. We were not born believing that, we were taught that, because everybody around us believes it. So we have that expectation in our life, and the expectation becomes a reality. We can challenge the legitimacy of suffering, we can raise consciousness so that dis-ease is no longer part of our expectation, not a part of our life.

At one point everyone believed that the world was flat. No one challenged it, it was a fact in everyone's mind, but did that make it true? No. Even if everyone believes something, that doesn't necessarily mean that it's true. We are challenging the belief in suffering. Stand back, get out of the mesmerism that just goes along with what everyone else believes. Is that what you want?

I want to go from goodness to goodness, with the expectancy of good that radiates out to others so they also can learn to expect good. I believe that's what we were created to have. I have to get off that human train, with its destination of suffering. There is Life beyond disease.

"Thou hast turned for me my mourning into dancing."
                                                    Psalm 30:11

DAY 118

You shall live!

Everything that exists exists as a manifestation, a result of the Presence of this Divine Life that fills all space, fills all eternity, does not know a vacuum, and is constantly revealing itself in various forms that we can understand, and various concepts that we can grasp hold of. God is as close as our hands and feet, God is as close as the breath we breathe, because all things are revealing this energy, this Source of all Life and goodness. We are not separated from it, as we have believed.

Believing we were separate, we created images of a God who was fierce. If we obeyed we were blessed, and if we disobeyed, we were cursed. This is seeing God as a god of both good and evil. It says in Genesis 2:17, "The day you eat of the tree of the knowledge of good and evil, in that day you shall surely die." And, in the day that you eat of the tree of Life, in the day that you consider God as Life, and everywhere you see Life, you see God, in that day you shall live.

When we feel so separate, we don't understand what we're supposed to be doing, no matter how hard we try. I thought, what's the use of trying? Here's the answer that came: *I never told you to try, I never told you to try to please me. You please me because I created you. You please me because you are an expression of my Life. You please me because you exist.*

I thought about my daughters. They please me because they exist. They please me when they're crying, they please me when they wake me up in the middle of the night, they please me when they're good, they please me when they're bad, they please me because they exist. It's the same for God.

"God will rejoice over you with joy...he will joy over you with singing."   Zephaniah 3:17

DAY 119
I am a manifestation of the Divine Life of God.

We get back out of life what we image God to be, and we're imaging God according to the character that we've developed. If your heart is a heart of purity and mercy and kindness, then that's how you see God. If your heart is hard and judgmental and opinionated, bloated with self-importance and pride and ego, then you must see God as being that same way. It's impossible to please that kind of a spirit.

God says, "You shall have no other gods before me." (Exodus 20:3) *You have to know me as I am, and I am easily known by that which I have made, that which you see. Don't let an image you've created be engraven in your consciousness, because whatever you allow to be in your consciousness is what you're going to be living.*

There is only one law, and that's the Law of Love. We don't have to partake of the knowledge of good and evil, we don't have to try to determine what's good, what's bad. As long as we move in the Law of Love and Mercy, tenderness, kindness and grace, then we will also experience it. All we have to do is say, was that a loving thought, was that a loving act?

Because we are one, for me not to enact the Law of Love toward you is for me to hurt and harm myself. We are one because we came from the same Source, and it's the same Life that flows through all of us. We are who we are because we have been made in the image of the One who made us. If I see you as a manifestation of the Divine Life of God, and I know that's what I am, then I know we are one.

"Thou shalt love thy neighbor as thyself."
Matthew 22:39

DAY 120
Accept the goodness that is all around us.

We carry a belief of being separate from God because we were told that--we weren't born with that belief. We were also told we were less than beautiful and holy and perfect, and we carry a vague sense of not being quite right, of not being quite where we ought to be. This leads us to accept suffering as a way to try to make the wrong right.

God says, "I've made everything in my image and likeness, and it's good, everything I've made is good. I am one with all that I've made." (Genesis 1:26,31) If you have a vision of being one with your Creator, and you know that is good, and holy, and pure, and happy, and whole, and full of Life and energy, then you're ready to go and love the world, do all that you can do, give all that you can give, enjoy everything there is to enjoy, be blessed.

We insist on that, even in the face of circumstances that say it's not true. We insist on it because it is the truth, the absolute God truth that doesn't change, no matter what the human circumstances might be. There is no greater way to bless your Creator or to be blessed than to accept and cherish and love and acknowledge the goodness that is all around us.

We can walk right out of the human knowledge of good and evil. We get what we believe, and we believe according to our image of God. If disorder comes, we can stand back and say, "This is an intrusion. This is not part of the sphere of consciousness that I live in, where God lives. I will not accept this, because God made me whole and complete."

"He has given unto us all things that pertain to life and godliness...that ye might be partakers of the divine nature."   2Peter 1:3,4

DAY 121
I must be able to see myself as God sees me.

This is my prayer: *Father, this thing has come against me, and it is an intrusion in your Life, in the Life of goodness and order and harmony. I know that it is not from you, and I do not want to entertain this as a reality. In order for me to be able to rise up into a higher level of consciousness, I must be able to see myself as you see me. Father, show me what you see, show me what you know when you look at me.*

If I stay with that prayer long enough, I will begin to take on a consciousness of goodness and purity and order, and I will lose my fear or dread of whatever the intrusion was. Before I know it, it just goes away.

If I don't make that prayer, then it's my own human mind trying to make something go away, and it is impossible then to be healed. You can't heal a problem with the same consciousness that created the problem. You have to defer to a higher understanding, and there is no other understanding higher than the human understanding but the Divine Mind, the Mind of God. We defer to the consciousness of Life, the consciousness of Love, the consciousness of wholeness, of perfection, of order. That prayer changes your consciousness, and you see the human picture take on order where there was disorder, wholeness where there was disease, abundance where there was lack and limitation.

I heard from a young man who heard me speaking about this on television. He said he had been in bed with a disease for the last three months and had suffered a lot. He prayed that prayer: *God, show me what you see when you look at me.* He woke up healed, that is, he saw what God saw. It is that simple.

"Will you set your eyes upon that which is not?"
Proverbs 23:5

DAY 122
We are a Spirit Being who wears a body.

The source and origin of all disease is a lack of understanding of the true spiritual nature of man. We are first a spirit being who wears a body, not a body that happens to have a spirit. Does the spiritual nature of man have an effect on the condition of our body? Does it have an effect on the condition of our mind and our emotions? Does the knowledge of our spiritual identity have any effect on our relationships, on our finances, on our careers, on our purpose and direction for living, on our happiness? The answer of course is yes, it not only has an effect, it is the source and origin of all that is.

We are first spirit, we are first life energy, and from there we take on a form. This form is our physical being. The flow of Life, which we call Spirit, has a direct connection and is directly responsible for the condition of the physical body. If this Divine Life or Spirit Life is flowing freely, unencumbered, unhindered, unobstructed by beliefs, by opinions, by judgments, by anger, by resentment, by fear, by the expectation of negativity, then we will experience wholeness, and we will experience goodness.

If the flow of Divine Life, or the flow of our spirituality, is choked down, by any of these things I mentioned, then we see dis-ease appear, dis-order appear, disrepair, confusion, chaos, darkness. We have choked down the absolute laws of the Spirit. The greatest of all these laws is the law of Love, the law of Mercy, the law of forgiveness, the law of gentleness and goodness toward one another.

"The fruit of the spirit is love...   Galatians 5:22

DAY 123

Love yourself because God loves you.

The Law of Love is a continuing acknowledgement, moment by moment, that we live in a state of spirituality and it is good. Our expectation of Life becomes good instead of dread and fear and wondering what's next. We don't wonder what's next, we expect good. That's the way it's supposed to be.

God's unfolding to the understanding of the mind of man has been a progressive unfolding. Much of our image of God has been passed down through the opinions of people, not God. Job had an image of an angry God, and he sacrificed day and night, and as a result of having that image of God, he suffered. At the end of the book of Job, his image of God changed, he saw God in a different way. He repented, he took on a new understanding of God, and his life was blessed, his health was restored, all was restored to him again. Whatever image we hold of God is what we will ultimately, not only experience in our life, but how we will act out our life.

When Jesus came bounding on the scene, he said that the whole law can be summed up in the Law of Love. Love God, love each other, love yourself. Love yourself because God loves you. God loves you because he made you in his image and likeness, and when he looks at you, he sees himself. He sees a perfect, complete, whole, balanced, orderly, being that came out from his own perfect, whole, balanced, orderly, Being.

We realize that Love is what directs us, Love is what formed us, Love is the impetus that gives activity to our being, it's what animates us.

"We love him because he first loved us."   1John 4:19

DAY 124

God pursues us.

God is Love and Mercy and Grace, and without that moving in our life we cannot possibly live above the basic human nature. When that becomes the responsible, motivating issue of life, that's our spirituality. It's not even up to us to get in touch with God, God pursues us. God pursues the unfolding of His nature to man, God pursues showering goodness upon us, God pursues unfolding His nature, His character, His image, His person, His understanding, to us.

How do we know what God is like? You can see God by how he reveals himself. How would you get to know anybody that you wanted to get to know? You would spend time with them, ask to know them, to understand what they're like, what their nature is. I get to know a person by the things that they reveal about themselves.

If I pass a field of flowers, I realize that is God revealing himself right there. That's God saying, I am beauty, I am order, I am harmony, I am peace, I am something that you can depend on to bloom, year after year. I will always be there, you can depend on me, you can count on me. I don't change.

I say to God, *I have erased everything I've ever been told, or thought I knew or believed, now you show me. Show me who you are, what you are, what you're all about, what this life is all about, how to live it, what's expected of me, how should I see others, how do I heal others?* After years of this, a whole new image formed on the canvas of my mind. A whole new image.

"With lovingkindness have I drawn thee."

Jeremiah 31:3

DAY 125
Be willing to let go of the old.

Can our understanding of God be corrected? Yes, but we can't correct it. We can yield, we can surrender, we can pray, we can ask, we can spend time alone, we can really search to understand who and what God is. We can really pray to understand how that translates into the physical body or how that translates onto the human circumstances and situations of our life. We can pray to understand those things and then we will, because we've opened up our heart.

In order to open your heart and make a prayer like that, you have to be willing to let go of the old. You can't put new wine into old wineskins, (Matthew 9:17), you can't put a new understanding in a mind already filled with what it believes is true and what it thinks is right. If you're going to keep defending the old, then you won't be able to take on the new.

Until we change the basic consciousness of man, we cannot solve the problem of suffering. Until we elevate mass consciousness, we cannot come out from under the rubble of sorrow and suffering. Can that be done? Yes. At one time there was not a man, woman or child on this planet who did not believe the world was flat. One man proved that it was not, and the old consciousness of a world that was flat began to give way to a new understanding, a new perception, a new image.

It's time to look at Life, to begin to understand what Life is. Where does it really come from? Who are we, who are we when we leave this body, who were we before we came to this body? Why are we? It's time to explore spirituality, just you and that Spirit of Truth.

"That which had not been told them shall they see, and that which they had not heard shall they consider."
Isaiah 52:15

DAY 126
God sees us in a continual state of goodness.

The Divine Life would, in its energy of goodness, soar through us, bringing to manifestation and bringing to revelation all the wholeness and goodness of God. When we choke down the Divine Life, the Law of Love, we suffer the consequences of the way we've been believing, acting, thinking, feeling. Is God punishing us? No, we just choked it down. We can unchoke it.

In the Bible there is a story of a man who, though he had much forgiven him in his life, he refused to forgive someone who owed him. (Matthew 18:23) He carried an unforgiving spirit, and he was thrown into a prison of darkness, of confusion and suffering, until he learned that he must forgive as God continually forgives us. He must learn to see others in that state of goodness, no matter their actions, just as God sees us in a continual state of goodness, no matter our actions. That's what true forgiveness is.

True forgiveness is not, "I think you're a bum, but I'm going to forgive you." That's a condescending, self-righteous attitude. I must see them as God sees them in that state of innocence and purity and wholeness and lovingness and inability to hurt another person, because I know that's how God sees them and how God sees me. That's how he made us, and he hasn't changed his mind. He made us that way because that's how he is.

It all goes back to our image of God. What is your image of God? Is your image of God goodness, tenderness, kindness, gentleness, purity, innocence, always making eveything perfect, always holding everything in a state of perfection, always loving everything?

"Now my eye sees thee."   Job 42:5

DAY 127

Life will not be denied.

The most amazing thing on the earth to me is how a little sprout bursts its way through the hard thick covering of, let's say, a black walnut seed. You can hit those seeds with a hammer, and not be able to break those things open, yet out comes this tiny seedling sprout, so thin you can almost see through it, and yet it had the strength to burst through the shell that encased it. And if that wasn't dynamic enough, this thin little sprout pushed away the heavy sod and clods of the earth and pushed its way toward the surface, toward the sun. It is phemomenal when you look at the molecuar weight of a sprout compared to the molecular weight of what it took to break open the shell, and to push the clods of dirt and stones out of the way on its way up.

This is Life that will not be denied. Every time I see something green growing up out of the cement, or coming out of a rock, I smile and think, "Life will not be denied. It knows no obstacle, no barrier, nothing can stop it from having its experession, because Life is God and God is Life. There is no energy, there is no power, there is no Source of Life other than that, and nothing to be compared with it."

The seed does not look at the earth or the shell that surrounds it as an enemy, nor does it look at it as though it were part of its identity. That's what we do. We need to see ourselves as the Life that never changes, that's eternal, that knows no barrier to its expression, no obstacle. Nothing can be thrown at Life that will keep it from dominating the situation, from eventually rising up and dominating and overcoming the situation.

"He abides faithful; he cannot deny himself."
2Timothy 2:13

DAY 128

*I have, contained within, everything
that could possibly be needed.*

In nature, the circumstances do not dominate Life. Everything in nature says, "I am the Life and that Life is Eternal and it is the only power. I'm going to exercise the energy of that Life, I'm going to keep expressing out of my true nature, and those circumstances will become subservient to that Life. I don't see these circumstances as obstacles that have come to destroy."

Focus on being the Life, and not letting the circumstances become part of your identity. We are not the circumstances, we are not vulnerable victims of whatever comes. Do not acquiesce to the circumstances. We are the Life that never changes. The circumstances and events come and go. Don't see them as dominating your life, then they will not appear as suffering.

You did not create the circumstances, you did not deserve them, you are not being punished. That does not have any bearing on the absolute truth of being, and who we really are. We are the Life. There's only one Life and we are that Life, and we are made in the image and likeness of that Eternal Life.

We do this simply by a change in our perception, a change in our attitude. We are not victims, we are not vulnerable. If something appears, step back in your thought and identify with who you really are, not with that event: "I am a completely separate entity from that event. I am a Life that never changes. I have, contained within that Life, everything that could possibly be needed to walk right on through this. This is not something trying to defeat me, an enemy coming against me, it is simply something I will walk right on through."

"You are ever with me, and all that I have is yours."
Luke 15:31

DAY 129

*Having peace in a situation is the fastest way
to find yourself extricated from it.*

Having peace in a situation is the fastest way to find yourself extricated from it. Not resisting the circumstances and yet not acquiescing to them either. It is possible to submit and yield to the Presence of God in your life, to the goodness and the Love that surround you, without submitting to the dis-ease.

The best way to see yourself out of an adverse situation is to surrender to God in it. That is not to say that God has caused it--there is nothing in the Divine goodness that can rain discord and confusion. Each seed can only reproduce after its own kind. God can only bring forth after his own nature, and there is no chaos or confusion or disorder in the heart and mind of God.

The first step is humility. It is saying, "I've been going the wrong way down a one-way street. I don't know what I'm thinking, what I'm doing, or why this has come into my life." We reap what we sow. We're going to get back what we're putting out, what we're thinking, believing, fearing. Circumstances are not sent by God, rather, we allow them through our fear, our imagery. But it doesn't have to result in a head on collision.

Submit to God in the midst of the circumstances. Do not submit to the circumstances. Don't roll over and let them walk on you, don't acquiesce to fear or to intimidation. Do not get into the drama of it. Submit to God in his goodness and his Presence and his Wisdom, and he will lead you out of it. Use the circumstances to enable you to gain a better relationship with God, an understanding of God. Use this as a time set aside for you to come into an understanding of your purpose.

*"Humble yourselves under the mighty hand of God,
that he might exalt you in due time."*   1Peter 5:6

DAY 130
Dive headfirst into a relationship with God.

My first wilderness experience was when my second daughter was born and diagnosed as mentally retarded. I dove headfirst into a relationship with God. I found the characteristics and attributes of this entity, this Presence, this Divine Source of all Life that we call God, to be completely different than anything I ever imagined or was ever told.

I found that the goodness and the Mercy that comes forth from that Being is constant. I found the faithfulness, the trustworthiness, the loyalty, the dependability, the Wisdom, the direction, the completeness, the peace, the Love, that come forth from that entity, that Divine Source of all Life that we call God. I learned that Presence was ever present with me, so that I couldn't go to the right, left, up or down, without feeling that Presence. I learned the faithfulness of that nature, because I learned that God cannot do anything but what his nature dictates and demands.

The Bible calls these times our wilderness experiences. All the people in the Bible had a wilderness experience prior to some dynamic outworking of spirituality in their life, some incredible success.

What do you do when you find yourself in it? You submit to the God of all Life, to the God who is the Source and origin of all existence, the God who is your breath, the God who is your Life, the God who animates your body, who sent you here with purpose, to fulfill that purpose in you. Have you stopped and surrendered to the God who leads and guides your life? Have you stopped and prayed for wisdom and direction?

"Can God furnish a table in the wilderness?"

Psalm 78:19

DAY 131

Doing is different than being.

God sent you here with a purpose, to fulfill that purpose in you. You may ask, how can I fulfill it when I don't know what it is? We don't fulfill it, it is God that fulfills the purpose, but he does it through us. That which is appointed for me to do, he will perform. (Job 23:14) You do have to cooperate with the efforts to bring this forth. The way you coooperate is you get to know the Author of this purpose, the Author of the life that you're living. You get to know this by relinquishing and surrendering to the Presence of this, while in the circumstance, in the wilderness.

Do we need this circumstance to do it? If we're not in a wilderness experience, we are out being very busy, living unto ourselves, making money, we're out doing good, doing bad, we're out doing. Doing is different than being. The concept of being gives you the idea of stillness and quietness. Doing is what we do when we don't want to be still and quiet and get into that state of being.

The sooner you surrender to the goodness of the Presence of this God who is the Source of your life, the sooner you wil learn what you need to learn. That's why He is called the lily of the valley. The lily is the truth that you will find down in the dark valley of your experience. When you find that lily and pick it and hold it to your heart, then you will be extricated right up out of that valley.

That's the resurrection principle. What goes down will come up, darkness will turn into light, winter will turn into spring, adversity will turn into goodness.

"What wilt thou have me do?" Acts 9:6

DAY 132

There is nothing that can stop the flow of Life energy.

The resurrection principle comes from the experience that Jesus had of the darkest night of his soul, when he was put to death and put in the tomb. During those three days, no doubt he acquiesced to the Presence of his Father, to the strength of the Spirit that led and motivated him and was the Source and origin of his life, no doubt he finally came to grips that there was nothing about his body that gave Life.

Life doesn't come from the body, it doesn't come from what's been created and what's been formed, it comes from the Creator that formed the form. He was able then to yield 100% to that Spirit of Life that animated and gave him Life. He realized that it had not been taken away, and death couldn't even hold a candle to it. The experience of physical death could not alter or change the Presence of this Divine Life, which is God, this Spirit of Life that flows and nothing can obstruct it, nothing can get in its way. There is nothing that the human thought or experience can throw out there that can stop the flow and the Presence of this Life energy and force. It's impossible.

Why do people die? Sometimes they die because they have fulfilled their purpose and it's time to go on to the next experience. Other times, unfortunately, they die because they are looking at their circumstance and they're saying, "This has power over me." If they end up experiencing death, they awaken a moment after they stop breathing and see that Life continues, and they are a continuing entity and always will be.

"If ye then be risen with Christ, seek those things which are above...set your affection on things above, not on things on the earth." Colossians 3:1-2

DAY 133
There is only One Life.

There is a Spirit of Life that has power over me, not circumstances. I refuse to give power to the circumstances. I can't be giving both power at the same time, and if I give this circumstance power, then I have taken the power away from God, or from the Source and origin of my existence, which I have no right to do.

When was the last time you stayed awake all night praying for daylight to come because you were afraid that the day wouldn't come? Never. You know why? Because you trust. You know that darkness will yield to the light and you know the light will be faithful to come. When was the last time you prayed all winter because you were afraid spring would not come? Never. You knew it would come. Some things we know that we know, because we believe that nothing will change those things. Now, if we could just learn that about our lives.

There is only One Life, that's what we are, and nothing will ever change and make that go away. Why not yield to this Life? If you surrender to LIFE, the Eternal Spirit of Life that brought you forth, and realize that the Presence and power of that is immutable, if you can yield to that in the midst of your circumstances, you will find yourself very rapidly coming out of those circumstances.

When you surrender, you have begun to come into a relationship of understanding of the true characteristics and Presence of this entity we call God. You are created in that image, so you will begin to see yourself differently, and see others differently.

"Not that we are sufficient of ourselves to think anything as of ourselves, but our sufficiency is of God."
                                                    2Corinthians 3:5

DAY 134

Yield to the Presence of God.

Yield and acquiesce to the Presence of God, and let that lead out. It takes consecration, it takes dedication, it takes desire, it takes discipline, it takes patience. Impatience makes us want to run out ahead and make something happen. How many times in my life have I run ahead of the Wisdom of God before it was opened up to me, and run into what I call my proverbial brick wall? I didn't let Wisdom open the way for me. I didn't have the patience to wait and let it happen. I ended up in situations I had no business being in. My business should have been to be still. My business should have been not to let the circumstances cause such fear that I could not get in touch with the Presence of the goodness of God right here with me. Fear led my life from one mess to another.

We must not let that which we fear dominate us to the point that we are running ahead of Wisdom. We must wait and say, in the midst of this, where I'm suffocating from fear, *I am going to yield to the presence of the Spirit of Life, to the Wisdom that sent me, to the purpose that was intended for me. God give me the grace and stength not to run ahead out of fear, impatience, or because of what other people are saying.*

People say, what are you doing, sitting back and doing nothing? I'm not doing nothing. I'm praying. Day after day, praying for wisdom and direction and the grace to be still enough for it to come. That is the most active, the most pro-active, the wisest, smartest, best thing that you could ever do for yourself in any situation. Gradually or instantly, comes the unfoldment of the direction or the answer, or the truth you are being told.

"The effectual fervent prayer of a righteous one avails much."   James 5:16

DAY 135
God is always enveloping us.

What can we do instead of looking at a circumstance with dread and fear of it enveloping us, or with blame or condemnation, or with the human effort of trying to figure our way out of it? These are the reasons we end up so entangled in things, that we end up making choices without all the pieces to the puzzle. What can we do? We can make a choice based on Wisdom, based on knowledge and understanding.

Stand back, pull yourself and your emotions and your focus away from the circumstance long enough to submit yourself to the Source and origin of your life, which is God. As soon as you know that right in the midst of these circumstances you are really enveloped by the Spirit of Life, by the Presence and the Love and the Wisdom and the understanding of your Creator, then the enveloping comfort and security that you will feel will bring peace. Peace will bring patience. Patience will finally bring the answers that you seek. When the answers come, you follow the lead, and you're out.

If we find our lives shipwrecked, the only reason for that is that we spend so much of our life not yielding to the ever-presence of God. We think this is our life, so we must figure out what to do. We must be clear, God is not the source of the circumstance, but God is that which is always enveloping us, right in the midst of the circumstance. It's like air, you just simply inhale. It's that simple to surrender to God, the Spirit of Life that surrounds you, that would fill you with understanding and strength and Life and direction and would extricate you out of whatever you were into. Because it is Light, it can't help but overcome whatever is darkness.

"The eternal God is thy refuge, and underneath are the everlasting arms." Deuteronomy 33:27

DAY 136
You can strengthen the energy of Life flowing through you.

When you walk into a dark room and flip the light switch on, what happens to the darkness? Did the light fight against the darkness? No, there is no conflict. There is no conflict of good and evil. Don't get absorbed in good and evil, instead turn away from all that and get involved with Life.

The only thing that blocks the energy of Life flowing is human struggle. Life is way beyond the human. Because it is so present and so strong, if you would just pause and look at it, think about it, let it manifest itself, you'd begin to feel the Presence of this generating energy. Just turn to it, acknowledge its Presence, acknowledge that it fills all space and cannot be denied.

Genesis 2:5 says that the herbs and the trees and the grass were in the earth before there was seed planted in the ground. This is the result of the Life that never fails us. It will not be denied. The Life which animates you is this Eternal Life, the same Life that gives life to the plants, to the birds, to the planets, the same Divine Order that never changes, that is always present. By realizing this, you actually enable or energize or strengthen and empower that Life.

Believe it or not, we can empower the Life of God in our circumstances. That's why in Revelation 7:12 it says,"Blessing, and glory, and wisdom, and thanksgiving, and honor, and power, and might, be unto our God for ever and ever." When we acknowledge the Presence of God it strengthens the influence of it on our lives. It just starts pumping that Life through us.

"Make a joyful noise unto the Lord all ye lands. Serve the Lord with gladness: come before his presence with singing."   Psalm 100:1-2

DAY 137

God is always speaking to you.

There is a lot to be said for the exercise of worship and praise, there's a lot to be said for prayer, there's a lot to be said for meditation. There's a lot to be said for the silent moment, the moment of recognition that I am surrounded by the energy and Presence of Divine Life, the Eternal Life called God. I am so surrounded by it and it is so powerful and so eternal that I can lean into it. I can stand still and let it embrace me. Let it impart Wisdom and understanding. Let it impart Life and strength and energy. Let it impart direction and purpose.

When there seems to be nothing but darkness surrounding you, you yourself have the power to energize, and to release the power of this Divine energy of the Eternal Life of God. You don't have to pray and beg, you don't have to get everybody around you to pray, to get God to do something for you. You don't have to get God to do something that he's already doing, that he never stopped doing. You're just not in touch with it. The only way to get in touch with it is to quit all that and be still. Then you realize that it's been all around you all along. Just be still and let it do it.

What can we hope to learn when we turn to this Presence, this enveloping Love and Wisdom? You gain the true knowledge of the attributes and characteristics of God. You come into an understanding that would produce a relationship based on truth. What actually comes to you is through Divine Inspiration, from the Presence of the Wisdom of God that is enveloping you, and speaking to you right now. It's always speaking to you, always has been speaking to you.

"Man does not live by bread alone, but by every word that proceeds out of the mouth of God."
Deuteronomy 8:13 + Matthew 4:4

DAY 138

Line up with reality.

Each seed reproduces after its own kind; everything comes forth from its own kind. We can only produce that which we are, that which we contain. A poet, out of the abundance of the love in his own heart brings forth the beauty of the words that he speaks and writes. A flower can only bring forth the fragrance that it contains and the beauty that it contains. A cat can't bring forth a dog. You don't put a carrot seed in the ground and wait for a celery stalk to come up. Each brings forth out of its own nature, and so does God. The Creator can only bring forth after its own kind. We are created in the image and likeness of God. (Genesis 1:26)

We cannot judge the nature of God by looking at humans. We must find another way of searching out the nature of God. When we find that, we can challenge anything on the human scene that does not line up with that. As we challenge it, we overcome it. Instead of living the life of a victim, of complete vulnerability to chance, instead of living life afraid of our own bodies, we can go back to the Creator and say, "How are you really, and how did you make us to be?" Then we can line up with that reality, and we will see a change in our circumstances.

Nothing can change the truth of God. We can experience something that's not the truth of God because we believe something different. If we believe it and that's what we perceive, then that's what we'll experience, but that does not change the truth. "Whatsoever God does it shall be forever, nothing can be added to it nor anything taken from it." (Ecclesiastes 3:14)

"Of his fullness have we all received."   John 1:16

DAY 139

What does God know?

Einstein caught hold of the Divine Intelligence of God, and he realized he was created in that Divine Intelligence. He realized that if he stopped looking at the limitations of his own human mind, his own human resources, his own human education, and just paused and yielded to what he knew was really true, then thoughts and understandings, perceptions and concepts and wisdoms began to dawn on his mind.

Do the same. Look away from the picture of limitation, and know that is not how God made us. Look away to what you know is true about God. God is beauty and order. God is Life, and that Life cannot be interrupted, that Life is Eternal. God is whole, complete, perfect. God is the intelligence of everything that he's made.

We can look at the body and say, this was made in the image of God, and therefore, irrespective of what we see with our eyes, irrespective of what every doctor believes, irrespective of what every book says, irrespective of all the advertisements, irrespective of everybody else's experience, we can challenge disease. We can say, this does not line up with the truth of God. God cannot change his own nature, nor can he change what comes forth from his own nature.

We do experience suffering. These human experiences come from the whole human thought that we're sent into. We are sent to this darkness of thought for the purpose of bringing with us the Light of truth and correcting human thought (not succumbing to it!) Realize an elevated way of seeing, thinking, and experiencing. It's the difference between the mind of man and the Mind of God. What does God know?

"My thoughts are not your thoughts, neither are your ways my ways, saith the lord."   Isaiah 55:8

DAY 140

What really surrounds us?

We cannot let go and have total reliance on God as long as he is perceived as being the progenitor of our suffering, or even as long as he's perceived as allowing our suffering to exist. This perception is saying that God is the author of, and has a good reason for, human suffering. How can we have total reliance on God if we don't trust God? How can we trust what we don't know? Take the time and the effort and the quietness and the prayer to find out what God is really like. Get ahold of the absolute Love and goodness of the nature of God. Then we have no concerns over what may come in life, because we know that nothing bad can come. We are enveloped in the goodness of God.

That's different than fatalism, which is having no concern over what comes because I know that it will be good for me, and whatever happens to me, God's in control. No. It's living in the abundance of all good, in supply, in relationship, in love, in health and strength and vitality, in wisdom and understanding and intelligence and joy and peace. That's the nature of God, and we're enveloped in it. The goodness of God can't be anything but good.

We don't fear circumstances or situations, because we see beyond them and see what's really here. There's a story in the Old Testament (2Kings 6) where Elisha's servant stepped out from their tent one morning and saw the entire Assyrian army surrounding them. He was terrified and ran into the tent to Elisha. Elisha walked out and lifted his eyes to heaven and said, "Father, show this young man what really surrounds us." His eyes were opened to see a host of angels surrounding them.

"Cause me to hear thy lovingkindness in the morning; for in thee do I trust." Psalm 143:8

DAY 141

Rise above the human condition.

We need to go back to the drawing board, and we need to say, "God, what are you like?" We need to stop listening to people and their beliefs and understandings, shut it all out. You have to get it on your own.

One gift Jesus gave us was the Spirit of Truth. He said, "You have no need that any man teach you." (1John 2:27) "For the Spirit of Truth that I'm giving to you will lead you into all truth and he will speak of me." (John 16:13-14) All truth, not just a little fragment here and there, but the entire scenario, if you just accept the presence of the Spirit of Truth that was poured out to mankind, and say, "That's where I want to get my information. I am going to erase everything I've ever known or heard, and I'm going to find out from the source and origin of Life what this is all about."

If you did that, gradually you would begin to see things differently, with a higher conscious awareness, a different perception. We need our consciousness purged, we need our thought process, our belief system washed clean, we need the whole slate to be erased. We need the Spirit of Truth to start all over with us and make us know and understand what really is true. If you are willing to do that, it's fun, it's exciting, it's adventuresome, and it's harmless. It will not hurt you.

Go in humility to the Source and origin, to the Spirit of Truth that was promised us, that would be with us, constantly speaking the truth to us, so that we could finally understand, and we could rise above the human condition that seems to have enveloped us.

"When the Spirit of truth is come...whatsoever he shall hear, that shall he speak...and shall show it unto you."   John 16:13-14

DAY 142

I'd like to start all over again.

The highest way to extricate yourself from any human condition is to go back to the source of your life and say, "What is this? What can be done about it? What are the truths that I don't know? What am I believing that isn't true?" We really don't know, we have no way of knowing. We have to be willing to say, "I really don't know anything and I'd like to start all over again." God honors that. You will begin clearly understand things.

All the characters in the Bible, before they set out on their purpose, had a period of time alone. They took time to be alone, because how can you hear or know clearly what the truth is if you are surrounded by the voices, the words, the thoughts, the beliefs, the concepts, that are entertained by man, by the same consciousness that you were in when you got into whatever mess you are in?

We all live in this atmosphere of human thought and belief. We can't find our way out of a condition by remaining in the same conscious scenario that everybody is believing, and expect to come out of it. You are better off going away alone, going back to that which created and formed and breathed its Life into you. You live as its Life, as an expression of its Life.

Go back and say, "What happened? This does not make sense to me. How could a perfect God create something imperfect? How could a God whose attribute is immutability (that means an unchangeable nature of perfection) bring forth something unlike itself?" Instead of bringing God's image and likeness down to the human condition, why not be willing to change what we're believing and get more in line with the truth of God?

"If any of you lack wisdom, let him ask of God, that gives to all liberally..."   James 1:5

DAY 143

Consciousness was elevated to the mind of God.

If you're still entrenched in the same consciousness that created a problem in the first place, you do not have the sense of wholeness, the sense of Divine protection, the sense of living in a state of abundance, that you need. If it is not something you have experienced, if it isn't in your consciousness, then you don't have the expectation of it.

When I was raising the children, those first three years I didn't have two pennies to rub together. One day, I didn't have 35 cents to send with my daughter so she could have chili at school. She cried, "Mommy, don't we have 35 cents?" I stood there in the kitchen crying, because I didn't have 35 cents to give her. When I went to move the sugar canister over, there was 35 cents under it, and I gave it to her. I knew, because of that and a million things like it in those early years, that my supply never came from a job, didn't come from my bank account, my supply came from God, who is the infinite resource, who is the infinite, abundant giver of all and above all that we can ask or think.

As time went on, that gradually began to change my consciousness, until today I live in the knowing that nothing I ever need will ever come from an external source, and that I always have it, I live in it. I can't outspend God and I can't out-give God. No matter how much God gives me, I can give it all away and I'll still have ten times more tomorrow, because my consciousness was elevated to the Mind of God and what he sees and knows is true.

"The Lord shall open unto thee his good treasure."
Deuteronomy 28:12

DAY 144
Feel the perfection of God.

We need to be elevated into a different way of seeing things so that our life experience can be changed into a new way of living. When my daughter was born and diagnosed as mentally retarded, there was nothing anybody could do. Then one day, before she was three years old, she was spontaneously healed, in an instant.

It happened because during those scary first three years of her life, I did a lot of praying. "God, is this the image and likeness of God? Is this what you've given me? This doesn't line up with what I see as true." I read in my Bible that all the works of his hands are perfect, and we are his creation, formed in his image and likeness. Why are babies born deformed or sick?

Gradually my understanding evolved and changed, until I saw and felt the perfection of God. I felt it all around me, I felt the wholeness of it, the strength of it, the beauty of it. I felt the continuity of it, I knew I could trust it. The sense that enveloped me was no longer a sense of human conditions, chance, accidents-- that was wiped out, and I do not contain that anymore.

What has taken the place of that is a sense of wholeness, a sense of goodness. I know I will always live in goodness, because I feel the goodness first and then goodness presents itself in my human condition.

With my daughter, I began to see and feel her identity to be more akin to wholeness and beauty and order and perfection than to being a victim of a tragic beginning. I began to see things differently, not with my eyes, but with my heart. I began to realize that there is a huge difference between what God sees as being true and what we are seeing.

"When that which is perfect is come, then that which is in part shall be done away."   1Corinthians 13:10

DAY 145

This is not how God is seeing this.

There is a Mind that sees through and beyond all this hysteria that we live in, and holds in Its thought the absolute truth of what It has made. It is to that Mind we must flee whenever we realize we are entrenched in a circumstance we don't want to be in. Simply pause and recognize, "This is not how God is seeing this, this isn't how he made it." We need to let the Spirit of Truth correct our thought. When it does, you're healed at the level of consciousness. Then when health comes to your body, it stays there, because you have that *sense* of health and wholeness. When strength is returned to your life, it stays there, no matter how many years are added on to your life, because strength is part of the eternal picture of the Divine Mind. It's part of this Life, this One Life that brought you forth. When finances improve, it stays good and gets better, because you have that *sense* of living in the abundant goodness of God.

No more do you see yourself as having to reach out and make something happen. You can't reach out and try to change the human condition on a human level without having your consciousness first healed and changed and corrected, because it is out from our consciousness that these human conditions come forth. When the perception is changed, the whole human picture is changed.

We are living a life that we are imagining--that is imaged in our mind. Is it put there by generations of human thought, or is it the eternal Mind of God? It is to the Mind of God that we must defer.

"We have received, not the spirit of the world, but the spirit which is of God; that we might know the things which are freely given to us of God."

1Corinthians 2:12

DAY 146

My true nature came forth.

I know someone who has been healed in her life of some very serious emotional, mental, and character problems. This person has been dramatically and beautifully healed and restored to her basic nature and character in which God created her, which is his image and likeness. It is good, it is pure and it is not a victim and not vulnerable to such a lifestyle. Now she has a self image and a self understanding and a self identity--she knows who and what she really is.

She made this statement to me: *I firmly believe that I was not healed. I now realize there was nothing in reality to be healed of, but instead, it all just dissipated into the air when I realized who I really was. And when I realized that the character that I strove to become was always and already mine, by virtue of the fact that I was created in the image and likeness of God. I was only acting out what I thought was true about me, because I did not know the truth. If I believed that I was healed, then I would have to believe that at some point that was reality, or that was the truth about me, but instead I know now that I only needed to understand and to know something that I did not previously know. As soon as I knew it and understood it to be so, then the true nature that I was created in came forth.*

Dis-ease is not something that needs to be healed, but there is something we need to see and know and understand that is different from what we have been believing.

"Remove from me the way of lying...I have chosen the way of truth."   Psalm 119:29-30

DAY 147

We live in God.

"In him we live and move and have our being." (Acts 17:28) Not in disease, not in vulnerability, not in a life victimized by our body or by circumstances. We live in God. We can choose to look away from the human circumstances and focus on Life, on the Presence of God.

Remember Daniel in the lion's den? (Daniel 6) If he had focused on the fierceness of the lions and the situation he was in, the fear would have caused the lions to eat him. But he didn't, he focused on the God that was ever present as his protector, the Presence of God that he had learned to live in. He knew that whether he was in the den of the lions or safe and secure at home, he was enveloped by the Presence of this God that he had come to know so clearly. He knew the Presence of God more than he knew the human circumstances.

"The works were finished from before the foundation of the world." (Hebrews 4:3) God is not changing anything that he has done. The way God made it is the way it is and it's perfect. So what is this circumstance surrounding us? It's hysteria, it's obsession, it's an attraction to misery. Dis-ease was never part of the creation of God. And it is not something he is using to teach us something. It is something we have to turn away from, or we will never grasp the truth.

A body is not healed by calling it diseased. Someone is not going to experience prosperity by declaring their poverty. It's impossible. It's like going to Houston following a Los Angeles map. You cannot find yourself going in the direction you want to go while you're still declaring yourself in another direction. It's impossible.

"My kingdom is not of this world."   John 18:36

DAY 148
Something can just disappear when a higher understanding comes to consciousness.

Judge righteous judgment. (John 7:24) What does that mean? Righteous judgment is what God sees through the eyes and mind of God, what he knows is true, what he knows he has made and created and formed and brought forth. Unrighteous judgment is if we declare something to be true based on what the human is seeing, on the five physical senses: what I see, what I've heard, what I've been told is true, what I see other people experiencing, what I can feel. Righteous judgment says, "Although I see this a certain way, my judgment in this situation will be according to what God has made and not according to what I see." The Bible is telling us how we're supposed to be seeing things.

Isaiah 25:7 speaks of a veil covering the faces of all the people. It says when that veil is removed, there will be no more sorrow, no more death, no more disease, no more suffering, no more tears. Not because something changed, but because a veil that was covering our understanding, covering our ability to see clearly, is finally removed. If we see something more clearly, then what we thought was our enemy is just gone. It's just not there anymore.

The veil is the distorted way that we're viewing Life and God. Dis-ease is declaring there is a place where Divine Order has been interrupted, where the government of God has been obstructed. That can't be true, and still have an omnipotent, all present God who is the Life of everything created. Don't give reality to something that can just disappear when a higher understanding comes to our consciousness.

"In that day...the eyes of the blind shall see out of obscurity and out of darkness..." Isaiah 29:18

DAY 149
The goodness of God is poured out...grab hold!

Humans insist on finding a reason for things happening. Our biggest enemy is insisting on finding a cause. As long as we give a cause to things, as long as we believe that we are part of the human law of cause and effect, then we try to create all these causes and we come up with these effects.

There is a higher law, the law of the truth of God, the law of Christ. Christ is the visible expression of the invisible God. We all are visible expressions of the invisible God. We were made in the image and likeness of God; everything that is made declares the Presence of the Divine Life of God, the Presence of Divine Order, the Presence of the self government of God. All of creation is the Christ. As Christ, we can choose to come under that law that is not subject to the law of cause and effect on the human level.

To "choose this" is to say, "No, I will not accept this. There is no reason for this to exist, I'm going to come out of it." One young man had a terrible stuttering problem the whole time he was growing up. He was embarrassed, kids made fun of him, he hated himself for doing it. One day, in desperation, he fell across his bed, put the pillow up against his face and screamed, I will never do this again. There is no reason for me to do this. God did not make me like this, there's no cause for it. He stood up, and he never stuttered again.

Call upon the truth, the absolute truth, the truth of the way you've been created and who you really are and what is available to you. The goodness of God is poured out. Either you grab hold of the goodness of God, or you miss it, but it's always available.

"If ye be led of the spirit ye are not under the law."
Galatians 5:18

DAY 150
We have always been in the mind and heart of God.

We believe that because disease shows up as a physical manifestation, the cause is certainly a physical cause. We have all been told that we get a cold because we have a germ. We don't believe that anymore, no one's ever found that germ. Then alternative medicine comes along and says you have an accumulation of metabolic toxins in your system, and that caused the immune system to break down, and that's why you got a cold, and that's why flushing the system out and rebuilding the system causes you to stop getting colds.

Even though that is a far superior and far more accurate picture on the material level, still there is another level of thought and understanding that we must pursue in order to break out altogether, to break out of seeing physical manifestations as having physical causation.

We want to see as God sees, we want to take on and understand the Mind of God, the vision of God. Why? Because God is the Source and origin of all Life. It says, "Whatsoever God has made shall be forever, nothing can be added to it nor anything taken from it." (Ecclesiastes 3:14) God made us in his image and likeness and has not allowed anything to come and be added to that, such as disease, death, unhappiness, poverty, isolation, purposelessness, nothing. Nor can anything be taken from us that God has given us, such as Wisdom, perception, understanding, Eternal Life. We have always been in the Mind and heart of God as an expression of his nature, and we are now, and we always will be.

"We look not at the things which are seen, but at the things which are not seen, for the things which are seen are temporal, but the things which are not seen are eternal."   2Corinthians 4:18

DAY 151
We serve an unlimited God with unlimited resources.

The physical body is no more than an objective manifestation of whatever you hold in thought concerning your image of yourself. Just as you are formed, the flowers are formed, the creatures are formed, the planets are formed, all from what God holds in thought concerning his own being. Everything is created for the purpose of expressing the reality, the Presence, the truth, the allness, the nature, of he who created everything in his image and likeness.

If we see God as the source of all Life, not just the spiritual Life, not just that which cannot be seen, but all that we see, then we come to a dilemma. We say, I have this body and it fell apart, but it says, "Whatsoever God has made shall be forever." (Ecclesiastes 3:14) What do I need to understand?

If you say, "My life depends on the health of my body, and that depends on how I feel, or on what the doctors say," you have just limited your life to the world's concept of the human body, when actually, your life is an expression of the Life of God, and your body doesn't define the condition of your Life.

We don't live in chance and probability, we live in God. In that we are safe and secure, whole and complete, and continually being governed by his goodness and his Presence, but *we have to know that*. The minute we look to something else and believe we're being governed by our body, then we're not serving an unlimited God with unlimited resources and knowing that huge provisions are constantly being poured out upon us in all kinds of different ways.

"It is the spirit that quickens, the flesh profits nothing."   John 6:63

DAY 152
God is not separate and apart from us.

I don't always use the word God. I use the word Divine Life, or Divine Love, or Divine Order. I do that because it is critical that we learn the true nature of what God is. It is also critical that we come to a place where God is not a being separate and apart from us, who we fear and who we do not understand, and therefore cannot trust. We must come to realize that this is not a personal being, it is a Spirit. It is not a male, it is both male and female. It is not an allusive being who created everything and then sits back, folds his arms, and judges how well we do. That is the vision I had growing up and what I believed was true. When I got into problems way over my head, I felt responsible, condemned, guilty, and very, very angry at being left to deal with things that were beyond my resources and beyond my ability to deal with.

I was at someone's bedside who was dying, and the family said, "It must be the will of God." I don't know how you can see a person in such a horrible state of destruction and believe for one minute that could come forth from the heart of Love. How can we pin that on God? It tells me we have no idea what God is. Why is it so critical that we find this out? Because as soon as we find it out, our life, our body, our finances, our relationships, then conform to the image that we now have cleared, and that we now hold as being true.

We are simply living out in our life experience what we image to be true about God, about our source and origin of our Life, about who we are, about where we've come from and where we're going.

"I shall be satisfied when I awake with thy likeness."
Psalm 17:15

DAY 153

My Life is hid in God.

My Life is hid in God. (Colossians 3:3) My Life comes from God. My Life is an expression of the Life of God. My Life is my spirit and it's what animates me, and it animates my body. My life declares the condition of my body. I will not let my body declare the condition of my life. My life is governed by God, who is the Source and origin of Life.

It says, "I am your life and the length of your days." (Deuteronomy 30:22) The body doesn't determine the length of your days, *I* am the length of your days, and *I* am an Eternal Being, therefore out of the substance of my eternalness, you come forth in that image. You too are an eternal being. That makes the body line up, but it's you who have determined what law you come under. You can either come under the law of what the Bible calls sin and death, or you come under the law of Life. (Romans 8:2)

Make some prayers to help you understand this, because gone are the days that we run off to other mortal men and women, or go to Rome or to Mecca or to Tibet, to find out what God is saying. Gone are the days when we look outside of the orbit of our relationship with God and the Spirit of Truth that was so freely given to us, that promised to lead and guide us into all truth and all understanding, into Life abundant, into wholeness, into Life eternal. It was a gift, it's here, it's now, it's a Presence that can be felt, can be heard, can be known, can be trusted. It will be faithful, it will speak the truth of God, and it will lead and guide us into all truth.

"Thou will light my candle: my God will enlighten my darkness."   Psalm 18:28

DAY 154

We are living the Life of God.

What we see is each one having an individual life, and that life is contained in a body, and the body determines the condition of that life. Then we live in fear, under the law of physical cause and effect that God never intended us to live under.

In 1Corinthians 11:30 it says, "Many are weak and sickly among you and many sleep because they do not discern the body of Christ." I prayed to know what that meant, because if I knew, I would understand why people were sick. Here's the reason: they are not realizing the One Life, which is the Life of the Father. They are not discerning that there is One Life, one expression of that One Life, and that Life is outside of the body.

This Life is too unlimited, too eternal, too immortal, too vast in its expression and its goodness and in its being, to ever be contained within a body or within any part of its creation. Rather, the creation is the visible manifestation of this magnanimous One Life, one Being, One God. In Colossians 1:15, it says the Son, Christ, is "the image of the invisible God."

We are living the same Life that Jesus lived: it's the Life of the Father. There is only One Life and only one Source of Life. There is only One Life with many, many expressions, two-footed, four-footed expressions, plants, planets, all kinds of expressions of the One Life.

In 1Corinthians 10:17, it says, "For we being many are one bread, and one body: for we are all partakers of that one bread." You look at one loaf, but you realize there are many, many pieces of grain that make up that one loaf.

"I pray that they all may be one, as thou, father, art in me, and I in thee, that they also may be one in us."
John 17:21

DAY 155

Peace begins to reign.

The One Life is God, and it is expressing itself as and through creation, and you are not even in the equation. That which you thought you were, the image that you held gets swallowed up by the reality of this truth. There is One Life. Fear goes, and a false sense of responsibility for your life to be led in wholeness and in order goes with it. Peace begins to reign. It is a whole different way of perceiving Life, a whole different way of living life. Joy and happiness and peace and the expectation of goodness overcome you, so you do not live in fear, or under the law of chance any longer.

There is a veil that covers the face of all the people. When that veil is removed, there will be no more death, no more disease, no more tears, no more suffering. (Isaiah 25:7) This veil is what we're all believing. The veil is seeing Life contained within the thing that's created, as though God could be contained within a finite form, as though the infinite could be contained within something that it has brought forth.

If that veil, that confusion, can be rolled away like a scroll, then what stands present before us is what has always been. The way we have been perceiving life needs to be rolled away, so that which is true can appear. There's nothing that needs to be changed. Behind that veil, you've never been sick, you've never had lack or limitation or tears, you've never known confusion and disorder. We simply have to understand that what God has made has always been and will always be. Behind that veil, the fullness of the expression of the Life that created you is in its full glory. "Of his fullness have we all received." (John 1:16) We have it all.

"When they shall turn to the Lord, the veil shall be taken away."   2Corinthians 3:16

DAY 156

Hear the voice of creation.

"The heavens declare the Glory of God and the firmament shows his handiwork. Day unto day utters speech and night unto night shows knowledge." (Psalm 19:1-2) We are encouraged to look at all that has been created and to hear the voice of creation. If creation was created to declare truths, then certainly, since we are also created beings of the same Creator, we have an inborn ability to hear and understand. Animals have an intuitive nature, they know how to birth their young, the newborns know to eat. They know where to go to get food, what to do when they're sick. This knowing comes from the Mind that created them. Why would we be any different? Why do we think we are separate from the Mind that created us?

Jesus spoke the words of our Creator. He said, "When I go I'm going to send a gift, the Spirit of Truth." (John 16) It's the same Spirit that spoke to him while he walked the earth. He said, "I will just take that Spirit that was given to me and I will pour it out upon everyone. You all will have the same ability to know, to perceive, and to do the works that I have."

We have not worked the works because we are not leaning in to this Spirit of Truth that speaks day and night, continually declaring to us anything and everything that we need to know, answering every question we have ever asked.

Try this. Think of a question you really want an answer to. Close your eyes, recognize this Spirit of Truth, ask your question. You will notice that before long you understand the answer. The answer can dawn upon your mind in a million different ways.

"Unto you it is given to know the mysteries of the Kingdom of God"   Luke 8:10

DAY 157
The human condition will conform to the truth.

We trust in our own ability, our own resources, rather than knowing that all around us the voice of truth is speaking. When we get into a state of stillness, no matter what may be bearing down upon us, when we have prayed until we have found the "rest of God," we know this truth: "The works were finished from before the foundation of the earth." (Hebrews 4:3) Everything that needs to be done has already been done.

We do not need to declare to God what needs to be done, how he needs to fix this. We need to realize, deep in our hearts, that what he has made, he made from his own image and likeness, in a state of wholeness and perfection and order and beauty and harmony and balance. In the Mind of God, and in the works of God, nothing has changed. God isn't scrambling around trying to find some resource to get us out of the mess we're in. That which has been made *is*. As soon as we understand it, then our human condition conforms to that truth. The only thing that will change is our understanding. It will conform to the truth, and the human picture will be corrected.

If you're still and you're quiet, you will hear a word behind you saying, "This is the way, walk ye in it." (Isaiah 30:21) This is a promise, so that we don't find ourselves in a situation that can consume us. There was never a situation created by God to hurt or consume us. The only way something could appear to consume us is if we are leaning into our own understanding, instead of being still and letting that energy build until the word of Wisdom and truth comes to clear the air for us.

"If I take the wings of the morning, and dwell in the uttermost parts of the sea, even there shall thy hand lead me."   Psalm 139: 9-10

DAY 158

The energy of Life goes before us.

What is fasting? In the Hebrew, the word fasting means "to cover one's mouth." The common understanding of that is not to eat, but the real meaning of the word is to stop talking. As we stop talking, we are no longer dissipating the energy building within us.

When a seed is put into the ground, the energy of LIfe begins to build and build, until finally it comes to a place where it breaks open that shell that surrounds the little sprout, allowing the release of the sprout to begin its journey upward. The energy of Life goes before that sprout and pushes off the heavy sod and dirt along its path. It goes before and clears the path for it, much as is spoken to us in Luke 3:5, "I will go before you and I will make the crooked way straight and I will bring down the tall mountains and make them a plain and I'll bring up the low valleys and I'll make them a plain."

When the Israelites came to the wall of Jericho, (Joshua 6) it was way too tall, too thick, too wide, too deep, for them to get around, over, or through. It was a seeming obstacle in their path. They did not take it personally, nor blame their past. They did not pass out shovels to dig under the wall, or hammers to burst through the wall--no human effort. They didn't question, "Why is it there, did I make a wrong turn?"

What they did was they got quiet. Knowing who leads this journey, knowing whose Life we live and that we are not personally responsible to have the answers, they said, "What do we do?" The answer was to march around the wall, not speaking a word, for seven days. The energy built and built, and on the last day they gave a shout and the walls fell.

"Be still and know that I am God."   Psalm 46:10

DAY 159

Effortlessly act out of that nature within us.

The animals get sick and they go down by the river and dig a hole in the mud and bury themselves in the mud so the coolness can break their fever, they just drink water, they don't eat, they chew certain herbs, they know what to do. They listen. They don't know they're listening, maybe, but they are following that which intuitively comes to their mind and heart. They are not struggling with their own intellect, trusting in their own ability to fix something, believing they are personally responsible for a life that they didn't create. All of creation declares this truth. It's time for the humans, made in the image and likeness of the Creator itself, to learn the basic foundational Wisdom of Life, which is, THIS LIFE IS NOT OUR OWN. That which formed it, that which breathed its Life into it, that which has a definite course for every Life to take, will also provide all that is needed for that Life.

Let us get into quietness, stillness and confidence. Let's learn that healing can only come as we enter into that state of quietness and rest, *knowing* that "The works were finished from before the foundation of the world." (Hebrews 4:3) In the silence, in the covering of our mouth, in not sharing our problem, not turning to and fro frantically from one person to another, one teacher to another, but in the stillness and quietness, let whatever is being spoken to us be absorbed deep into our spirit, until it becomes part of our nature, until we are effortlessly acting out from that nature within us. Stay quiet and let these truths go deep into our souls. Let them change us.

"We have this treasure in earthen vessels, that the excellency of the power may be of God and not of us."
2Corinthians 4:7

DAY 160
Seeing the Christ.

We want to understand the human body as it was intended in the Mind of God, as it is yet held in the consciousness of God. Once we see how God sees our body, then we will realize not only how impossible it is for it to disintegrate into something less than that, but how simple it will be for us to find restoration and healing and a rebuilding of what was intended to be. We can know God by studying the human body and realizing the spiritual nature of each aspect of the human body, just as we can understand God by studying nature, by studying anything that has been created by God.

We can spiritualize the body, look beyond the visible, beyond what is seen. We can understand the nature of each aspect of the human body as it relates to the nature of God, who made it in his image and likeness. Since God is Spirit, we can know that though we appear as tangible and mortal, we are actually spirit beings made in his image. We are beings of Light with an energy-magnetic field. That's what flows through us and makes us work.

"The body is Christ." (Colossians 2:17) The word Christ means the visible expression of the invisible God. It's anything that's been created, in the earth, in the universe. If you look at that which has been created, and you insist on understanding and seeing the Life that formed it, then you are seeing the Christ.

Look at a flower, see the beauty of it, and realize that must be the nature of God. God must be beautiful. Look at the seasons, and see the order. God is absolute, perfect, unchangeable order. We look at what God has made, and by what he's made we know him.

"God made every plant of the field before it was in the earth." Genesis 2:4-5

DAY 161

There is Life within every creature that cannot be touched.

Instead of looking at the body as tangible, mortal, flesh, bones and blood, look at the dynamics of it, to understand more of the nature of the God that made it in his image and likeness. Then we will understand our oneness with God. We will understand the Divine nature of our being. See our body as the Christ, the visible expression of the invisible God.

To realize our true spirituality is to realize our indestructible nature. Our body cannot be interrupted, it cannot be maligned, it cannot be destroyed, it cannot be altered. We go beyond man's limited understanding, into that which is eternal and never changes. We have not been experiencing the absolute truth, we have been experiencing what we've been believing. We can change what we believe.

I saw on television a show about a man who heals horses, physically and spiritually. He was asked, "Do you ever meet a horse you cannot heal?" He said, "No, I don't believe that. I know there is a life down deep within that horse that cannot be touched, no matter how broken this horse has become, no matter how abused this horse has been, no matter the damage done, there is that Life down within every creature created that cannot be touched. If I can reach that, then I can heal anything, because that will release the energy from that core Life, and it will heal the animal."

If we can get past focusing on the damage to the human body, if we can touch the core Life, that eternal Life, then we can see a healing. I have seen it and I know it's true.

"That life is the light of men."   John 1:4

DAY 162

The mind of God controls the entire creation.

Think of the brain as a visible manifestation of the Mind of God. The Mind of God controls the entire creation, just as the brain controls the body. God sends messages to creation, because he has purpose and order and direction for everything that's been made, just as the brain sends messages to animate every aspect of the body. The mind of God holds everything in Divine Order, just as the brain holds everything in the body in order.

We, as every other aspect of creation, automatically receive impulse and understanding from the Mind that formed us. Instead of looking to the physical brain, we go beyond what is visibly seen and realize this is a visible manifestation of the invisible Mind of God that governs and controls every aspect of this body. If that is true, where is there room for disorder and disease?

Think of the heart, which supplies life to the rest of the body--the life is in the blood. If there was any cell in the body that was not receiving blood, that cell would very soon die. The heart is that visible manifestation of God that supplies Life to every aspect of creation. If God is responsible to supply Life to every aspect of creation, where could there be disease?

Think of the liver, our chemical factory. It knows what every cell and system needs and it supplies those needs on a continual basis, without hesitation. We don't need to know what we need, the liver knows. This corresponds with the Divine intelligence of God, who is cognizant of everything that is needed. God goes before us and supplies the needs we have before we even know we need them. How can we then believe he dropped the ball and allowed us to get sick?

"I will lead them: I will cause them to walk by the rivers of waters in a straight way."　　Jeremiah 31:9

DAY 163
"Take no thought for your life."

Let's look at the immune system. It is the great protector. We don't need to direct it nor does it consult us,
but simply day and night, it is ever present to protect us
from things we don't even know we are needing protection from. We have no concept of the vast supply of
protection that goes on continually, that we never think
about, we never have to worry about. It simply does it.

The human immune system is a visible expression of
the Presence of the invisible God, and that particular
aspect of his nature, which is constant protector. God
does not get worn down, he doesn't get overused and
abused, nor do we have to direct, instruct or give
thought to it. Matthew 6:25 says, "Take no thought for
your life." Why can we take no thought for our life?
Because we have this Divine protector, in the form of
the immune system. The real truth beyond the visible is
going on day and night without us realizing it. It is
constantly in operation and it's eternal. It can't be
destroyed or interrupted.

The white blood cells declare the nature of the
Christ. They lose their life but it makes no difference,
because of the joy of fulfilling what they are sent to do.
Even though the visible expression has been lost, the
invisible is dynamically alive.

I'm sent for a purpose, and no matter what the cost
is, I've come to serve my Creator. It's a joy to complete
my purpose. In yielding to our true nature, and in yielding to the invisible God behind the visible scene, we
find the joy of giving. That is the white blood cell. It
doesn't have to be the physical life, but any aspect of
life we lay down.

*"Greater love has no man than this, that he lay down
his life for his friends."* John 15:13

DAY 164
Choose to see all things as spiritual.

Choose to see all things as spiritual. Choose to see the Life of the thing, not just the thing. We're trading one creation for a greater creation. When we start looking at the body this way, we begin to see ourselves as higher created beings, spiritual beings. In that context, we are indestructible. We are not to be maligned, we are not to fear, we are not victims, we are not vulnerable. We are the immutable expression of the indestructible, eternal, immutable God, never changing, perfect, complete, expression of God itself.

Instead of looking at the body as many different aspects, just look at the whole thing and understand oneness, understand wholeness. When God looks out upon us, he sees the wholeness of himself. He doesn't necessarily see the individual expressions and all the dramas of each individual life, but he sees the whole expression. He sees beyond the visible, and he sees himself. He sees what he's made in his own image and likeness, he sees the continuity, the never changing, the ever present, the eternal. He has no problem getting in touch with and maintaining absolute oneness with the true life that is within everything that is created. Neither should we have trouble getting in touch with that.

As we continue to practice seeing the spiritual beyond the visible, seeing the life beyond the form, understanding what it is declaring about the Creator and understanding that is the Presence of what's really here and now, beyond the visible, we will get in touch with it. The more we practice this, the more we begin to see everyone's spirituality, as well as our own. That is how we come into true knowledge of God.

"I have seen your face as though I had seen the face of God, and you were pleased with me."   Genesis 33:10

DAY 165
Stop seeing evil, confusion, as having any power.

How do we get from where we are to knowing our lives are an expression of God's goodness and wholeness and completeness? The very first step is to believe it more than you believe what you see with your eyes. Our eyes see what our hearts have already believed. You have to believe the truth. The truth must edge out the confusion. We must pray until we know from where we've come. We must understand our Divine Source and origin, not because I said it, or you've read it somewhere, but because you have prayed, and you have stayed with it long enough that it has actually gotten in your heart and changed your perception from within. Then nobody can take that away from you.

The next thing is that you must know that Life is stronger than death. As a matter of fact, death has no strength at all. *It is merely a belief in the absence of Life. It is merely a belief that there is some space where Life does not exist.* You must believe that wholeness and health and strength and vitality, which is the expression of Life, is stronger than disease, chaos, confusion and interruption in your body and in your life.

Dis-ease is no more than believing that there is a space or place that Life does not occupy. Yet Life is God and God is Omnipresent and occupies all space. If God occupies all space and is the Life of all that lives, then tell me where disease has place and space to occupy. We must stop seeing evil, confusion, darkness, as having any power over us at all. We must come to see that the goodness of God is ever present and fills all space and is all around and about and from within us. We must see that is the power that governs and controls us for good.

"Let every soul be subject unto the higher power. For there is no power but of God."　　　　Romans 13:1

DAY 166
We have been created to LIVE.

It's the Mind of God that we're really seeking. The thoughts held in the Mind of God are freely being shared with us, we're just not hearing it. We're filled with all this other hooey phooey that's been thrown at us from all directions. Though God speaks day and night and is constantly declaring to us his Presence, and our protection as expressions of his Life, covered by his goodness, we don't see it. We're too filled with all the other nonsense in our heads.

God is good. Evil judges itself, brings upon itself its own destruction. That's the law of sowing and reaping. That's the law of what goes out comes back, what goes around comes around, for good or ill. It's the truth, and it was designed that way so evil would self-destruct. Notice that evil is *live* spelled backwards.

God tells us, "Do not partake of the knowledge of good and evil, what's good and what's evil. Become involved in my Divine Life that is only good." If God tells us not to, then he hasn't gotten involved in it either. We don't need to be doing that, we need to be showing mercy on all, and we need to choose to see the Life of God and the goodness of the Presence of God in all of his creation. That's what we're here to do. We're here to see the good, we're here to see the Life, to see God everywhere. We're here to honor God by believing the truth.

Life will not be denied. Out from the rubble of what we see with our eyes, and out from the rubble of the fear that has gripped our hearts, always comes forth the eternal manifestation of the endless Life of God. We have been created to *live*.

"Not rendering evil for evil but contrariwise blessing, knowing that ye are thereunto called."　　　1Peter 3:9

DAY 167
The Life of everything created is God.

I received this email from a woman who had surgery: *The night before my surgery, I bought myself a red rose so I'd have something nice to look at during my recovery. Before going to bed I admired the rose, and I prayed about the upcoming surgery. I asked God to help me see myself as he sees me. I thought, wouldn't it be nice if he looks at me and sees the same beauty that I see when I look at this rose? I admired the rose for a week, and after ten days, it was crispy dead in the vase. As I was about to toss it out, I noticed it had sprouted some tiny green shoots, which soon developed into little leaves. I left it for a few more days, to see what would happen. By the end of the second week, the rose had produced two tiny buds, which then opened into peach colored roses. The original rose was red! In all my years of buying roses, I've never had one even sprout, much less bloom again in a different color.*

That is Life declaring its existence. That is Life that will not be denied. That is the declaration that out of the appearance of death comes forth the indestructible, unchangeable, eternal Life that is God. That is the declaration that the Life of everything created is God and it cannot be interrupted, nor can it be destroyed. That is what animates you, what gives you breath. That is what created and formed you, that is what sent you here to this earth, and that is what has a purpose for your existence. That is what will never change. That is the true Life of you.

"O bless our God, who holds our soul in life."
Psalm 66:8,9

DAY 168
We exist in Divine Consciousness.

We are first a spirit being. We are then an aggrega-tion of thought, feeling, judgment, belief, and then, only then, forms the physical. Our body is a localized bundle of energy in a vast universe of energy. We are light beings. God is Light and we are made in the image of God. Remember in the Bible (Matthew 17) where Jesus was transformed into an energy field that could be seen by the disciples? Their eyes were opened to see what was always true. They were able to see past the solid physical and realize the true Source of Life, the true Source of energy that animated the physical being. This Light energy is what forms the physical being.

We are also localized bundles of consciousness in a Divine Consciousness. Think of the Mind of God, Divine Consciousness, the consciousness where all things origi-nate, the consciousness of perfect harmony, balance, beauty and perfection--we exist in that divine con-sciousness. "In him we live and move and have our being." (Acts 17:28)

Lift your mind and your thoughts above the physical enough to understand that we are basically thought, energy, knowledge. These are transformed into material substance. It was the thought of God that formed the world, and it's the thought of this localized bundle of consciousness which we are, that forms *our* world, our physical world. That's why thoughts are able to create good or to destroy. That's why thought is so incredibly important. That's why you hear so much about what we meditate on, what we think on, what we dwell on, is what we are magnetizing to ourselves. It's true.

"God said, Let there be light, and there was light.
God saw the light, that it was good."   Genesis 1:3-4

DAY 169

How prayer is answered.

Energy is a flowing vibration. Whenever there is a block in the flow of that vibration, or energy, or light, then there is malfunction. How do we keep this energy flowing?

We are elevated through spiritual readings, through time in silence, through time with nature, through meditation. Whenever we are elevated to an atmosphere of spiritual consciousness, we feel energized, we feel the dynamics of the presence and the flow of this frequency through us. When we are elevated to Divine Consciousness, this frequency, this molecular vibration, is speeded up to the point that we feel the energy. That's when we feel faith, and hope. That's when we barely whisper a desire or intention and we know that we know that it's to be fulfilled.

When we are not in that high atmosphere of thought, our desire, our intention, comes from desperation, frustration, fear, from a sense of lack and limitation. We can whisper and shout it until heaven drops down to earth and we are not heard and we don't get what we're praying for. As we are lifted into Divine Consciousness, into that realm of expectancy, into the atmosphere of Divine thought, into the Presence of God, then with barely a thought and with barely the faintest whisper, you know your desire will be fulfilled.

The energy of Life, the dynamics of the Spirit of God, flowing through anything in creation, brings, "exceedingly, abundantly, above all that we ask or think." (Ephesians 3:20) It magnetizes to itself all the other aspects of its own Life. That's how prayer is answered.

"Thou shall decree a thing and it shall be established unto thee: and the light shall shine upon thy ways."
Jeremiah 22:28

DAY 170
Allow Life to flow to its greatest potential.

When we think of anything flowing, it is clear that the channel of flow has to be open, it cannot be constricted or obstructed or blocked. If it is, in order to get it flowing again, those things must be removed.

In order for anything to flow, the area which it flows through must first be emptied out, so that fresh life energy might course through it. No two things can occupy the same space at the same time. Jesus said you have to first empty out the old wineskins in order for new wine to be poured in. (Matthew 9:17) In order for fresh life to flow through, whether we're talking about the body, the cells in the body, or about the heart, mind, or emotions, first what is occupyiing that space must be emptied out.

If your emotions are filled with anxiety, which blocks the flow, a new fresh thought from the Mind of God cannot flow through. If you want to learn something new, you first must be willing to empty out the old concepts for the truth to fill your mind. You don't have to be afraid of letting go of anything, because that which is true will come back. Trust that the Spirit of God is not going to allow anything to be put into the soil of your heart and mind that isn't true. Ask, "Is this true? That which is true I would like to hold, and that which is not I would like you to carry away."

It's like traveling from Egypt to the Promised Land, traveling from darkness to light, into the fullness of the understanding of God and your relationship to him. How far will you go? If you say, this far will I go and no farther, you don't grow anymore. How do we allow the flow of energy of Life to flow to its greatest potential?

"He opened the rock and the waters gushed out; they ran in the dry places like a river."   Psalm 105:41

DAY 171

Make room for the energy of Life.

How to open up? By giving. Once we are willing to pour out from our substance, on any and every level, then we have made room for the energy or the flow of Life, the vibrations, the frequency, the Spirit of Life, however you talk about it.

Take something simple, that we do automatically. Whenever we exhale, we are giving carbon dioxide out into the atmosphere, and the plants take it up and they give off oxygen. That's a symbiotic relationship, meaning that we both give and we both get. As we take up the oxygen that they give off and we give out the carbon dioxide that they take in, the cycle of Life continues.

When we give love, we are acting as a magnet for love to come back. If you want love in your life, you give love. If you need compassion, then you give that to anybody and everybody that you see. As you pour that out, you become a magnet for that flow of energy to flow through you. The energy of Divine Consciousness contains everything that we could possibly give out. If you give kindness and mercy and gentleness and good-ness to people, if you compliment, if you build someone up to make them feel more confident or happier about their moment or their life, then that is contained in the energy you have just made space for. It's like exercising, it does not wear you out, but in fact energizes and strengthens you. As you expend energy, you are allowing more energy to flow through you.

You can make a decision today that you are going to give something to every single person that you see, even if it's just a kind thought, a prayer, a blessing, a compliment, a smile.

"Freely ye have received, freely give." Matthew 10:8

DAY 172

"Cast your bread upon the waters."

What is your intention for giving? If your motive for giving is so that you'll get, you've missed the point. If you do things to be rewarded, your intention is self serving. The Bible says that if you do things to be seen of men, you've already received your reward. It says, "Don't let your right hand know what your left hand is doing." "Do things in secret and your father will reward you openly." (Matthew 6:1-4)

If you give from your heart, because it's joyful to give, to bless another, to meet a need, in giving we do receive. If we're not receiving, we're not giving from our heart. We're hoarding and we don't realize it's clogging and it's stagnating, and it's become like a lagoon where the river doesn't flow and it gets trapped and turns to slime. It's not a healthy place to be. It's not being in the center of the flow of the river of Life, where there is only incredible energy and wholesomeness and health and happiness.

The word affluence comes from a word meaning to flow. Affluence of health, affluence of wealth, affluence of happiness and peace, everything that we think we want is flowing to us right now. "The sun shines on the evil and on the good, and the rain falls on the just and on the unjust." (Matthew 5:45) But does it flow through, do we get the benefit of it? Not unless the channels are open that it might flow through us. We want to constantly look for ways we can give and open up. As you give, you're casting your bread upon the waters, and it comes back to you. (Ecclesiastes 11:1)

"What have you that you did not receive?"
1Corinthians 4:7

DAY 173

I choose to see goodness.

How do we choke down the flow of Life? One way is by judgment, and we all do it. All day long, unconscously or consciously, we are forming an opinion. It comes with the human consciousness, because the human consciousness was formed by turning away from the consciousness of pure Divine Life, and partaking of the knowledge of good and evil. That's what the tree of the knowledge of good and evil is. It means we are forming opinions and judgments, categorizing everything, right and wrong, good and bad. That clogs up the works faster than anything else.

Genesis 2:17 says, "In the day that you partake of the knowledge of good and evil, you shall surely die." We are in this progressive process of degeneration until ultimately we die. How do we stop the process of continually going toward death? We stop judgment. That takes an act of grace. It's a moment by moment check-ing your thoughts and choosing. *Father, I choose to see Life. I choose to see you. I choose to see goodness, wholeness. I choose to see the light of this person, the eternal light. I choose to see the eternal goodness which is you, and not to see what this person is doing, and not to react to it in any way.*

When we do that we're opening channels of flow through us beyond anything we could ever imagine. We haven't imagined it because we don't do it. How many of us have made a concentrated point of praying non-stop, if that's what it takes, to not form judgment or to release judgments that have already been formed? Open up the channel for the incredible river of Life to flow.

"The Lord is in the midst of thee: thou shall not see evil anymore."   Zephaniah 3:15

DAY 174

Let it go.

It's not what happens to us, it's not what comes into our experience, it's what we do with it when it comes. We can't stop somebody from saying something ugly, something that hurts us, but we can release that judgment. We can determine, I will not resist this attack, I will not hold on to it, I will not form a judgment, I will not defend myself, I will just let it go. That's a choice we can make.

When negative things come at us, we can say, I don't choose to visit that space and place. Sometimes we have to do that over and over again, we have to bless that person or circumstance, we have to see the good in it, we have to pray for the good to be seen, pray for the good to flow through it, in order for us to be released. If we don't do that, we suffer the consequences, because the hurt, the anger, the anxiety, clogs us up, shuts down the flow of Life through us. We gain weight, we get depressed, we take on disease, poverty, fear, loneliness. We ask, "Why has this come upon me?" Because you shut down the flow of the river of Life that contains every good thing in abundance, exceedingly abundantly above all that you can ask or think. (Ephesians 3:20) You shut it down and you didn't even know you were shutting it down.

How do you build it up? It comes through silence. Do not speak. Spend an hour every day alone and quiet--or even ten minutes. Don't move about. Don't dissipate the energy that builds up during that silence. You will feel the Presence of the Source of all Life, you will feel that energy, that vitality within you.

"Better is a handful of quietness than both hands full with travail and vexation of spirit."   Ecclesiastes 4:6

DAY 175

Get a clear vision.

It's not what you do, it's what you know, because experience starts at the level of belief. One of the first prerequisites to coming into a higher state of consciousness is an extreme self honesty, a deep self exposure of your fears, thoughts, beliefs. In order to have old thoughts removed to make room for the new ones, you have to be willing to have them exposed to you. You have to be willing to say, "This is how I've been thinking, but I choose not to think this anymore. I choose not to believe this. I choose not to hold that opinion."

When you want to jump from one consciousness to another, you're pushing against the entire world belief. The change depends on the confidence that you have in the vision that you have. Let me recommend that through prayer, through your conversations with God, you request a clear vision of where you're going.

When the Israelites wandered through the wilderness, they got a clear vision of the Promised Land, a land flowing with milk and honey, a land of great abundance. Because they kept that vision before them, they were able to endure the difficulty that they experienced in their journey. It's imperative that you get a vision, your own vision, of what life would be like, life abundant, life in peace and harmony, life free of dread.

Once you put out that desire fervently, and you stay with it, something will come to you, a very special vision to you. Write it down and refer to it, because you need to keep your eye on the path. You need to keep you eye on your hope, because as soon as you look away from that, it is difficult not to believe that the circumstances have preeminence over that truth, that vision.

"Where there is no vision, the people perish."

Proverbs 29:18

DAY 176
"Lay the axe to the root of the tree."

We are accustomed to fighting a physical problem with a physical solution. The "weapons of our warfare" (2Corinthians 10:4) are not material, they are spiritual. That means they are in our thought process, in the world beyond what is seen. It's in the world of thought where all human experiences originate. We're going to the root of whatever the problem seems to be. The root of it is going to be in thought. You want to lay the axe to the root of the tree. (Matthew 3:10) You don't want to just keep lopping off branches, one branch after another, dealing with circumstances always only on a physical material level.

You don't want to tolerate an affliction, you don't want to cope with it, or worst of all, submit to it. Once you've done any of these things, you've invited it into your experience. You've opened the doors and the windows and said, "Come on in. I don't want you, I haven't invited you, you're an intruder, but I've been duped into believing you belong here, and I have no way of extricating myself from you." You've learned to cope with an unwelcome visitor that is systematically destroying your house.

You have to be absolutely convinced that this is an intrusion. You don't choose it. It is not an act of God, it is not God's nature. From the purity and goodness of that being who brought you forth, only purity and goodness can come. If you have trouble with that, ask for the understanding of the true nature of God. Once the answer comes to you, you will have it forever.

"Our weapons are mighty through God to the pulling down of strongholds, casting down imaginations, and every high thing that exalts itself against the knowledge of God."   2Corinthians 10:4-5

DAY 177

"It is He who has made us."

Be sure you do not believe that whatever has befallen you has come because of your DNA or genetic code. As soon as you fall into that, you have denied your spirituality. You have seen yourself strictly and only as a material, mortal being--another world belief that we have accepted. If you see yourself as a material being, you see yourself as your body. You are not your body. You wear your body. You are completely separate from that which you wear. You are a dynamic consciousness that's not even found within the body. You don't live in your body and you are not your body. You live in your consciousness. That's what defines you.

If you realize this, you will then realize that you have an incredible amount of power over how your body behaves and how it defines itself. As long as you think you are your body, you will be subjected to it, to whatever it does. It's the boss. It declares whether you live or die, whether you're happy or sad, whether you're in pain or free fom pain. It dominates your experience.

If you see yourself as separate from it and simply using it, then you will realize the strength of who you are and you will realize you can direct it. If you see yourself as a DNA, you are always looking for the cause of disease within the body, denying your true life, that eternal substance that goes on and on forever and ever, and always has.

Creation comes from one Creator. "It is he that has made us and not we ourselves." (Psalm 100:3) Forget the concept of being born and replace it with the concept of being sent, sent to this physical plane for a purpose.

"Awake, awake, shake thyself from the dust.
Arise...loose thyself, o captive daughter."   Isaiah 52:2

DAY 178

"None of these things move me."

Disease does not come from anything you did or didn't do, such as, getting your feet wet, or being exposed to someone who had a cold, or not getting enough sleep, or eating something you shouldn't have eaten, or not taking vitamins. As long as you see yourself as a physical body, and you believe you live in that body, then you will feel vulnerable and susceptible to all these things. But once you get that first awakening in consciousness of being an eternal being, separate from the body, not subservient to it, then you will understand you are not susceptible. We come to a place where we realize that "None of these things move me." (Acts 20:24) None of these things have any power over me.

The minute we feel anything disturbing us, we try to come up with a reason why it's there. As soon as you give disease a reason to exist, you have just allowed it passage into your life. You have just empowered it over you, you have given it authenticity, you have validated it, you've agreed to it. The strongest thing you will ever do, the most dynamic thing you will ever do, is to resist taking on a disease, to push it off your land and out of your house. If you have inadvertently allowed it in, you can refuse to give it a cause. As soon as you've given it a cause, you've given it life, you've given it a place, you've empowered it, given it a right to be there.

Say, "I am not subjected to the circumstances and events that are hurled at me, I live above those. I am not a body and I am not living inside this body, vulnerable to whatever comes along."

"In the world ye shall have tribulation, but be of good cheer: I have overcome the world."   John 16:33

DAY 179

Declare the truth.

Disorder, dis-ease, has no valid reason to exist. Do not allow it a reason. Listen to your thoughts, to what comes to mind as a reason for it to be there. Write that down, and the next one and the next one. Go down that list and declare the truth against every one of those thoughts and world beliefs. By declaring the truth you strip disease of its power, of its influence, of its right and ability to exist. Find the truth that cancels each belief out, and you will strip it of its power.

Upon what basis can we deny these unchallenged beliefs that the human consciousness has accepted?

First, your true Source of Life is Divine.

Second, you have been made in the image and likeness of your Creator. That includes wholeness, completeness, perfection, balance, order, harmony, intelligence, and no changeableness.

Third, the God that made you is good. God is Life, Life is God. Life defines the body.

Fourth, you are under the government of this Divine Life, which is your Life. The Divine Life of you is not subject to human or material conditions.

Can you imagine living your life anticipating goodness only, looking forward to each day with the expectancy of only goodness? Can you imagine living a life where the expectation is fulfillment, direction, energy, strength, vitality? Can you imagine expecting Wisdom and intelligence in every situation, just knowing you live in all that? That is our true life, what we were created to live in. The way to get there is to not look at ourselves, but look at the source of our existence.

"It shall be called the way of holiness...the ransomed of the Lord shall return with songs and everlasting joy upon their heads." Isaiah 35:8,10

DAY 180
What you need is already available to you.

Why do some people get healed and others don't?

What if you were very cold, and yet the sun was shining, and those in the direct line of the sun were very warm, however you were in the shade? You can stand in the shade and pray to be warmed up, continuing to declare how cold you are and how much you want to be warmed. Yet, the answer, the provision for you, is already available, it always has been, it's eternal. It's impartial, but you must receive it. How do you receive it? You leave where you are and you walk out into the sun. The sun did not shine because you asked it to shine, the sun was already shining. The warmth was already there, what you needed was already available to you.

The provision for everything that creation could ever have imagined to need, is already operative, already available, already here. It's already here exceedingly, abundantly above all that we could ask or think. (Ephesians 3:20) Some people are receiving and other people are not, and the only difference is that some people have made themselves more receptive to receiving, and other people have inadvertently and unknowingly shut off their receptivity.

How do you shut off receptivity? One way is to think you are not worthy, or you have not earned it. This is misunderstanding the nature of God, whose nature is to give. Another way is to believe the physical world governs your body, rather than knowing your Life is God's, who brings Life to every cell and holds everything in perfect order.

How to open it up? Ask, "Where am I shutting down?" As soon as the answer comes, Life begins to flow.

"I send you to open their eyes and to turn them from darkness to light."   Acts 26:18

DAY 181

Life is the Presence of God.

The flow of Divine Life through all creation, that formed all of creation, is full of energy, an eternal energy. It doesn't depend on human circumstances, situations, events or people, in order to be full of energy. Nothing can take that away, nothing can alter or change it. It is also infinitely intelligent, so we don't tell it where to flow and how to form and what to form, but we get in line with it. When we line up with that will, with that intention, with that intelligence, when we allow that energy to flow, then our life will take on the abundant joy, the abundant blessings, the abundant health, the abundant anything and everything that we could possible imagine, that we could possibly need.

We first have to know that it is available, and we have to line up with it. The scriptures say we must first realize that God is. We must realize he *is*, not will be, not will come, if, when, and how, not a has-been, but *is* right now. "He is a rewarder of them that diligently seek him." (Hebrews 11:6) He is a rewarder of one who diligently seeks him, not diligently begs for the same thing over and over, but diligently seeks to find out how we might better *receive* the goodness of God.

Life is the Presence of God, not something we do. God, to express the dynamics of his own nature, formed creation, and through creation his nature is being expressed and understood and lived out. Life is a continuing experience, it's impossible for Life to end because Life is God. Each of us is God in expression of himself. It is the energy, the Life, the thoughts, the heart of God that animates our bodies and motivates our thoughts. We are spirit beings having human experiences.

"Is he not thy Father? Has he not made thee and established thee?" Deuteronomy 32:6

DAY 182

God fills all space.

Grief is a belief in lack, limitation or loss. Any sense of loss, lack, or limitation comes from one vantage point: the object that we think that we have lost, we have put in the place of God. We thought that love and companionship came from this person, we thought that safety and security came from this job. We thought that our needs were being met by something on the material human physical plane. If it seems to have left, then we perceive a vacuum in that space, and that's a frightening experience. We thought that the strength and health of our life came from our body, and so when we no longer felt the strength and health of our life, we thought our body was falling out from under us, and therefore that our life was falling our from under us.

We need to see that God is what fills all space, is the Divine Mind, is all the immutable attributes, is the unchangeable, undeniable presence of that which is "exceedingly abundantly above all that we could ask or think" or desire or intend.(Ephesians 3:20) It is the Presence of that which causes us to experience companionship and love, it is the Omnipresence of the allness of the giver of all that there is to give, that fills our need. In that space where there seems to be loss, God still lives. The true Source and origin has not been removed, and therefore in that space will appear something else, because the Divine energy is still there.

When you're letting things go, recognize the beauty and the order and the goodness of your life. Focus on your ability to enjoy life, to hear the birds sing, to watch the flowers grow. Focus on what you have to be thankful for, that which has not changed.

"Am I a God at hand and not a God afar off?
Do I not fill heaven and earth?"   Jeremiah 23:23-4

DAY 183

Deep inside there is joy.

We can take the whole bundle of the human life, the human understanding, the way that we perceive things to be, our judgments, our opinions, our beliefs, all the pain, sorrow, suffering, and all the good, and all the hope, and all the happiness, and fold it into a little bundle, put a ribbon around it, and give it back to our Creator. In exchange, we get the unobstructed, unhindered, unchallenged flow of the Life of God. In that exchange is a whole new identity, a whole new life, a whole new hope, a whole new perception and outlook.

You may have to do that more than once in your lifetime. Every time we are faced with something, we need to heal it, to give it back to the Creator, and take in turn the joy of the Divine Life that can't be interrupted. Do not step over the problem, don't try to hide it, don't pretend you've dealt with it. We suffer because we don't know how to do that exchange, and we haven't done it.

Recognize that the human experience is not your true life, though it feels like it, looks like it, and that's what you've always thought. You need to set it aside, make a conscious moment of walking away from it. Then open your arms and your heart and invite the eternal infinite Divine Life, full of all the wonders and beauty and experiences that you feel you need. Invite that into the space you have emptied out by removing the old human. Say, I *am ready now to know, experience, feel and be all that I have been created to be.* Watch your life change. Watch and feel that energy as it begins to flow through you. Feel hope surging through you, smile, laugh, because deep inside there is joy.

"God answers him in the joy of his heart."
Ecclesiastes 5:20

DAY 184

"Joy comes in the morning."

If you have struggled with situations that have gone on for a long time, it may seem as though there is no end in sight. You may have resigned yourself to living in that state of helplessness and unhappiness, because you seem to find no avenue of change. There was a time in my life I felt the same way, but I'm here to tell you, the day comes when the light shines again. I'm here to tell you the sun always comes up. "Weeping may endure for the night but joy comes in the morning." (Psalm 30:5)

How do you know it's going to end, and you're going to be better off than you were? How do you know you're going to be happier, more secure, more whole, more directed? How do you know this thing's going to end? What built my hope back up was when I understood the resurrection principle.

In Genesis 8:22 it says, "While the earth remains, seed time and harvest, cold and heat, summer and winter, day and night, shall not cease." In Jeremiah 33:20-21, it says, "If you can break my covenant of the day and my covenant of the night, that there should not be day and night in their season, then may also my covenant be broken."

God's promise, God's covenant with us, is that we share his Life, we share his joy, we share his wholeness, we share his Wisdom, we share his understanding, we share Love, we share all the wonderful attributes of God. His promise to us is Life.

Many of us are wondering when that promise is going to be fulfilled. When I was in the long winter of my life, I realized that no matter how long and cold it was, the spring was going to come. I didn't doubt that.

"The hills may be removed, but the covenant of my peace shall not be removed."   Isaiah 54:10

DAY 185

The Light will arise.

Spring is God's message to the earth. When was the last time you stayed up all night praying that the sun would rise again, out of fear that it might not? When was the last time you prayed your way through the winter that spring would come, because you feared it might not? Spring will come.

The resurrection principle is that every twenty-four hours the earth is blanketed by night. The Light always appears. Even though the seed looks dead, from that appearance, LIFE always appears.

In some instances, we feel trapped, we're in pain, we're frightened, we're alone. One day we come to the realization that we are not ever alone. The night gets dark and long, but we know the sun will always shine. We know that effortlessly it will drive away the darkness. At the appointed time, your light will arise.

I don't believe that suffering comes from God, but I do know that in order for us to move from one experience to another, there has to be a paradigm shift in consciousness, in understanding, in expectation. There has to be a shift to a higher level of understanding. Sometimes that's an uncomfortable time, but it doesn't have to be suffering. "In his presence is fullness of joy." (Psalm 16:11)

Suffering comes when we take it personally, when we personalize it and think it's our problem. Suffering comes by way of the perception that we've given the situation. You can go through a situation that seems dark, but when you're looking down the road knowing that the day is going to come, the daylight's going to break, spring is going to come, then you know you can ride this thing through. All is well.

"Behold I make all things new."   Revelation 21:5

DAY 186
Inside is the Eternal Life of God.

Suffering can come because of fear of the unknown, fear that things won't change, thoughts that you have caused it, thoughts that God, who is your only hope and anchor right now, laid this on you. If you knew that when it's over you were going to see, know, and understand, that you were going to have avenues of opportunity, avenues of joy, that you never imagined, that you were going to have changes in the whole picture of your life--if you knew that absolutely, and had no doubts, you would not suffer.

When you put a seed in the ground, that seed will appear to die. It's put in this dark earth with no air, no sunlight. It's alone down there. It looks like it's dead, but inside of it is the Eternal Life of God. A Life that will never ever be changed, be destroyed, be interrupted, be dominated by anything outside of itself. That same Life is in every one brought into the earth.

You are like that little seed. Be cognizant of this Life that's within you, that is ready to burst out into the open. Like a seed, all of a sudden, the outside finally cracks and splits. Maybe that's what you're experiencing right now. That breaking is not to destroy, but to bring forth Life. Out comes that little sprout. It's not the strength of that little seedling that pushes aside all the dirt and rocks, it's the strength of the Eternal Life within it. So it is with you. It is that Eternal Life within you that can never be changed or altered, never be challenged, never be overcome. It is not by your efforts, but the effort of that eternal Life within, pushing against whatever the circumstance that seems to be entombing you in darkness.

"I shall put my spirit in you and you shall live."
Ezekiel 37:14

DAY 187

The Eternal Life is revealed.

A little seed put into the ground is nowhere near the beauty and the magnitude and the glory of the flower in full bloom when it arises, or a cornstalk with all of its ears of corn, or a hickory tree with millions of nuts coming, all from one little seed. This is the hope. This is the resurrection principle.

When we experience problems in Life they're here to make a change, to bring forth good. We're about to have a complete vision change, a different perception of truth. It has to be glorious. It has to far surpass what we were living out from when we went into this experience. Forget what happened, how it happened, why it happened, and look toward what is coming. Look toward the spring. Look toward the light of the early morning sun as it effortlessly and without a battle pushes aside the darkness of the night. Think about that seed, identify with it, realize the Life as it pulsates down deep within you. Let it build, let it grow, let it find its avenue of expression, and it will.

All of nature goes through this exact same process, and so do we. It's an unfolding of the Eternal Life of God. It's the process whereby the Eternal Life is revealed. It's our hope. It's the covenant God made with us. Look toward what we're aiming for, not toward the darkness and despair in front of us. Look toward Life, look toward the spring, look toward the fullness of the manifestation of the Life that's within you, that is finding yet another explosive outlet of expression. You will feel a joy rising up in you, and you will begin to see the Light of Life again.

"Let not your heart be troubled, neither let it be afraid."   John 14:27

DAY 188
Receive from God every imaginable goodness.

There is no power available to us in this human existence that comes close to the power of prayer. It is a gift
given to us, to communicate with the Source and origin
of our existence, God, as well as to be communicated to
by God. Prayer is an intimate communication, an intimate relationship, an intimate moment between the
Creator and that which has been created. It is the
response of Life back to its Source and origin. There is
nothing of more value to the human being as we live out
this human consciousness, as our ability to enter into
that realm of consciousness that we call prayer. Here we
can not only communicate our needs and desires and
thoughts and feelings to God, but we can actually receive from God direction, understanding, focus, healing,
supply, abundance, and every imaginable goodness that
we could ever need.

There is only One Life, the Divine Life. It fills all
space throughout infinity and all eternity. We all contain
the fullness of that Life. We come from the realm of
pure understanding, of pure light and truth and illumination, as a part of this One Life, for the purpose of shining the Light of truth into this dark human consciousness. There is no blueprint, nothing we can humanly
follow, to know how to get from where we are to the
fulfillment of what we came to do, but we have this
experience called prayer, where we can both communicate to and be communicated to by God. This is our way
of knowing the direction of thought and action that we
are to take.

*"I pray thee, show me now thy way, that I may know
thee, that I may find grace in thy sight...And he said,
my presence shall go with thee and I will give thee
rest."*   Exodus 33:13-14

DAY 189

"Thine is the Glory."

Start your prayers with the truth about God. Don't start with the problem, because the problem is but an image that proceeded from the human consciousness. I would not ask God to share in that convoluted image and then fix it.

Instead, I might make a prayer that says, *I realize the truth here, though it does not seem evident, is that this person stands in the wholeness and completeness and Divine image and Glory of God, and nothing can take that away, no human circumstance, event, or belief. I know this, I believe it with my whole heart.*

I have to feel the truth, not just rehearse what I know is true. So I might say, *Show me what I need to understand more clearly. Show me what I'm holding on to of the human consciousness that would be blocking this feeling, so I can enter into the feeling where it becomes my whole experience.*

"When you pray, enter into your closet, and when you have shut your door, pray to your Father which is in secret, and your Father which sees in secret shall reward you openly...Your Father knows what things you have need of before you ask him.

Our Father which art in heaven, hallowed be thy name. Thy kingdom come. Thy will be done in earth, as it is in heaven. Give us this day our daily bread. And forgive us our debts as we forgive our debtors. Lead us not into temptation, but deliver us from evil:

For thine is the kingdom, and the power, and the glory, for ever. Amen."

Matthew 6:6-13

DAY 190
Let your prayers come from a sincere heart.

If you were developing a relationship with somebody that you loved and wanted to love more, and know more, you would not pick up a book to find out how to communicate with that person. You would communicate out from the depths of your desire to know that person better, and to love that person more. That's how it is with God. If in the depths of your being, you desire God, and fervently want to understand him more, or you fervently desire to have him move in a situation where you desperately need help, it's the depth of the longing and the desire that causes the answer to come.

God is a being that fills all space, and is constantly available to whoever will partake of it. We just need to become partakers of it. We need to stop worrying whether we've earned it or whether we're worthy. Let's settle that right now, we can't earn it. You don't earn the air that you breathe, you don't earn the sun that beats down on you, you don't earn the rain that comes . It's not a matter of worthiness or earning, Love is just there. That's how it is with God.

God is an available experience, full of Wisdom and purpose. There is a way to avail ourselves of this: by sincere and fervent communication through prayer. Let your prayers come from a sincere heart. Turn to light and understanding, and see the whole thought of God as impartial, Omnipresent, Omnipotent. Some see God as an energy, but it's difficult to develop a relationship of trust with an energy. God is a Being with whom we can develop the kind of communication that causes us to know him and trust him.

"Call unto me and I will answer you and show you great and mighty things which you know not."

Jeremiah 33:3

DAY 191
Surrender the human mind to the mind of God.

People say they're praying about a problem, but nothing happens. They are really more thinking about the problem, worrying about it, obsessing over it. It's on their mind day and night. They're analyzing it, they're trying to figure out the path that will produce the desired results. They're trying to figure out, with the human mind, the Wisdom of God. Quite naturally, there is no change in the human situation, because there is no prayer there.

Prayer is not the human trying to figure out the best way to handle it. It's not the human trying to analyze any given situation, looking at it from all different points of view. If that's where you're at, the best thing to do is to turn from that frame of mind and choose instead the Divine Mind of God. Stop all the analyzing and be willing to surrender the human mind to the Mind of God.

When you do this, by surrendering the human mind, you're getting in exchange all the wisdom and understanding of the Divine Consciousness. You can't beat that! Once you've done that the answer will come. There will be nothing to stop it, and nothing could stop it. That answer will produce Life for you. It will be a solution that you probably never thought about. It will be a solution that will bring Life to this situation, whatever the situation is. But not until we lay down all the thinking, all the worrying and all the figuring, which comes from human pride and human fear. This causes you to understand more of God, your Father, your Creator, your Source, and the Life you truly are. This enables you to develop a relationship with God based on truth.

"There is a spirit in man, and the inspiration of the Almighty gives them understanding."   Job 32:8

DAY 192
God is there to lift and correct our thought.

While God does not put anything on us, the Mind of God is there to lift us out of it and correct the human thoughts. In praying, God's power, God's understanding, gets focused in our thoughts. What God sees and what God knows becomes impregnated in our own heart and soul and mind, until we start seeing and feeling and perceiving things in a completely different way. When that happens, we see the uninterrupted constancy of God. Now we would never accept into our experience whatever it was that we once accepted, because we would not have that human perception that allowed the problem to start with. Prayer is us taking on more and more of our true nature.

Even if you have others praying for you, it is terribly important for each individual to carry their own situation from beginning to end, with God guiding and leading and directing. In the process of doing this, we are raised to an entirely different, higher, clearer, purer, more illuminated understanding of truth and of God, as God truly is and as we are in him. We don't want to depend more on other people's prayer than we are on our own.

Remember Einstein said, no problem can be solved by the same consciousness that created it. Eventually you must have a change of understanding, a change of perception, so that the problem, once healed, can never return.

"May the God of Jesus Christ, the Father of glory, give unto you the spirit of wisdom and revelation in the knowledge of him, and the eyes of your understanding be enlightened, that you may know what is the hope of his calling."   Ephesians 1:17-18

DAY 193
Let the energy build and build and build.

How do we get to a place where we can actually hear what God is saying? As in any communication, if one person does all the talking, and there's no listening , there's not much of a relationship, there's just one person talking. It's imperative to come into an understanding of the relationship that you have had since before the foundation of the world, and you will have long after. You acquire this not only by speaking, but mostly by listening.

What I do is read, knowing my mind will wander if I just sit. I read either the Bible, or something I feel led to read at that time. I read until I feel the Presence of God. We're told to enter into the closet, shut the door and pray in secret, and the Father who hears it in secret will reward us out in the open. (Matthew 6:6) Our prayer is not something we share with other people, because as soon as we speak that which we heard in secret, the energy of it dissipates. We must hold deep in our heart those times, and be very quiet and still about it. It really is an intimate relationship, an intimate communication, something to hold in our heart and let the energy of the words build and build and build in our experience, until finally it recreates the human picture.

God is always speaking to us. There is no time, day or night, that God is not continually speaking, continually imparting truth, understanding, knowledge, and Wisdom to us. It's not a matter of trying to overcome God's reluctance to speak to us. God is not reluctant to do anything. Love is not reluctant. It is impossible for Love to withhold or to be reluctant to do or to say anything. Love continually pours out from itself.

"Precept must be upon precept, line upon line, here a little, there a little."　　　　　　　　　　Isaiah 28:9-10

DAY 194

Enter into the Presence of God
with a heart of thanksgiving.

Enter into the Presence of God with a heart of thanksgiving. That can be hard when you think the body is ill, your pockets are empty, and the kids are hungry. What do you have to be thankful for? Don't get confused and thank God for the disease or the poverty, God didn't send that.

Thank God for the Presence of God that has never left you. Thank God that that Presence is good, pure goodness. Thank God for the faithfulness of God, that when you make yourself available he will cause you to be able to hear and to know. He will make the change that is necessary. That is what you're thankful for. You're thankful for the true nature of God and the Presence of God and what you know is true about God. You are not thankful for the misery. You might be grateful that the experience caused you to press in to know God better, but that's different than being thankful for the problem.

Thankfulness increases the awareness of the Presence of God. In your thankfulness, you are reiterating your understanding of the nature of God, your awareness of the faithfulness of that nature. You become more receptive to what you're going to hear. A heart of gratitude opens wide the heart to receive the goodness of God and the solution to the problem.

"Make a joyful noise unto the Lord, serve the Lord with gladness, come before his presence with singing. Know that the Lord is God, it is he that has made us, and not we ourselves. Enter into his gates with thanksgiving and into his courts with praise: be thankful unto him and bless his name. For the Lord is good, his mercy is everlasting and his truth endures."

Psalm 100

DAY 195

Go to One who knows something you don't know,
and can do something you can't do.

You don't want to bring into prayer a rehearsal of the problem. You don't want to carry your burden into the holy place. You won't find yourself in the Presence of God while you are rehearsing all the imagery and all the fears surrounding the situation pressing on you. Because in the pure truth of God none of this is true. The Mind of God sees what he has created. What he has created is whole, perfect and complete. It can't lack anything, it can't experience limitation, it doesn't know boundaries, it doesn't know obstacles.

You are an eternal being and have always been an eternal being. There is One Divine Life, and you, as a part of that Life, have been sent to this area of dark-ness, this human consciousness that has imaged all sorts of suffering and fear. We come from the Divine Life with a fullness of understanding and Wisdom and knowl-edge and perception, to bring that to bear on humanity so we can lift them up out of it. That is the real pure truth, no matter what else is appearing.

We perceive problems in Life when we become ensnared in the human consciousness, forgetting who we are, forgetting that we've been sent for that purpose. When we get caught up in the confusion of the human condition, we experience it. We don't want to carry that back into the pure conscious realm. When we pray we want to leave it behind.

Come to prayer with an attitude of humility. You are going to Someone who is wiser, who is of far greater intelligence, who has a clearer perception, who knows something you don't know, and can do something you can't do.

"God gives grace to the humble."   1Peter 5:5

DAY 196

What is it that I don't see?

One of my favorite prayers is, *God, what is it that you know about this situation that I do not know, because if I knew it, I wouldn't be in this situation? Impart to me what you hold in mind and thought.* As soon as I understand it or see it, that situation is going to be cleared.

If I'm having trouble seeing another's wholeness and completeness and the truth of their being and who they are, if I can't see past the situation and see the fullness and wholeness of the goodness of God, then I need to pull away from that situation and go to God in prayer and say, *What is it that I don't see? What is it that maybe I know with my mind but not with my heart? What is it that I might be holding in my heart that would be blocking me from perceiving the truth in this situation?*

If I'm looking at a person who believes they have a disease, and I'm unable to see their wholeness at that moment, I'm about to get pulled into the same confused belief (which is total unbelief), of who they really are. If I agree with them, "Yes, you do have a disease," or "Yes, you are poor, yes, you are alone," then I have just empowered the problem and I have become part of the problem.

One of my favorite scriptures is Psalm 119:19: "I am a stranger in the earth. Hide not your commmandments from me." Hide not your understanding--you sent me here into this strange consciousness, this strange atmosphere of thought, quite unlike the Divine thought I enjoyed before being sent here. Lest I get swept along into it, I must continue to go back to my true home in the Presence of God, in prayer.

"Receive thy sight."   Luke 18:42

DAY 197

Be willing to let go.

Jesus said, in Matthew 4:17, "Repent, the kingdom of God is at hand." What did he mean? Repentance simply means to turn to a different way, different than the way you've been going, to turn away from a certain thought. It's being willing to let go of your old human understanding, being willing to make space for new understanding.

I might know a lot of truths in my mind, but there is something going on in my heart or I would not be experiencing this situation. If I have a problem that I can't seem to walk away from, there is a belief or thought, an obstruction of flow to the presence of the truth. Your mind is so full of what you already think you know, you are not making space for the new understanding to come. Be still, be humble, in that state of, "I don't know, but you do, and I know that you'll let me know." That attitude allows a Word to be spoken to you where you can hear it and receive it. You get into the Kingdom of God, this correction of thought, through this attitude of humility.

If you want to be freed from a situation, go directly to God first. Don't run around looking for people to fix it. And don't go to God thinking you already know the answer. We can't gain something without first being willing to let go. It's important to go with an empty heart, an empty mind and an empty hand. We want to unload things that are taking up the space that should only be occupied by the truth, by the Spirit of God. Don't be afraid to admit you've been wrong. You don't want to hold on to self-righteousness, justifying, rationalizing, you want to be willing to let it go.

"As the heavens are higher than the earth, so are my ways higher than your ways and my thoughts higher than your thoughts." Isaiah 55:9

DAY 198

"Before you called I answered."

Something I hear a lot is, "Put up your sword." (Matthew 26:52) Let go of the resentment, let go of the situation, quit rehearsing it, around and around in your mind. To receive mercy, you've go to be willing to let go of human reactions. You've got to be willing to give the mercy you need to receive.

God keeps no score card. He doesn't look to see when you've been bad or when you've been good. Divine Love cannot withhold itself, it is continually pouring out. The problem is us. If we're acting or thinking or feeling in a way that is unmerciful, or ignoring the Presence of God, then we are the ones blocking what is being poured out. It's there, but we've thrown up a wall. Prayer enables us to get focused in our thoughts and in our receptivity to that which is being poured out.

The sun shines on the good and evil alike, and the rain falls on the just and the unjust alike. (Matthew 5:45) The birds sing whether you're listening or not, the flowers bloom whether you notice them or not, the seasons change whether you care or not. That's the nature of God. God does not withhold and cannot withhold. It's pouring out upon us more than we could ask or think this very second, and always has. The moment you're ready to turn to receive it, it's there.

In Isaiah 65:24 it says, "Before you called, I answered, and while you were yet speaking, I heard." Infinite Love says, "I've been speaking to you ever since you were born, I've been pouring out my blessings, you just haven't noticed. The moment you pause to notice, you will experience it."

"Let us come boldly unto the throne of grace, that we may obtain mercy, and find grace to help in time of need."   Hebrews 4:16

DAY 199

It is God's will for you to be whole.

Is it God's will for you to be whole and complete and perfect? It's not only God's will for you to be that way, you already are that way. You were created that way. That would be like me saying it's not God's will for me to be a girl. Of course it's God's will for me to be a girl. I am a girl. Of course it's God's will that I be perfect and whole and complete, full of the majesty and the Glory of God. I am. I was created that way. That's the substance of my being. That's who I am, what I am.

We have been sent here to bring order and Life and understanding. If we get caught up in the maze of the confusion of the human consciousness, then we just need to, in prayer, be willing to let all that go, and to be reminded of who we are and why we are here, where we've come from and where we're going. Once that happens, we're clear again. It doesn't go any deeper than that. Never has your identity been changed or altered simply because you got caught up in some human belief. Nothing can change it. The only thing that can be improved on is our ability to know, to understand and receive, so that we can fulfill what we've come for.

The very fact that you desire something is God speaking to you. Your desire is his will for you. God impresses things on my mind to want, so that I, in prayer, put myself into a position of receiving. That's part of his plan and purpose for me. The right desires that are in your heart are really the words and attitudes of God being interpreted as your human desire. You and God are One heart.

"We pray that you may stand perfect and complete in all the will of God."   Colossians 4:12

DAY 200

"Acquaint now thyself with him."

"Acquaint now thyself with him, and be at peace: thereby good shall come unto thee." (Job 22:21) That means you need to know the nature of God. If you don't understand the nature of God, then you're going to be hard pressed to have with God any kind of a relationship of trust and the expectancy of good. You'll be hard pressed to be able to open your heart and receive all the oneness and all the goodness that is all around and about us to receive.

You can pray, *God, teach me about you. I have heard all these things, but now I want to hear it from you.* There's a big difference between reading about something, and actually being there, or between having a dream in your heart and living the fulfillment of that dream. And there's a big difference between knowing *about* God and knowing God.

The only way we're going to get to know God is, once again, that word repent. That means to let go of what you think you know. Be willing to say, *you teach me about you, help me to see you, help me to know what's true, help me to know what I can trust. Help me to know who I am, why I'm here, where I've come from.*

Through that kind of intimate communication and desire to know, desire to come into that kind of a union, you can absolutely know God as he loves you. Then no knowledge can be withheld from you, so great is your understanding and your depth. That can only come by asking for it, and you can only ask for it and receive it by learning to let go of whatever else might be taking its place.

"He satisfies the longing soul and the hungry soul he fills with good." Psalm 107:9

DAY 201

There is always, always an answer.

Fear is a huge obstacle to being able to receive. Where there's no fear, there's confidence. And where there's confidence you realize you already have the answer. The presence of confidence comes from the absence of fear. It comes from knowing the nature of God. Maybe you don't trust the depth of your understanding of God. Don't worry about that, because it's God's understanding that you're leaning into, not yours. Don't worry about what you know or don't know. There is always, always an answer.

Fear comes because somewhere deep inside you're still believing that this thing is more real than your true nature. Or that this thing is more real than the Presence of God. That this thing is more able to overpower you and to hurt and harm you than God is to correct it. Or fear comes from believing deep inside that something you thought or did caused this to happen. In fact, we don't have that kind of power. We don't have the power to make something bad happen.

We can believe that something bad happened, but we can't change the allness and the completeness of our experience, where nothing bad can happen. That's why prayer is so powerful: it corrects that. You need to realize, not only your present perfection, but the present perfection of God who created you, who you walk and talk and listen with, who you are in the presence of, who flows through you and animates your very body, who causes your mind to desire and to be drawn back toward the eternal truth of God.

"Fear not, for I am with you: be not dismayed, for I am thy God; I will strengthen you." Isaiah 41:10

DAY 202

God is drawing you back.

Why do you think you want to understand? That's God drawing you back. What is the answer to fear? Declare the nature of God, and fear will go. Sit down with a pen and paper and write down everything you can think of about God. Write down the word immutable. That means unchangeable, his nature does not change. He doesn't change based on anything you do or don't do. Write down the word good. The Anglo-Saxon word for God is good. All we're dealing with is goodness, pure goodness. Go down the list: Love, Life, Wisdom, knowledge, understanding, compassion, Mercy, forgiveness, every thought of the nature of God that comes to your mind. Look that over and pick out two or three and meditate on those, think about what it's like to deal with that pure nature. Think of how you can come to depend and have confidence in it. Soon fear will be gone and peace and assurance will fill the space.

In addition, be willing to let go of old thoughts about God that you've accumulated and are holding onto. And finally, the most important thing you can do to release the grip of fear is to give back to God your life. The biggest stumbling block is that you are still seeing your life as something separate from the Life of God. You're still seeing you as the owner of it, therefore, responsible for it, and responsible to figure out what to do with it.

Remember that prayer is the most powerful tool that we have. It will, if approached with desire and humility, answer every question. It will respond to every human circumstance and situation. There is nothing that it cannot, or has not, or will not, heal.

"Pray everywhere, lifting up holy hands, without wrath and doubting."   1Timothy 2:8

DAY 203

Faith is knowing the truth.

Perfect God can only form perfect creation. Out from the midst of the perfection and the wholeness and the allness of God comes all that he has formed. We have to believe what we don't see. We must start with realizing that though we don't see perfect man, God could make nothing less. It is not in the nature of God to bring forth something inferior or imperfect or diseased. We see these things, but remember that faith is knowing the truth and choosing to believe it, in spite of what our experience and our eyes and the feeling realm might be dictating to us.

I want to make a choice today. I choose to believe perfect God can only create perfect man. I'm aware that I don't see that. I'm aware that most people around me don't seem to see it either. But I believe and know that God sees it that way. If I can line up with the Mind of God, if I can enter into the knowledge and understanding that God retains about his perfect creation, then I can enter into the realization, as well as the emotional feeling that produces. I can experience a healing today.

This is so near and so available, we can walk away from what has enveloped our life, simply by this exercise of effectual prayer. I am not holding out a promise that I have not seen happen hundreds of times. If we see the perfect God and the perfect man that he's created, then we're going to be able to enter into this effectual prayer that brings dynamic results every time. God has removed the veil. Now we see the absolute present Glory of God, and us in that image.

"I am the almighty God; walk before me, and be thou perfect."　　　　　　　　　　　　　　　　　Genesis 17:1

DAY 204

Look into the heart of God.

There are truths we must come to understand, we must acknowledge as true, we must make a choice to believe, make a choice to know, in spite of what we might be experiencing. We choose to know that God made us after his own image and that is perfect and whole and complete.

I stand here in humility, choosing to believe and to know what the mind of God embraces eternally, the "knowing" that never changes, despite the human condition and situation.

If we can line up with that, we can experience the healing we're looking for. We have to perceive creation as God perceives it. We have to, by the grace of God, be able to look beyond what our physical eyes see, and see with our heart, the truth and the allness and the perfection and the beauty and the order and the Glory of all that is made by God.

Out from the substance of perfection can only come forth perfection, wholeness and completeness. That's how God sees his creation, how God sees us. That's not how we see ourselves or how we see each other, but we need to correct that. That's the perception that must be healed in order for the body to be healed, the finances to be healed, the family to be healed, the relationships to be healed. Whatever is disturbing us will be healed as our perception is healed, as we learn to look beyond the physical evidence into the heart of God. When our perception is renewed, changes begin to happen. Solutions come to us, things open up, doors fling open.

"Behold I have set before you an open door and no man can shut it."   Revelation 3:8

DAY 205

Feel the Presence of God.

   Radical prayer comes from a radical knowing and a radical choice. Radical means getting to the root of something. To get to the absolute root of our existence, we must look at where we've come from and from whom we've come. We must realize we are created by God, we did not create ourselves. We didn't evolve from our parents, we didn't evolve from genetics and DNA, we are formed and created by a perfect Creator.

   It is our perception of the physical and our clinging to it that keeps it clinging to us. When our perception changes, that which we begin to perceive as true is what begins to unfold in our experience, and cling to us. Human effort dissolves, for only the change in understanding produces the change in effect.

   When we enter into a time of prayer, we want to start with the realization of the nature of God. Then it's going to dawn on us that what's true about God is what's true about us. We enter into prayer realizing that we stand in the very Presence of God. He's all around and about, fills all space and place. God is the all and the only. The more we say that, the more we think it, the more we perceive it, the more we meditate upon it, the more we begin to feel it, and the more we realize that the truth is greater than this affliction that has declared itself to have a place and power over us. If God is the all and only and fills all space and place, then where is there room for something other than God to exist? You begin to feel the Presence of God all around, everywhere you look, just with that one truth.

"All things shall be subdued, that God may be all in all."   1Corinthians 15:28

DAY 206

Start with God.

You enter into prayer knowing what God knows, not dragging along your problem. You are not saying, "God, here I am with this disease, with this big problem." By the time you have built that up in your mind, even said the words, you have denied the allness and the Presence of God. You have instead put yourself in the presence of the image and idea of dis-ease.

Start out with God, not you. Start by realizing who this is that you are approaching. What are the characteristics of this Being that you approach? *I am approaching something that is only good and can only give forth good. God is faithful, that means I don't have to overcome God's reluctance. I don't have to worry about whether I've been faithful enough, God is faithful. God is merciful, God is kind, God is ever present, God is the all and only Presence that fills all space. I stand in the Presence of God believing to receive that goodness, that allness, that completeness, of God.*

As I allow that to fill my being and my thought and my heart and my soul, I begin to embark on the altitude of effectual prayer, that changes the circumstances, that allows us to receive and to know Him, which will correct and change any situation. Let's close the door on disease robbing life from our bodies. Let's reverse the picture back to its original state. The Divine Mind and consciousness and goodness, out from which we have all come, is the only governing factor for our lives. It governs us in goodness and harmony and balance and order and perfection.

"You shall return to your former estate."
Ezekiel 16:55

DAY 207

You are standing in the fulfillment of the goodness of God.

The Bible says, when you stand praying, believe you have already received that for which you pray, and you shall receive it. (Mark 11:24) When you really do believe that you've received and that you are standing in the wholeness and completeness of fulfillment of all the goodness that God would have for you, then you see an immediate change on the human scene.

How do you get to that belief? By the knowledge of the truth. What is the truth? Perfect God, perfect man. Look beyond the human condition and realize the allness of God right where that condition denies it, right where it dishonors the Presence, the truth and the Glory of the wholeness and fullness of God. Right where it declares that disease or poverty or sadness or despair exists, we can say "No." If God is all there is, is the all and only, then we declare that, we honor that, right in the face of all these other declarations that declare they are a power capable of destroying the truth of God. We're not going to deny it any more. For too long we have given all our power to this human imagery, which comes forth from the convoluted beliefs of the human mind. Too long we have worshipped at that altar and suffered the consequences. Too long we have denied and dishonored the truth, because we have not known, and have not been told. If we start with the absolute truth of God, we deny and defy the human condition to declare otherwise. You will be amazed at the changes that happen.

"Ask and you shall receive, that your joy may be full."
John 16:24

DAY 208
Take on the Divine Life.

"It is he that has made us and not we ourselves."
(Psalm 100:3) We have come not to do our will but the
will of Him that sent us. My life is not my own, I am no
longer going to cling to my own concept of my life and
try to make it turn out to be what I want it to be, and
try to be personally responsible to see that all these
wonderful things, including health and wholeness and
happiness and fulfillment, all come to pass in my life.
I'm going to instead recognize that the life I live is not
my own. I didn't create it, I didn't choose it, I didn't
send it here, I didn't have a purpose for it to come. I
am not the governing factor of this life like I think I
have been. I choose to surrender this life back to that
which has full ownership of it, and always has.

It is He that has made us. It is He that has sent us. It is
He that has a purpose for sending us. We willingly listen
because it is this prayer, this attitude of prayer and this
altitude of prayer that will correct any situation. We
take our life and our concept of it, the personal ownership, the me-mine-I, and we wrap it all up and we
exchange it for His Life. We loose ourselves from it. We
give it away, we give it back to him.

There is one Life and that is the Life of God. The Life
of God made visible on the human scene is called Christ.
We choose to take on the Divine Life, the Life of
Christ, because that's the Life that motivates us,
animates us, gives us breath and Life and purpose and
direction and hope. We take on that Divine Life as our
very own nature. By choice.

"Having made known unto us the mystery of his will,
according to his good pleasure which he has purposed
in himself: that he might gather together in one all
things in Christ." Ephesians 1:9-10

DAY 209

Walk in newness of Life.

Taking on the Divine Life, we are taking on the Life of Christ. That Life is already perfect, already whole, already complete, already healthy. It doesn't know anything but health and wholeness and completeness. It is already about its "Father's business."(Luke 2:49) It already knows that it "can of its own self do nothing." (John 5:30) It already knows that it must listen and respond, in order to realize the fulfillment and the purpose for which it's been sent to this earth. It already realizes that it has "come to do the will of Him that sent it" (John 5:30) and not its own will.

We don't have all this new stuff to learn, we only need to get rid of our old concept of my life, me, mine, and take on the new. After we have completed that exchange, we are walking in newness of Life. When we walk in newness of Life, we're walking in a Life that does not know pain and suffering and sorrow and lack and limitation and loss and loneliness. We don't experience this anymore because the life that experienced it, we have exchanged, we've walked away from it, we have let it go. It was only in the human consciousness anyway. We have taken on that which is Eternal and Divine, that which we really came to express.

Now you can stand praying "believing you have already received."(Mark 11:24) Now you can stand with a whole new perception, seeing through the eyes of Christ, seeing through the Divine Mind. Now you stand in your own completeness and see the wholeness of others and realize their healing as well. Now you can fulfill the purpose for which you have been sent, which is to bring healing and wholeness to the world.

"This corruptible must put on incorruption, and this mortal must put on immortality." 1Corinthians 15:53

DAY 210

Let go of the old nature for a higher nature.

In the Old Testament, the Israelites were told that before they approached God every day, they were to offer a burnt offering, an offering of a bull. (Deuteronomy 12:6) Spiritually, that is the bull nature of the human, that insists on its own life. This is my life, my will, my way, my mind, my achievements, I own, I possess, I decide, I want, I'll get, I'll do. That is the bullish nature of the human, contrary to the lamb, which is the nature of Christ, the submissive, obedient, gentle, meek, desiring to fulfill the purpose for which it's been sent.

Every day we let go of that old nature, the strong will, for a higher will, a higher nature, the nature of the lamb. We do it everyday because we forget. As we interact with people, we find we are unknowingly taking on the old human consciousness. Every day we need to refresh the unloading of that old nature. Every day we make a concerted moment of choice to let go of the old and to receive and take on that which is our true nature, in which we have truly been created, the eternal nature we will continue to live out for eternity.

That's the one we should be carrying while we're here, because that's the nature that will keep us separate from disease, suffering, the human scene. That's the one that will cause us to live in victory and in wholeness and that's also the one that allows us to fulfill the reason we've been sent, which is to deliver and free others. We've come to heal.

"Let this mind be in you which was also in Christ Jesus."   Philippinans 2:5

DAY 211

We are the visible manifestation of the invisible God.

God so loved the world, and so desired the ultimate perfection of all that he made to be visible, to be expressed and to be experienced, that he sent forth his word, his understanding, his mind, his heart, his will, his purpose, and he put it all in a bundle and sent it in a man called Jesus. That man came to reveal the heart of God, the Mind of God, to give purpose to our lives and direction to lift us out of the messes that we find ourselves in.

Remember that everything in our experience starts as thought, a state of consciousness. If we had the conscious awareness of God right now, we could not be consciously aware of disease or aloneness or sadness or fear. We could not have any negative emotions because "In his presence there is fullness of joy, and at his right hand are pleasures forever more." (Psalm 16:11) If we are experiencing that which we would not, we are still living in the human consciousness. When that consciousness is changed, the physical appearance is altered.

How can thought translate into physical manifestation? We were in the mind of God before we were created and that thought took on form. Jesus is called the Word of God. Thought become the spoken word and the spoken word became flesh. The prerequisite for bringing forth a higher consciousness, the Mind of God, the heart of God, the perfection, wholeness, order and balance, is bringing forth the Christ. The Christ is the visible manifestation of the invisible God. The whole of mankind was made to be the body of Christ. There is One Life, the visible manifestation of the invisible God.

"We being many are one bread and one body: for we are all partakers of that one bread." 1Corinthians 10:17

DAY 212

Let us walk in the Spirit.

"If you be led of the Spirit, you are not under the law." (The law which results in defeat, despair, disease and death.) "The fruit of the Spirit is love, joy, peace, patience, gentleness, goodness, faith, meekness, temperance: *against such there is no law.* If we live in the Spirit, let us also walk in the Spirit." (Galatians 5)

We have been created and sent by God, created in his image and likeness, as Spirit Beings. Though we seem to wear a body of flesh, we are indeed Spirit Beings, because the image of God is Spirit. If I am led by that knowledge, if I walk in that knowledge, if I allow that to be lived out in my life, then I am not under the myriad of laws as a human being. I am of a higher law.

"The law of the Spirit of Life in Christ Jesus has made me free from the law of sin and death." (Romans 8:2) There are two laws in operation. One is the law of the Spirit; we are Spirit Beings, part and parcel of the Christ existence, the body of Christ, the visible manifestation of the invisible God. We have been sent to be visible manifestations of the invisible God, to heal the physical world as Spirit Beings.

The other laws are human laws. As humans we live as though we are strictly mortals victimized by the laws of humanity, for instance, the laws of disease. The only escape out from under the human laws is to find ourselves under another law, the law of the Spirit of God. Those that are led by the Spirit, who recognize they are Spirit Beings, are under the law of the Spirit of God. This is what governs their lives. They have answered the call, said, "Yes, I recognize that I have been sent with a purpose and I have come to understand and fulfill that purpose by being sensitive to who and what I am."

"As he is, so are we in this world."   1John 4:17

DAY 213

Arise inside.

When praying for someone, recognize that though you may be looking at a very weak, frail human who seems to be subjected to the laws of humanity, beyond what you are actually seeing with your eyes is the true substance of everyone created. Beyond is Spirit, is Christ. No matter how they look, feel, act, believe, know, don't know, or say it isn't so, it doesn't change it.

That substance of Christ within you can reach out and join with the Christ within this person who is suffering. In quietness and silence, close your eyes and with a heart of intention and desire, reach out, take the hand of the true nature, the Christ nature of this person, and join with that Christ. Acknowledge that the true substance of this person is strength, wholeness, health, vitality, abundance, goodness, happiness, joy, completion. Everything wonderful is not coming, it already is. That is the true substance that this person has been created and sent as. There is nothing that can come against that acknowledgement and that understanding, when joined with another in a heart to heart knowing.

Awake, awake, from the sleepiness, from the dullness of mind that has been imposed upon us by the whole human consciousness. If you are under a law of human consciousness and human belief that is causing you suffering, there is a way out from that right now, a way of escape. It's to acknowledge and realize that there is but one Creator, not many, and that Creator has brought forth all things out from the substance of his own being. Therefore, everything brought forth is as perfect as the Source that brought it forth. If you are not in that state, awake. Stand on your feet, arise inside.

"Awake, awake, put on strength."   Isaiah 51:9

DAY 214

Is this what you want?

Years ago I heard a lecture by a Catholic Priest. He had liver cancer and was in the final stages of the disease in a hospital, dying. He hadn't been on his feet in days. Suddenly he heard, "Is this what you want?" He said, "No, this is not what I want." Then he heard, "Then get up, because this is not who you are." He got up, ripped off all the monitors, IVs, oxygen, and was getting his pants on when the nurses came running in. They thought he was delerious. He said, "I'm going home, I'm alright." They didn't want him to go, but he signed a release of the hospital, got a cab and went home. He had a few weeks of fighting the exhaustion, weakness, all his symptoms, but he remembered what he heard. "This is not who you are."

Within three weeks he had recovered his strength, not by anything he did, but by what he continued to acknowledge, by what he began to really understand. Now he's looking perfectly normal, smoking cigarettes, drinking coffee, and telling everybody his story.

This story is true, and it's true about hundreds of patients that I have known in the last forty years. We can walk out of the law of humanity, the law of disease, the law of poverty, the law of sadness, the law of despair. All these are laws of man, laws of human consciousness, that affect us because we believe that's who we are.

We are made up of much more than this. Our substance is the image and likeness of God, it is the Christ, the visible expression of the invisible God. We're the expression of the One Life of God.

"Ye shall be holy, for I, the Lord your God, am holy."
                                                    Leviticus 19:2

DAY 215

Your life will change forever.

I've learned not to look at things, but to look at the Life of the thing. Not to look at people, but to look at the Life of the people. I've learned to stop judging after what my eyes see. I've learned to look at the Life that created and formed and motivated and animated this thing. I've learned to look for the characteristics and the attributes of the Divine Life that are shown forth by the Life of this thing or this person.

Only after learning this are we able to fulfill the purpose for which we've been sent, and free people, all of humanity. Romans 8:22 says, "The whole creation groans and travails in pain together..." waiting for the manifestation of the sons of God. That's us, all of us. As we begin to acknowledge and recognize who we really are, we begin to free up a creation bound under the laws of disease and death. It says, "The lion will lie down with the lamb, and there will be peace in all my holy mountain." (Isaiah 65:25)

What does that mean? That means the consciousness of man will be lifted to the consciousness of God. Our whole thought will be elevated to know and understand and acknowledge the truth. Is this so far out? Is this impossible? People say, this can never be. It will be. It will be as soon as we arise into this. We've been talking about it for two thousand years and more. It's time to stop looking for something to happen in the future and stop worshipping something that happened in the past, and start taking hold of what is now.

Let's tuck this into our hearts. Ask, "Father, is this for me? What is my part in this?" Look out, your life will change forever. Everything you see will be different.

"Arise, shine, for thy light is come and the glory of God is risen upon thee." Isaiah 60:1

DAY 216

Love is the answer.

Jesus told a parable about inviting people to a wedding feast, but they could not come because they had so many other concerns. They couldn't bother to come to the marriage feast that God set out before them. (Matthew 22) This means the spiritual union, spiritual oneness, between our souls and the soul of God, which turns out to be the same soul. We are just multitudes of expressions of the same soul, but we don't know that at first. It takes a union and a marriage and a commitment, a consecrated commitment of clinging to the soul and the Mind and the heart and the true understanding of God, in order for that marriage and union to take hold.

In the parable, God, the Father, sends out invitations to come to that kind of an experience, but we all have so many concerns. We say, "I just can't do it." If you can't do it for your mother, if you can't do it for a friend, then you're not doing it for God. It says in Matthew 25, when you've done this for the least of my brothers, then you've done it for me. You bind your heart and soul in an act of mercy and compassion and love to reach out for another. You can't come into a union with God, unless you come into a union with a manifestation of God, what he has created.

Whenever I have seen people spontaneously walk out of destruction, there was Divine Love present, an experience of love they could hold on to, in the form of a person who made sacrifices of love, or someone who prayed to seek the truth for that person, to see them as they have been made. Love is the answer. Truth is necessary, but behind those words there needs to be a heart and a life that's willing to prove those words.

"We that are strong ought to bear the infirmities of the weak, and not to please ourselves." Romans 15:1-2

DAY 217
Be swallowed up in goodness and love.

God is an absolute being of pure goodness. It's an Eternal Infinite Being that just is. If we want to experience the goodness of that Being, we need to let our perceptions and our thoughts and our heart be enveloped by the thoughts of the Mind of God: the goodness, the purity, the wholeness. Line up with that as our perception, as that which we believe is true, as what we say is reality. Then our experience will produce that reality. That will be our perception and our reality will change to the good.

Let good and Life and purity of thought, and wholesomeness and giving encompass you and envelop you in thought: *This is God and I live in this. This is the Life that flows through me and this is the Life that I walk and talk and live and love and laugh and breathe in. It's all around me. This is my perception of reality.* Then my reality begins to take on the nature of what I have been believing and experiencing in my thoughts.

What gives disease and death and sorrow and suffering its strength? Feeling condemned, feeling guilty, feeling inferior. This is how we unconsciously attract suffering, we feel we deserve it. We need to set that aside, clear our thoughts, and ask, "What is God?"

We are a part of that, always have been, we've never separated from it. We need to feel ourselves enveloped in that Presence and in that reality. We need to claim and hold to that new and true and pure and clear understanding of our relationship to God. Get a vision of the allness and the oneness of God enveloping us, swallowing us up in wholeness and love.

"I am persuaded that neither death nor life... nor things present, nor things to come... shall be able to separate us from the love of God." Romans 8:39

DAY 218

Open up the flow of Divine Love.

What is the difference between human love and Divine Love? Human love ceases to be human and becomes Divine when it is poured out in an unselfish manner. You must give from your heart, whether it's your money, your time, your compassion and mercy, forgiveness, grace, or whether it's your effort to see past what the other person is seeing about themselves, to see their wholeness and completeness. By giving you've opened up the actual flow of Eternal and Divine Life, Eternal and Divine Love. Contained within that is the abundance of all good. As soon as you give with that spirit, with that heart, with that attitude, strictly for the good of another, you will find much more good in your own experience, because you have opened the door, and let this Divine nature begin to flow.

If you give in order to experience more good for yourself, then it was a manipulative motive, and the spirit of it was not pure. That's not love, that's just a mode of getting something for your own sake. That becomes self love, and we slip back into the human.

Another thing that seems to block the flow of Divine Love is the belief that we are supposed to imitate that which we see as Christ. We can't imitate it. If you are trying to imitate, you are trying to take this human nature and trying to make it Divine. You can't do it. It's constantly climbing up a hill that you never get to the top of. That produces a sense of failure and condemnation, confusion and dis-ease. That's not what it's about. It's not a human do-over.

It's about trading one life for another. It's about letting go of the human life in exchange for the Life of God.

"To whomever much is given, of him shall much be required."　　　　　　　　　　　　　　Luke 12:48

DAY 219

The true nature of your being already contains all that is.

We come, sent by God, in his image and likeness, already containing all that he is. That's the Christ Spirit. The true nature of your being already contains all that is.

We were intended to take the whole human life as we perceive it, and lay it at the foot of the altar of God and say, "Here, this is a product of the human consciousness, humanity's best thought without God. Take this, and I gladly release the flow of the Christ life, the Divine Love from within me."

When it says, "You are the righteousness of God in Christ" (2Corinthians 5:21), it's not talking about something you are going to be, it's something that you are. When it says you are "complete in him" (Colossians 2:10), it's not something you're trying to attain to, it's simply something that you are. But the only way to experience these things is to walk away from what you thought you were, from the whole human belief system. These are heavy burdens that do not allow us to experience the Christ Life.

We must understand that Divine Love is the nature of us, that God resides within us, *as* our true being. As we allow that to flow, contained within that nature is the fullness and the abundance of everything that we could possibly need. Once we get the pump flowing we begin to experience the abundance of the true, Eternal Life that we ought to be living right now, not waiting for some heavenly experience which is at our fingertips, as near as the breath we breathe, as near as the words we speak. It is you, it is me, and it is all of us. Every one.

"I will dwell in them and walk in them and I will be their God and they shall be my people."

2Corinthians 6:16

DAY 220

God is all in all.

We must come to the mystery of God, see that God is all in all. (1Corinthians 15:28) It's not the human *and* God, with humans reaching out to God, trying to get God to fix our problem. Are we living in the human experience or the Divine? If we let go of the human life as humans have defined it, and say, "This is not the life that I came to live, I did not come to live under the human condition with all of its frailty and confusion. I'm going to lay all that down and allow my true nature, the Christ nature, to begin to flow. I'm going to let Love flow."

How do we do that? We don't. We pray and it begins to flow. If you think you have to do it, that's the human doing it. My daily prayer is that unobstructed, unencumbered Divine Love be allowed to freely flow. Watch it happen, watch your thought softening, watch your judgment of people and events taking a back seat, watch Mercy begin to flow. Hear the grace that begins to flow from your mouth. Feel the compassion and Mercy that you begin to feel for another. Watch as things begin to unfold out from your own being. Become a beholder of the Divine Life and the flow of Eternal Love that flows through you.

When we read that "Divine Love always has met and always will meet every human need," (Mary Baker Eddy, *Science and Health*, p. 494), we don't see it as something outside of us coming to meet a need. When we hear, "Knock and it shall be opened to you" or "Ask and it shall be given" (Matthew 7:7), we're not looking outside anymore, but for something to happen to us on the inside. The flow of Eternal Love contains everything, beyond anything we've ever imagined.

"Is not my help in me?"   Job 6:13

DAY 221

Divine Love flows out from you.

The flow of Divine Love produces healing. That flow is not something external flowing to you, where you have to be worthy to receive it, or where you have to have everything all in order, or where you have to overcome your belief in God's reluctance to give to you. It is not Love coming from an external being, it is Love flowing out from you. It feels very much like, and is, *you* loving, you giving just for the sheer joy of giving. You can tell that it comes from the Christ nature, not from the human nature, because there's no effort, there's no thought. You get to that by choosing to exchange all that you have been functioning in, for your higher nature.

When people have a problem and they're running here and there, they're not really running for some magic pill or some doctor's wand. What they're really looking for is Love and Mercy and compassion. It's the Love and compasssion flowing that heals. They're looking for someplace where they can realize true compassion, Mercy, grace and Love. In that experience, which is a Divine experience, they will be made whole. They may not know that in their human consciousness, but the Spirit within them drives them forward looking for that.

It's available within our own being. It's available coming from those around us, because we all live in this huge soup of Divinity, of the Eternal Love and compassion and Mercy and grace of God. As we let that Divinity flow, we let ourselves love others. We will see healings all around us.

"The Lord make you to increase and abound in love one toward another." 1Thessalonians 3:12

DAY 222

Let go and be part of the flow.

John 12:32 says, "If I be lifted up, I will draw all unto me." When Divine Love is lifted up, when out from the center of your being you allow the Love of God to flow, any way it wants to, in any direction, you will see healings everywhere. "The wind blows whichever way it will blow" and it's not up to us to know which way the wind is going to blow. (John 3:8) But it is up to us to let go and be a part of the flow of that wind, let it carry us. Let that Love flow wherever it wants to.

That river is going to either flow out, or it's going to be like the Dead Sea, flowing into this big cesspool of selfhood, my concerns and wants and needs, my disease, my fears. If it doesn't flow out, it becomes like a dead sea. That breeds disease. Once the river stops flowing out, it causes dis-ease. The human situation always produces lack and limitation and hardship and negativity, as long as we live in that human realm. It's a dead end, it's a dead sea, it won't flow.

The block in the energy flow comes from thought, not from something physical. That's what needs to be set aside so Love can flow. It's done by prayer. *I deliberately choose today to let go of all my human life and allow the Christ mind, the Christ Love, the Christ compassion, the Christ Life, to flow..*

You don't get what you need by accumulating, you get by giving, by pouring out. It says God will meet our needs, which he will, always. But it's up to us to let God flow. It flows from us. The origin of Eternal, Divine Love is within us.

"He sends out his word and melts them, he causes his wind to blow, and the waters to flow."   Psalm 147:18

DAY 223

Get the true picture of Love flowing.

In the book of Revelation, chapter 22, it talks about the river of Life pouring out from the throne of God. Where is the throne of God? It's Emmanuel, God with us. Where did God choose to make his habitation? In us, not in the human, but the Divine. The Divine is all around and within us. We have to stop seeing ourselves as a solid entity, stop seeing ourselves as a body, because then we can't get the true picture of Love flowing uninterrupted.

We think in terms of inside and outside--there's no inside or outside of you. Do you know that when you're a baby you're 90% water, and when you're an adult you're 75% water? What holds the water together? Why doesn't it pour out? It's not because you're a solid entity, it's a molecular holding that holds it all together. That adhesive, cohesive quality is God.

The energy and the Life and the thought and the compassion and the Mercy and the grace of Divine Love all flow through you unencumbered. It doesn't see a solid entity. It's as near as the breath you breathe, it's all around you, you're walking and talking and living and breathing in it. It's flowing through you as if you were not there--you, by your human definition. We let go of our definition and yield to the flow of this Love. That's how the outpouring of Divine Love heals. It contains within it all the nature, characteristics and attributes of the Eternal and Divine God.

"He showed me a pure river of water of life, clear as crystal, proceeding out of the throne of God and of the Lamb. In the midst of the street of it, and on either side of the river, was there the tree of life...and the leaves of the tree were for the healing of the nations." Revelation 22:1-2

DAY 224

Enter the rest of God.

Jesus did many of his healings on the sabbath day. "Sabbath" is a Hebrew word meaning rest. In the book of Hebrews, chapters 3 and 4, it talks about the rest of God, and how to enter into the rest of God. When Jesus did his healings on the sabbath day, what he was saying was that our healing, any reestablishment of order and perfection and wholeness, will come when we have entered into a place of rest, when we have let go of the turmoil and the tension and the fear that accompany so many of our problems. How do we get from that very human response of stress and worry and doubt and fear to that state of peace that is of God?

The sabbath should be every day. Every day we should live in that peace and rest of God. Every day we should avoid the thought and the confusion that accompanies the human response to any negative situation that would produce dis-ease in our minds and our bodies and our lives. When it says, "The sabbath was made for man, not man for the sabbath," (Mark 2:27), it means that the rest of God was given to us. It is a gift. It is a place where we are to live, day in and day out, 24/7. It is a place where we continually recognize that God is the director of our lives. We stop feeling a personal sense of responsibility to extricate ourselves from any given mess. What do we do when we find ourselves in there, and how do we shift over to that rest?

I remember, this life is not my own. "It is not given unto man to direct his own steps or to know his own way." (Jeremiah 10:23) I humble myself under the mighty hand of God, (1Peter 5:6), and I wait, until I am in a state of peace and rest.

"One that has entered into his rest, has also ceased from his own works as God did from his." Hebrews 4:10

DAY 225

I humble myself under God.

"Humble yourself under the mighty hand of God that he may exalt you in due time." (1Peter 5:6)

"Whoever exalts himself shall be abased, and he who humbles himself shall be exalted." (Matthew 23:12)

I humble myself under God, not under the situation, not under the people and places, not even under my own inadequacy, just under God. I continue to humble myself until I'm in a state of peace. Until I'm content with every day, until Life is all I see and know, until I am grateful and joyful for all that I am blessed with and all that I have. I don't look at what I don't have, I don't look at what someone else has. I am content.

We are here to give, we are here to obey a Supreme Being, we are here to humble ourselves and to take on the Life of Christ. That is the core doctrine of Christianity, and also Islam and Judaism. What God exalts is people willing to love. People who let go of personal selfhood as their god, for the good of the whole. The love that says, I am no longer in self preservation mode, I am in giving mode.

We did not create ourselves, we do not belong to ourselves, we belong to another. The key is in recognition of that, and the humility it takes to turn ourselves in another direction. Everything we reached for is let go, we are at the point of no longer caring, we are content with our life and our days, content with the joy of our human experience. Once you're there, everything you had let go of is yours, not something you grasped, but as a result of the Life you are living, of the Spirit motivating that Life, of the Love and joy flowing through that Life.

"We brought nothing into this world and it is certain we can carry nothing out."　　　　　1Timothy 6:7

DAY 226
Become enamored by the incredible perfection of the human body.

When I was in nursing school, I devoured medical textbooks. I spent multitudes of hours pouring over those books. God himself was forming in my mind and in my heart a concept of the human body. When I read about it, I actually fell in love with it. I was enamored by the incredible perfection of the human body. I was in awe at the intelligence of every cell, every system, every organ, how they worked independently and yet were interdependent. How they seemed to know what to do--they were always bent on maintaining the balance, order, harmony, and integrity of the body.

The idea that anything could go wrong with the body became more and more absurd to me. There was nothing about the body that could not kick itself into a compensatory mode and fix itself. There is no reason for the body not to be an eternal experience. Since then, a physicist got a Nobel prize for proving that every cell is immortal, and determining that if the fluid within and without every cell in the body was kept pure and kept flowing, that cell would live eternally.

Back then, at twenty years old, I reveled in hearing the mind and the heart and the Spirit of God teaching me, causing me to see the beauty, the order, the harmony, the balance, the perfection, the immutability, the infinity, of that which God has made. Every year it's gotten more real to me, more of a reality than all the diseases that could stand against that truth and declare themselves to be a power, a presence and an entity that could interrupt that. As that vision governed my heart and mind, I saw incredible healings.

"Let it be healed."   Hebrews 12:3

DAY 227

Experience the Glory of creation.

If the body is so intrinsically whole and perfect, if it is the visible expression of the invisible God, if it is the Divine intelligence, the eternal, immutable intelligence of God in a visible form, if it does declare the true nature of God in all of its beauty and harmony and order, then what causes the experience of disease?

Stand back and, instead of feeling like a body, look at it objectively, knowing who made it, who sustains it, whose energy and intelligence flows through it. Stand back and feel the beauty and the order and the presence of such perfection and realize you are experiencing God by looking at one of his beautiful formations. It's much like looking at a rose. You experience God when you look at the horizon and you see the sun coming up or going down. You experience God every time you look away from your own human, fearful, limited thoughts. You experience the Glory of creation.

Why not look at the body, which has also been created by the same perfect and intelligent being, that which is unchangeable. Stand back and think about the beauty and the order of God who made this in his image and likeness. Then you understand that disease is simply a lack of seeing that, a lack of taking the time to experience the truth of what Life in the body is. Once you have experienced that, you will never acquiesce to the power and the presence of something less than that. Disease declares that disorder is more present and powerful than Divine Order, that disharmony is more present and powerful than the eternal harmony of God. Stand back and see the reality of what God has created.

"I have created him for my glory, I have formed him: yea I have made him." Isaiah 43:7

DAY 228
The Mind of God is as near as your own mind.

The Mind of God is the intelligence that flows through you. Put aside all that you have been educated to believe, all that you have seen, all that you have feared, and consider that the thought of dis-ease might be a hysterical mass mesmeric thought. It's like a herd of cattle that hear something--a twig snaps in the woods and the whole herd starts running. Only one or two heard the snap of the twig in the woods, but when one starts running, they all start running. The more they run, the more they think they have something to run away from. Pretty soon they all run over the cliff and are killed, over what? Nothing. Over every mind being mesmerized by a belief in something that we are supposed to be fearing, instead of seeing the truth.

The Mind of God, that sees and knows the beauty and the order and the immutable perfection of all that He is, and all that He expresses throughout all of His creation, is a near as your own mind, to declare and allow the formation of the truth to come to your vision, to your understanding. You have to want it, you have to ask for it. You have to be still. You have to want to know what God knows, want to see what God sees, want to see the reality of what God has created.

What is the nature of God from which everything comes that has been created? How can that which has been created have a nature so contrary to the nature of that which formed it? It can't. "Each seed reproduces after its own kind." (Genesis 1:11) That is a law of God. God made that law, He's not going to break it.

Are we going in the direction the world is going? Let's challenge it, and eliminate disease at its root.

"Come out from among them and be ye separate, and I will receive you."   2Corinthians 6:17

DAY 229

I'm looking at the wholeness of God.

Envision a world without disease, mankind living in the joy and the peace and the harmony and the love and the wholeness and the perfection and the order that we were created to experience.

We have changed the truth of God into a doctrine of man, and say that we can't experience heaven until after we die. Never mind all that, Jesus came and said that the Kingdom of God is right here among you. Just repent and enter into it. (Matthew 4:17)

Repent means quit looking at what you're looking at, quit believing what you're believing, and turn around. Turn around and look at something in a different way, because it's all around you. It's within you, he said. (Luke 17:21) There should be nothing to keep you from entering into it, except that you're looking in the wrong direction. You are calling real that which is not real. You are reacting to what you're seeing and what you're envisioning out of fear, out of the expectancy of suffering and disease.

The healings I have seen come from a deep sense of the intrinsic wholeness of the individual, when I know that I'm looking at the wholeness of God, and denying all of the evidence to the contrary. If the patient shares in that deep intrinsic sense of wholeness, that deep down refusal to accept disease as part of their experience, something in them says, this isn't right, this isn't from God, I don't need to accept this. I'm know this isn't true. I'm going to stick with that deep sense of wholeness, and that sense that this is an intruder, an invasion, and that which is within me is greater than that which has come against me. (1John 4:4)

"He calls those things which be not as though they were."   Romans 4:17

DAY 230

God is all in all.

In Isaiah 14:12-17, it says that in the day when the veil is lifted and we are no longer groping around in the darkness of our own imagination and fears, and we actually see things the way they are, we'll look at this enemy that has so tormented us and caused so many tears, so much fear, and sorrow and suffering, that has dominated our very existence, has kept joy and peace away from us, robbing us of our inheritance...we're going to look at it and we're going to say, "Is that all that was?"

When you get a vision of the allness of God and realize it is the very expression of your life, your body, your existence, your mind, your emotions, your purpose, your direction, all that you're experiencing and all that you're giving, when you realize it is all in all, (Ephesians 1:23), you look over at this thing that's seemed so huge and you say, "Is that all there is to it?"

A gentleman called me to share a healing he had by listening to my radio broadcasts. He had been a severe asthmatic since he was six years old, but when he heard these truths, he knew this was true. He applied it, agreed with it, and this condition went away.

When truth is applied, the condition, whatever it is, goes away. Where did it go? It didn't go anywhere, because it was nothing to start with, except in our own imagination. It turns out to be a whole educated system of belief based on nothingness, and we've all bought into it. But now we reach out for a higher vision, and a higher reality, and we are able to say, "Is that all it was?"

"He makes the devices of the people of none effect."
                                                    Psalm 33:10

DAY 231

Trade it in!

There's no sense hanging out with despair to try to heal anything. There is no sense in going back into our childhood or into our teens, to every circumstance and situation that caused us disappointment, grief or despair.

The problem is we learn from infancy to define our life, and our happiness or our sadness, according to external situations, circumstances, people, and events. When we allow ourselves to be that vulnerable, when we let our emotional system be built on circumstances, on situations, we never take control of ourselves. We never make a decision to choose what we're going to feel, what we're going to think. We never hold to a decision and choice of how we intend to view life. So, from the time we're little, we're victims of whatever happens, just by the omission of that kind of a choice.

In my mind, the only thing to do is to trade in our grief, sadness and despair for joy. Make a choice, and make a decision, to trade in our experience of life as we have defined it, with all the negative emotions, for the Life that God has for us. Trade in the human definition of life for the Divine definition of Life. Watch and see what happens--it's incredible.

Dis-ease comes from a shut down in the free flow of Life through us, free flow of the intelligent energy of the Creator that formed us. When that free flow is restored, health is restored. Rather than trying to deal with everything on a physical level, or an analytical level, just take whatever it is and trade it in for what you really want, and for what God wants for us.

"You shall go out with joy and be led forth with peace; the mountains and the hills shall break forth before you into singing, and all the trees of the field shall clap their hands." Isaiah 55:12

DAY 232

Choose joy.

A woman came to one of our Monday night meetings, and hearing the phrase, "just trade it in", she said those words went down into her soul and shook the foundation of her being. Then and there she made a conscious decision and a choice to trade in the despondency, sadness, grief and despair, and all the physical symptoms that happened in her body as a response to all that negative emotion. She traded in the panic attacks, the anxiety, the mood swings and emotional instability that we hear 80% of the people in the U.S. are suffering from. They're a result of the misery and sadness of years of unresolved emotions that we hold in our emotional system. We hold them in our hearts, and that shuts down the free flow of the Life of God through us, causing disease and sadness to settle in.

She decided right then and there she was choosing it, and from the next morning on, it was gone. After forty years of grief and sadness, all of a sudden she woke up full of joy. She woke up full of happiness and confidence and an excited expectation for the day. Only a couple of times in the past few months has sadness tried to creep in, and she catches it and says, I don't choose you anymore. I choose joy. I've traded you in for the Life that God has predetermined that I should live. Joy comes right back again. Her physical health is restored, her emotional health is restored. She now has a life that's worth living. She's not just plodding along, she's not trying to analyze every thought, she's not looking back, blaming other people, she simply took the whole package and traded it in.

"Weeping may endure for a night, but joy comes in the morning."   Psalm 30:5

DAY 233

A life for a Life.

A woman wrote to me of her experience of a healing from lymphoma. After trying every route offered, physical and mental, including a bone marrow transplant, she said, "I quit. I gave up any investment, any personal interest in the outcome. When I finally surrendered, the peace I experienced is beyond understanding. And I was healed. Listening to Michele, I was reminded to return to my original belief system, that God is the Source of my Life, that Life is good and whole and complete, full of joy and the expectancy of good. To return to my belief that God will lead me and let me know where to go, and when. I can finally get out of the way."

When she gave up, she didn't give up to the disease, didn't acquiesce to the disease, *she gave up all the self-effort*. She laid it all down and said, "Here is my life as I am experiencing it. I'm trading it in for the Life of God, the Life that God holds in His heart and mind for me." She traded a life for a Life.

That's what the cross of Christ means. At the cross, the human mortal concept of life is traded in for a Divine Life. All of our suffering, all of our fears, we give back to God, offer it, give it away, lay it down. You remove yourself from it so you can receive newness of Life, a true Divine Life, a true free flow of the Life of God, the heart of God, the Mind of God, the Presence of God. You will enter into a whole new Life.

We can only do that if we realize that it's not God who chose this miserable life, God had nothing to do with this choice, it's something of human creation. Then we can lay it down and make space for the greater Life, God's very Spirit, the only Life.

"Of him and through him and to him are all things."
Romans 11:36

DAY 234

Let it come from God.

All that we will ever need in our life comes from the goodness of God. It is a constant pouring out without anything to block or stop it. We look at the avenue through which it comes and think it is actually coming from that, rather than realizing it is simply an avenue. Even if that avenue shuts down, it's going to keep on.

Money, jobs, careers, education, all these come from God. If you send out resumes and you're not hearing back, so what? It doesn't depend on them. It's coming from God. Let it come, receive it in your heart, whatever it is, however it turns out, whatever avenue it takes you to, just receive it. Don't look to people, places, things, circumstances, events, or anything on a horizontal, human level. Look to God and something will open up. A new avenue will appear that you didn't even know about. Let it come from God.

It's the same with love. Let it come from God. Just feel the Presence of Divine Love. Feel the enveloping, all encompassing Presence of the Love of God. Walk in it, feel the joy of it, see it everywhere you look. Be thankful. A human avenue of love will appear.

We can't let other people or things dominate our existence. We've got to put God in his rightful place, as the giver of all Life, every avenue of existence, and the answer to every need that could be imagined. God abundantly pours out all the time and always has. If you haven't experienced it, that's because you've been looking at the human scenario to supply it. Don't look at the human. God governs everything. Let's leave it to God.

"Blessed is the one that trusts in the Lord and whose hope the Lord is. For he shall be as a tree planted by the waters."   Jeremiah 17:7-8

DAY 235

Pray for the Wisdom of God.

What is the conscience? It's that voice within that speaks faithfully, directing and guiding, or roaring at us when we're ignoring it. Our conscience is given to us. It's like having a best friend that's always with us to nudge us along, keeping us on the right path. It teaches us, so that whenever we come into a situation where we're veering off unknowingly, maybe reacting, or taking on somebody else's idea of right or wrong, this guide says, "No, that's not right, try this." We come to trust that guide, and we find that our way stays very smooth in front of us. We can expect good things to come into our life. We can expect peace in our life.

How do we know when our conscience is leading us? Sometimes our justifications and our desires get us confused. We don't know what we're doing. The only way we would know is to be silent and not move, and pray for the Wisdom of God. When we don't, and we go our own way, we have a guilty conscience. Whether it's right or wrong, we feel guilty because we didn't wait to find out. We let self will and desire and demands lead out, so we feel uncomfortable inside.

But if what we're doing is because love is flowing, then we have a clear conscience. If we're not motivated by love, but by self will, then we have a guilty conscience. If we feel guilty, then whatever we're trying to do will fail, because we're unconsciously sabotaging it. Guilt is a good thing. Guilt is the conscience saying, "Whoa, wait a minute." If we do what is needed to fix the problem, we're clear. Guilt only becomes a problem when we refuse the direction of conscience-- that's unresolved guilt, and that's death to us.

"Be ye not unwise, but understanding what is the will of the Lord." Ephesians 5:17

DAY 236

Listen to your heart.

Often, things feel right when we are considering them in our head only, but when we consider something with our heart, it doesn't feel right. If you're wise enough to stop and listen to your heart, if you let your heart direct your way, you will never go wrong. You may be out there all by yourself for a while, but that path will open up and you will be blessed and good will come.

When I say, let your heart direct you, it's Divine Love that's directing you. It's really the heart of God that's directing you. It's the mind and heart and purpose and intention of God that speaks to our heart, our con-science, and says yes or no. The head is filled with a lot of stuff, but not our heart, because Gods speaks to us through our heart, not through our will, not through our mind, not through our education, but through our heart, through that still small voice. We don't want that to become a roar. We want to learn to fine tune it so that we respond to it immediately.

Guilt is not an enemy. The enemy is that you're not listening to it, you're not going to the Wisdom of God to find out how to resolve it. Running from it becomes an enemy. You hate the feeling so much that you run from it, instead of stopping and turning around and facing it square on. Ask God, "Why do I feel like this? Tell me what to do to extricate myself from this. What can I know? What can I believe? What can I understand? What can I do, what can I say, where can I go?" There's always a way to choose something better, you just have to go to the right Source to find the way.

"Commit thy works unto the Lord and thy thoughts shall be established."   Proverbs 16:3

DAY 237

Take it to the heart of God.

Any time we do anything against the Law of Love, without seeking the guidance of Divine Wisdom and following it, we are opening ourselves up to guilt. There are two ways to relieve ourselves of guilt. One is to attract suffering like a magnet, until we've suffered enough that we finally figure the slate is clean. A guilty conscience attracts misery, and until the slate is clean, we're going to suffer the consequences.

There is an easier way out: listen to what it's saying, and have the courage to obey it. There is forgiveness when we've done something wrong, and we can experience a sense of worthiness. The true cause of suffering is living under a sense of unworthiness. It may not be anything you've done, it may be something you've believed. Maybe your religion has told you how unworthy you are, and maybe you carry around a sense of unworthiness just for being alive. You're not alone in that.

Take that to the heart of God and say, *What do I do with this? I know you don't think that way about me. You created me in your image and likeness, in the likeness of Divine Love. When you look at me, you feel Love, you see Love. You created me to be an expression of your Love. What can I do about these feelings?*

Just doing that, just that exercise in prayer, will heal you of any sense of unworthiness. The acceptance of the Love of God will come flooding into your soul. You will rise up in such confidence in life and such expectancy of good, and such joy. All the hurts and the pains and the sadness and the misery will vanish. Goodness will be the portion of your days, just by doing that.

"Thou knowest that I am not wicked...thine hands have made me and fashioned me together."   Job 10:7-8

DAY 238
Come to understand the Mind of God.

There are principles of God, laws, commandments, things that we must come to understand. As we do, our way is made much easier, the path is much smoother. We run into negative experiences much less frequently than we did when we were just stumbling through life without an understanding of these principles.

Psalm 119:19 says, "I am a stranger in the earth. Hide not thy commmandments from me." I have felt that way, not wanting to grope through this very uncomfortable experience called human life without some kind of a road map. God, being God, with infinite intelligence, Wisdom, understanding and knowledge, would certainly have some rules or laws or principles that I could know, and if I kept them, my way would be a lot smoother.

God dwells in a kingdom--a spiritual atmosphere of thought, of Divine characteristics, the unseen world all around us. We use the word kingdom to describe certain principles that we need to understand in order to be comfortable in our relationship to God. We want to walk in Wisdom, we want to walk in purpose, we want to fulfill that which we have been sent to do. Our Creator has breathed his very own Life into us because he has some reason. To understand that reason, we pursue a relationship with this Creator, God, who is all in all.

We come to understand the Mind of God. When we apply the principles in the Mind of God, we see that which is visible take on Divine Order, infinite perfection, we see it take on what we would expect to see from something created by God, sustained and governed by goodness.

"The counsel of the Lord stands for ever, the thoughts of his heart to all generations." Psalm 33:11

DAY 239

The Kingdom of God fills all space.

I see two distinct avenues of existence, a physical avenue, and a spiritual avenue. Our experience depends on which we choose. Let's look at the characteristics of the spiritual kingdom, governed by goodness. We want to understand the laws, the principles, the cause and effect of that realm, just as we have learned the cause and effect of the physical realm. In the spiritual realm,we see absolute and unchangeable characteristics, a nature that does not alter itself. I like that, because I can trust it. I can be sure of God, whose nature does not change to meet any human circumstance.

One principle of the Kingdom of God is, it is absolutely whole and perfect. It does not contain evil, distortion, confusion. "God is light, and in him is no darkness at all." (1John 1:5)

Another principle is its infinite intelligence, Eternal Wisdom, knowledge and understanding, beyond the human mind, and yet it is willing and desires to share all that it contains. I can avail myself of this any time I ask for it, any time I am willing to set aside my own finite intelligence, wisdom, knowledge and understanding.

How do these principles of the Kingdom of God relate to our experience in this life? There is a way to live, if we choose it, where Life is our experience, and not life mixed with death. Not good and bad, sick and healthy, prosperous and poor, a roll of the dice. The higher principle is in the spiritual world, heaven, the Kingdom of God. It fills all space, it's eternal and infinite. The whole visible world has been formed from it. To understand our Source sheds Light and Wisdom on what we can expect right here and now.

"The kingdom of God is righteousness and peace and joy."   Romans 14:17

DAY 240
What do we know about the spiritual realm?

What do we know about the spiritual realm? One thing we know is that it's infinitely perfect. It's immutable in nature, so that perfection cannot be interrupted. Another thing we know is that the spiritual realm is Wisdom, knowledge, understanding and intelligence, way beyond the human mind, way beyond anything we could achieve in our understanding without it.

We know that it wants to share all of its attributes. It wants to flow freely through this physical realm, this physical, visible world. It wants to express itself in all that it has made. That's why it made everything, so it could express itself through all that's visible, including your life, including your body.

What blocks this flow? First is not knowing there is a spiritual world around and about us and that we have come from that, and we are to take on the attributes and characteristics of that from which we have come. And not knowing that it flows freely and desires to share and express its nature through and to us.

Second, we need to avail ourselves of it, turn away from what we have been embracing in thought and reach out to understand, to know and to have a relationship with this spiritual realm, this kingdom. We're going to turn away from our human level of thought, where we only understand man's wisdom and man's definitions of life. We're going to go deeper into the definitions of this spiritual realm from which we've all come.

"The kingdom of heaven is like unto a merchant, seeking goodly pearls: who, when he had found one pearl of great price, went and sold all that he had, and bought it."   Matthew 13:45-46

DAY 241

"Let this Mind be in you."

How do we have a relationship with God? The Bible says, "Let this mind be in you which was also in Christ Jesus." (Philippians 2:5) He knew that he was equal with God, knew that he started as part of that nature, and out from that being he was formed. Yet, he took upon himself the nature of a servant.

I am a servant in that I have chosen to put myself under the authority of the Wisdom and intelligence, knowledge and understanding of the Mind of God. I have chosen not to follow my own self will. Why can I trust what I can't see? Because I also understand that the nature of God is good. I can trust that no evil will come from him, only good can come. When I know that, it enables me to take on the nature of a servant. I can put myself under the authority of something that's always going to be good, that's always going to be wise. I know it has a purpose for me and it's going to be good.

So, I can freely obey that which I feel in my heart, after I have submitted my mind. I don't follow my heart until I've submitted my mind, my will, my perception. It is my nature now to be a servant, to obey. I wouldn't think to break out, I don't want to suffer the consequences of breaking out and coming under my own authority. The law of cause and effect is too harsh. I don't want to go back to that. I like this better. The law of cause and effect says if I go the wrong way, I'm going to collide into something. That sends me to a higher law, and I don't have to wonder whether I'm going to obey or not, you bet I am going to. It's second nature now--actually it's the *only* nature now.

"Forget not my law, but let your heart keep my commandments: for length of days and long life and peace shall they add to you."   Proverbs 3:1-2

DAY 242

Take on the Divine Life of God.

Jesus became obedient, as a servant would be, and through his obedience to the higher nature, through his absolute humility and obedience, regardless of what it cost him, he was elevated to the relationship of the son. A son knows everything his father knows, understands what his father is thinking, feeling, his direction and purpose.

These Biblical relationships are to help us understand the thought that we must take on in order to avail ourselves of the nature of this atmosphere of thought, this kingdom, this realm of perfection from which we have come and which would flow freely through us, enabling us to live a life which is higher and purer than we have been living.

Now I've been elevated to sonship, where I know the heart of God. I've walked with it enough, heard it enough, seen the consistency enough, to know that God is Love. What Love wants is to express his own Life through all that he has visibly formed. God is God, and we're creatures he created, so what he has purposed, he's going to get. He's either going to get it through your blood, sweat, tears, and suffering, or you're going to submit to that desire and let that Life of his flow. You're going to let that flow through your affairs, through your body, through your finances, through your career, through your family, through your relationships, through your thoughts, through your desires. Your life will take on a much purer expression, because it will begin to take on the Divine Life of God.

"The mountains shall drop down new wine, the hills shall flow with milk, all the rivers shall flow with waters and a fountain shall come forth of the house of God and shall water the valley." Joel 3:18

DAY 243

Let Life do what it will.

There is another relationship with our Creator which is the highest of them all, and that's an intimate love relationship. God is the giver of Life and we are the receiver. The male/female relationship is a visible manifestation of the highest relationship that Divine Love would have with all that it has formed. This is the kind of love relationship, the kind of intimacy, where it's just you and Divine Love, you and the heart of God. It's you wanting and experiencing and living in his voice, his direction, his thoughts, his feelings, and you expressing that Love out to creation, out to others.

Do you serve a God that you fear? You can't love something you are afraid of. Love means, I trust you with everything, I understand your nature, I understand the purity, the goodness of it. I understand that you do not hurt, you do not afflict.

If you want to understand the Mind of God, the spiritual nature of things, and you're wondering how, it's time to return to your first love. You've left your first estate, and it's time to return. (Revelation 2) What you do is submit to a love relationship, first as a servant, then as a son, and then as an intimate marriage, a oneness with God.

You submit your will, you give over any investment in the outcome of a situation, because you understand the goodness and the explosiveness of this Love that is surrounding and enveloping each one of us. The Life of God is so pure, if you submit, that Life flows into whatever your situation is. You let it do what it will, and what happens is goodness, order, perfection.

"Rise up, my love, and come away. My beloved is mine and I am his."   Song of Solomon 2:10,16

DAY 244
Step aside and defer to another's good.

There is cause and effect. We are not just victims that live randomly under the law of chance and probability. It looks like that, that's how the word accident ever came to be. The truth is, nothing that happens, for good or ill, happens accidentally. It's not just a roll of the dice. You aren't just lucky or unlucky. The human existence is influenced by the presence of unseen principles of Life.

On the human plane we define life as a self centered scramble, as survival of the fittest, and we find ourselves not having the good that is promised us. We find ourselves in ill health, in poverty. We live in a very limited good.

There is a greater goodness that is available for us today, this instant. In the Kingdom of God, this invisible kingdom that we live and walk and talk and breathe in, the main principle is that we attain good by how much we love, or how much we give, or how kind and gentle we are toward one another. If we step aside and defer to another's good, regardless of what it might cost us, that fulfills a spiritual principle, and we are blessed by good coming to us.

In order to avail ourselves of this goodness, to be able to receive it, we must be able to open up the hardness of our heart, the limited way we see and expect things. We do that by learning the principles of operation, the laws of this kingdom that are so directly connected to us. We live our life out from it. That's why, by not keeping these principles, we are negatively affected, and why, conversely, by keeping them, we are blessed.

"By love serve one another, for the law is fulfilled in one word, thou shalt love thy neighbor as thyself."
Galatians 5:13-14

DAY 245
I am never outside the fullness of Divine Love.

"There is One God and Father of all, who is above all, and through all and in you all." (Ephesians 4:6) God, being all in all and everywhere, being Spirit, fills all space with its Presence, its characteristics, its nature, and we are as near to that as the breath that we breathe. From that atmosphere that's all around us, we have come and have been formed. It is that Life that flows through us, carrying with it all of its goodness, all of its love, all of its harmony and balance and order and perfection and beauty and vitality and strength, all of its knowledge and Wisdom and understanding. Everything that we attribute to God is within this river of Divine Life that flows throughout all of eternity.

If we are living in a state of thought or experience less than this description, then we have not understood the principles of this Divine Life. We have inadvertently violated the principles of this Life, whose main characteristic is Eternal and Divine and Infinite Love. We have forsaken the law of Love.

The New Testament says that all the law is wrapped up in this one law, the law of Love. (Galatians 5:14) It's not human love, which by definition is self serving. Divine Love speaks in a different voice. This voice says, "It is my nature to love, to give, I don't look for anything in return, because I do not need anything in return, since I am the fullness of all that is. I can love you with no concern whether you love me back, because I am never outside of the fullness of Divine Love. I always feel love, when I'm alone, and when I'm with others. Out from that abundance, I can love."

"Let us love one another, for love is of God and every one that loves is born of God and knows God."
1 John 4:7

DAY 246

God is the supply of my good.

I can give and not be concerned about getting back. That's why it says, in Luke 6:35, "Lend hoping for nothing in return." How can I do that? Because my supply doesn't come from you. I can give and I will never lack for giving to you. The more I give, the more I will have, because the more I give, the more I open up this free flowing channel of love. As it flows through me, it contains the abundance of all that I could ever imagine.

God being the supply of my good, I do not need to look to another. If you fail to give to me, or if I go to work and I fail to get enough to meet the needs that I have, I am not resentful or upset by it, because it doesn't come from that source. I go to work to give, to offer my services and my self for Love, and to give the best that I have. What I get in return is a bonus. I get from God, who is the direct Source. That never, never falters or changes.

You say, "Then why am I lacking?" You're lacking because you're looking toward a person or a situation to give to you. As long as you're looking at the stock market, your job, your inheritance, your parents, or people who owe you money, as long as you're looking in that direction, then you will feel lack and limitation. Not only that, you'll feel resentful if it doesn't come when you think it should, or if it isn't meeting the needs that you have. It will never meet all your needs, so you will live in fear and in stress and anxiety, wondering when it's coming and when it's shutting down, when it's going to be there and when it's not. There's no end to that. Look to God!

"Love not the world, neither the things that are in the world...the world passes away, but one that does the will of God abides forever."   1John 2:15,17

DAY 247

Look to God.

When we look at our bodies as the source of our health and our life, we are in trouble. Our body might or might not feel very strong and healthy that day. It may or may not have all systems working on all eight cylinders that day. But if we look to God, to this invisible Presence of the Divine Life that flows through us, as being our life and the Source of our strength, and we *only* look to that, then our body will line up with that.

Now we have taken our body out from the place of being the progenitor of our life and the determining factor of how we're doing in our life. We've put God there where it belongs. Our body has to respond in like kind. We say to our body, line up! The Life of God, the Divine Life, the eternal, infinite, unchanging, uninterrupted, rich, strong, beautiful, whole and perfect Life of God, is the very substance of this body that we wear. So we say, "Line up, body," and it does, no matter how un-lined-up it's been.

How do we get to this place? What are the principles that we can follow, like a roadmap, that will enable us to live in this place? How do we recognize when we have violated it? How do we counter our steps, go back and pick up where we messed up, get back on track and going again?

This is a simple way to live. The human thought does not offer it to us as an option. All we ever learn is the human law, the human standard, which is sub-standard to the principles of the Kingdom of God. There is a higher way to go. Go to what God says these principles are. Go to the Mind, the Wisdom, of God.

"You shall walk in all the ways your God has commanded you, that you may live and it may be well with you."   Deuteronomy 5:33

DAY 248

God is the only Source.

"Thou shall have no other gods before me. Thou shall not make unto thee any graven image or any likeness of any thing that is in heaven above or that is in the earth beneath, or that is in the water under the earth."
(Exodus 20)

How easy it is to have another god, how often we do this. We might put an employer, a job, as the Source of our supply, putting that before the realization that God is the only and infinite Source of all the supply we could ever need. That is a graven image, that is having another god before us. We might put our body above the place of God by saying that from our body come the issues of life or death, instead of from God who is the Life of the body.

What about worrying about losing someone's love? What about worrying about someone passing away? What about looking at people as the source of our comfort and our love and our companionship and our sense of being loved, our sense of belonging, our sense of completion and fulfillment? That is putting someone in the place of God to us. We put that person in the place of the kind of love that should be reserved for God. I'm not saying that we don't need people, but as we realize that God is Infinite Love, we will experience a never ending Presence of Divine Love, a feeling of completion, a sense of belonging. We might be alone, but we never feel alone. With that as our main focus of love, the Source of love, our heart is always filled with Love. Then we become a magnet, attracting to us the love of others.

"The Lord direct your hearts into the love of God."
2Thessalonians 3:5

DAY 249

Seek first the kingdom.

If nothing else stood between us and the Presence and the Life and Love of God, then we would gain everything in our human experience. Everything that is visible comes from that realm. As we only look to that, and don't put anything else in that place, then all the other things we need will appear in our life.

Matthew 6:33 says, "Seek ye first the kingdom of God, and his righteousness, and all these things shall be added unto you." In Matthew 6:25-29 it says, don't concern yourself with what you get and how much you have and how much you don't have, "consider the lilies of the field, not even Solomon in all his glory was arrayed like one of these."

John 12:32 says, "If I be lifted up, I will draw all men unto me." "I" is the Eternal "I", the Love and Life and Being and Presence and Person of God. Let that be our first and foremost vision. You'll know when it's not, because you will begin to lack. You will lack peace, you will lack harmony, you will lack joy, you will lack a sense of free flowing love out from you to others. This is because you put something else in the place where only God should reside.

If you do that, step back and say, that is idolatry. That is putting something else in the place of God and bowing down to it, letting it rule my life, my peace, my confidence, letting it rob me of joy. There is a Presence in the kingdom, all around and through you, that never stops pouring out its goodness. It never stops talking to you, never stops showing you the way. Just listen.

"If God so clothes the grass of the field shall he not much more clothe you, o ye of little faith? Take no thought...for your heavenly father knows that you have need of all these things." Matthew 6:30-32

DAY 250
Stop. Ask. Wait.

What if something undesired appears in your body? The first thing to do is turn to God and say, *You are my Divine Life. You are the substance and the flow and the energy and the animation of my life. I have this thing appearing, what should I do about it? It's contrary to what I know is true, it denies the truth, but I will state the truth and I will know the truth, and I will cling to the truth with my whole heart.*

Then whatever you feel in the quietness of your heart led to do, you obey. There are many instances where we are directed toward other people's help, but to put that first, before you have acknowledged the truth, before you have asked for direction, before you have waited for it, is idolatry, because you have put all your hope in man. We cannot hold another person account- able for us because that is putting that person in the place of God, and that is putting ourselves under the authority of human intelligence.

Stop, declare the truth about Life, where Life comes from, whose Life is really being lived in this body. Direct your attention to the Divine Life that flows through you, that's uninterruptible, that's whole and perfect, that denies this infirmity. Establish where your allegiance lies. If you wait, you will either realize the symptoms have disappeared, or you'll be led to do something. Whatever it is, your confidence will be not in the person you've gone to, not in the path that you've been led down, but with the God that led you down that path. That makes all the difference in the world in how it turns out.

"The loftiness of man shall be bowed down, and the Lord alone shall be exalted."   Isaiah 2:17

DAY 251

I have nothing to fear.

Do you put your seatbelt on because it's the law? Or do you put it on because you think if you get into an accident you won't be hurt ? One is life to you and one is death. One magnetizes life because of obedience to the law, and the other magnetizes accidents because of fear, because you've already put yourself under the authority of the law of chance and probability.

Putting yourself under the law of God says, *God is the government of his Life. He is self sustained, self governed and that's the Life that flows through me and that's the Life that leads, and that's the Life that is unfolding as my own Life. I have nothing to fear. I don't fear germs--germs came forth from the same life, the same Divine Source from which everything came--they are my brothers, and they can't hurt me. They are of the same substance and that substance is altogether good.*

If you view germs as evil, you've just put yourself under the law of chance and probability and under the authority of that germ, and your interpretation of the life of that germ and what it could do to you. If you see everything as good, then you will see everything as coming forth from the same created being and it will be altogether good unto you. You will not fear.

Life is God. There are not multitudes of little lives, but one gigantic, all consuming, all inclusive, eternal, infinite, perfect, whole and beautiful Life of God. From that everything physical comes, including germs. I can bless those germs and they're not going to hurt me, never have and never will, because I recognize that everything comes from the same source, and it's good.

"Blessed are the pure in heart:
for they shall see God."   Matthew 5:8

DAY 252

What is required of me?

If we do not understand and keep the laws of the Divine Life of God, we shut down the flow of Divine Life, and we end up suffering the consequences. Then we create lots of reasons and physical causes for why things happen. Those things only exist for those of us who live on that level, who choose not to understand that we are Spirit Beings, formed by the one Creator. If we do not line up with the nature of our spirituality, we violate the Source from which Life flows through us, and we shut down that Life. Then we become vulnerable to anything and everything, because we've fallen headlong into the consciousness of humanity, leaving higher Wisdom, leaving our Divinity. We've slammed the door on the very flow of the Life.

We can spend our whole life studying cause and effect in a lesser realm, or we can leave that and say, "I'll study to know and understand from where I've come from, why I'm here, and what is required of me in order to keep this spiritual life and energy and strength and wholeness and goodness flowing." We don't have to live under chance and probability, there is a higher law, our spirituality, or the law of the Kingdom of God.

By allowing that flow to be kept open, you will see the fulfillment of the purpose for which you've been sent. The highest human experience is to realize, I've done what I came to do, I've done it well, with my whole heart, there are effects because of it, and they're good. I blessed people, I helped people, I made people happy, I helped show them the way.

"One who looks into the perfect law of liberty and continues therein, being not a forgetful hearer but a doer of the work, shall be blessed in his deed."

James 1:25

DAY 253

Express the true nature of God.

"Thou shalt not take the name of the Lord thy God in vain." (Exodus 20) The word "vain" means vanity, taking something unto myself for my own personal gain or good, in a selfish, self-absorbed state of mind. It's me, myself and I. It's being consumed by my own selfhood. The word "name" here means the nature, the characteristics and attributes, the purpose of God.

We have been formed in the image of God, "Of his fullness have we all received." (John 1:16) The intention is that the Light and Glory of the fullness of God be more and more revealed through our person as we walk this earth. It's a fact of being that contained within us, in our true spiritual nature, is the whole nature of God, as well as clear knowledge of his intent and purpose and will for having sent us here. It's contained within, and the idea is to get that river flowing out, not take that nature and consume it for our own purposes.

Jesus came to show us the way for this name to be revealed, for this nature and purpose and intention to be fulfilled. If we watch the way he lived his life, then we will understand that is the way we ought to be living our lives, in order for the nature that's within to be freely flowing and expressed.

Jesus taught a way of humility and meekness and obedience. Although he knew he was equal with God, he took upon himself the nature of a mortal. Through a lack of exercising his own will, through the lack of exercising his own self preservation, the nature of his spirituality was able to freely flow, and the true nature of God was able to be expressed.

"I have declared unto them thy name, that the love with which thou has loved me may be in them, and I in them."   John 17:26

DAY 254

Greater works shall you do.

Jesus was able to be who he was, the Christ, which is our calling as well, and he was able to do works that no other human has ever been able to imitate since. Although he told us in John 14:12, "greater works shall you do," it hasn't happened. The reason it hasn't happened is that we are not following the way that has been told us, the way Jesus followed.

Jesus started out birthed in the humility of a stable, and lived in obscurity for thirty years as a carpenter's son. Remember when he was a young boy, he got lost from his parents? He went to the temple where he was found teaching the rabbis and the teachers of that day. Way back when he was a child, he had the Wisdom of God flowing through him freely. What did he do with it? He submitted it back to the purpose and the Wisdom and the intention of God. He humbled himself. He knew what he had, what he knew, but he submitted it, and he became obedient to his parents. At any time, if he was to do his own will, he could have broken out from under that authority, but he would have never been what he turned out to be, had he broken out and done his own thing.

Look at the contrast between the way Jesus fulfilled the purpose for which he'd been sent, and the way that we are doing it now. It's no wonder we are not seeing healings. The only way we're going to make it work is to follow the way that was outlined for us, the way that Jesus did it. He said, I am the way, watch the way I'm doing it, because greater works than this are you to do. "As my father sent me, so send I you." (John 20:21) This is not just for Jesus, this is for the entire Christ sonship to fulfill.

"I am the way, the truth, and the life."   John 14:6

DAY 255

God leads out.

Moses knew his purpose. He had a passion in his soul, wanting to see the freedom of his people, to see the Israelites out from under the Egyptian bondage and slavery. Much like we feel when we look out at a world that is crying out in confusion and darkness and suffering, and we know this is not what God intended. We see bondage, and we would run out and do anything to break that, but we must be obedient. We must not set up our own little shop, so to speak, and try to draw people. This is not the way of God. The way of God is that God leads out. We take on a spirit of humility and meekness and obedience. The way to authority and dominion is always on our knees.

If we break out from under that obedience and the patient waiting for God to lead out, if we break out before the work has been done within our own nature, then we're taking the name of God in vain, and we're not going to get the results that Jesus got. We may be doing a lot for our selfhood, but not for the purpose for which we've been sent. The way is the way of obscurity, of humility. It's a heart that says, "I don't know, teach me."

Are we willing to deny our selfhood, stay in a state of obedience, waiting, until this flicker of hope and light starts bursting through and God says, *This is where I want you to go and this is what I want you to do and this is what I want you to say. I will go with you and the power of heaven will be upon you. Every word that you speak will come to pass, and every person you reach out to heal will be healed. Do it in my name.*

"God called unto Moses out of the midst of the bush...and Moses said, Here am I."   Exodus 3:4

DAY 256

The power of God can flow.

We have come to heal. We have come to restore. We live in a world that is engulfed in pain. We have come to lift consciousness above that, so that all might be free. The way we must do it is to follow the way Jesus did it. Not because he wanted us to worship him as a man. He didn't exalt himself. He said, "Don't worship me, worship God." He told us to follow him, not to set himself far above us, but because he wanted us to fulfill the reason for which we've been sent.

He wanted us to humble ourselves, to deny the temptation to exalt ourselves. Only when there is nothing left of the person, the selfhood, only then can God be all in all. Only then can God flow through us. Only then can the presence of God be known and felt by those to whom he sends us. Only then will their lives be restored and their bodies be healed. We were sent. Jesus said, "As my father sent me, so send I you." (John 20:21)

"Even the son of man came not to be ministered unto, but to minister, and to give his life a ransom for many." (Mark 10:45) What did Jesus mean by "give my life"? Give up my will, my demands, my desires, my hopes, my dreams, even the ones that God put in my heart. Keep taking them back to the altar and keep saying, not my will, but your will be done. Not my way, but your way. (Mark 14:36) We can't make our own way.

The sooner we submit, the sooner we learn that our foremost reason for being here is to honor God, to live in a state of submission to Him, in obedience, to be good and kind, to fulfill our obligations, to give with our whole heart and soul, to be quiet, and not magnify ourselves, then will God be all in all and the power of God can flow.

"Before honor is humility."　　　　　　　　Proverbs 18:12

"Thy will be done."

Moses went to the wilderness for forty years. He was eighty years old when he finally had the experience with the burning bush, eighty years old when God sent him to deliver the Israelites from the Egyptians. By the time God sent him, all that ego was gone, that wanting to stand exalted before people. He said, "What can I offer them? I can't even speak before people. I have nothing to offer." (Exodus 4) By that time he was content being a shepherd on the back side of the wilderness, tending the sheep, taking care of his family. All his high and lofty ambitions were gone. He had spent so much time alone that he had become peaceful and comfortable. Then he hears the voice of God. God says, "Now you are where I can use you. There is no more of you, of self, of will."

Moses said to God, "Do not send me unless you promise to go with me and be my mouth and speak the words and be the power. Let me always know what is your will, what is your intention. I, as a person, cannot stand before the magnitude of pain and suffering. I can't measure up to this, I am not equal to this job."

Do your time learning humility, meekness, obedience, learning, "Not my will but thine be done." (Matthew 26:39) No matter what it costs you, be willing to pay the price. What you're not willing, ask God to make you willing. You finally come to a place where you just give up on the whole thing, and you say, "If I'm not supposed to do anything, then I'm not going to do anything. But I'm not going out in front before God sends me. Thy will be done."

"As the clay is in the potter's hand, so are you in my hand."   Jeremiah 18:6

DAY 258
Partake freely of the tree of Life.

To repent means to turn the other way, turn away from what we're seeing, from the way we're going, and go another way. If we do not turn the other way in our thought and our belief and our attitude and our actions and our hearts, then we cannot take on the new way. Repentance should be an ongoing experience between you and God, all day long. Every time we catch ourselves thinking something that's critical, that's exclusionary, every time we catch ourselves having an attitude of defensiveness, every time we catch ourselves being offensive or being offended, every time we think a thought that is less than loving, less than merciful, less than healing, then we can catch it and say, "That's not what I want to feel, that's not what I want to believe, and that is not my true, new, nature in Christ." This is the simplicity of repentance.

Then we can enter into that new realm of conscious awareness, the Presence of God, which is all around and about us. Revelation 22:14 says, "Blessed are they that keep the commandments of God, for they shall enter in by the gate and shall partake freely of the tree of Life."

All the things of God, the nature of God, are our inheritance and our new nature, in Christ. What does "in Christ" mean? It means to be in, immersed into, the entire Mind, Spirit and heart of God. The very same Mind, Spirit and heart that possessed Jesus, that held him captive to his purpose and to his God. "In Christ" we share the Spirit of God.

God sent us here "in Christ." "In him we live and move and have our being." (Acts 17:28)

"Blessed be God who has blessed us with all spiritual blessing in Christ." Ephesians 1:3

DAY 259

Enter into the rest of God.

"Remember the sabbath day, to keep it holy."
(Exodus 20) Sabbath is a Hebrew word meaning rest.
We keep the commandment holy by maintaining a quiet,
calm, trusting heart, knowing God is in perpetual control. "We who have believed do enter into his rest...
for the works were finished from the foundation of the
world...for he that is entered into his rest also has
ceased from his own works, as God did from his."
(Hebrews 4:3,10)

True rest is a place of absolute quietness and confidence, where you are receiving all that God is and all
that God has, with no fear and no concern for your
personal good. You are living enveloped in the Presence
of God, knowing you are an inheritor of his nature and
his goodness, all that he is and all that he has. All that
you will ever need is yours at this very moment.

How do we enter into it? By choosing to know and
believe that all of the purposes of God have been finished from before the foundation of the world.

In the mind of humanity, it doesn't look like anything
is finished, does it? We see suffering, poverty, strife,
but in the Mind of God it is not so. God sees all of his
works completed and in a perpetual state of perfection.
If you'd like, you could see the same thing today, because God sees it today. You could see the allness and
the fullness of God. You could see the Glory of God. You
could see a world made bright and holy. You could see a
new heaven and a new earth. (Revelation 21:1) Everything has already been done. We only need to enter into
that realm of awareness called the Presence of God.
Entering into God's reality is entering into his rest.

*"Is not your God with you? Has he not given you rest
on every side?"* 1Chronicles 22:18

DAY 260

It's up to us to enter in.

Are you in the sabbath rest of God? You know when you're not in there, because you're still striving to get your personal problems fixed. The best thing to do is what we do with the monkeys and dragons, (my dream related in my first book). Turn away from the personal thing that keeps your mind so lassoed on this low earthly conscious plane of understanding, and desire to see as God sees, to know as God knows.

"The works were finished from before the foundation of the world." (Hebrews 4:3) There is nothing yet to be done, except to enter into that reality. Enter into his Presence, declaring that truth and knowing it is true, asking for that veil that covers your eyes, the veil of mortality and humanity, to be lifted so that you too can see and enjoy and understand and perceive. When that experience comes, you will look back at the human situation and see that it has been put into Divine Order. You will see it in its perfection, in its wholeness and in its holiness. You do not have to, nor should you, try to fix something on the human scene when it's already been fixed. If you're still trying to fix it, whether by praying or repeating affirmations or running from here to there, getting on this program, taking these pills, if you're still in that striving, then you are not seeing from the Mind of God. You are in the condition that is called in the Bible, unbelief. You are not in God's rest.

Jesus healed people on the sabbath day to declare that healing and the bringing about of Divine Order, comes from entering into that state of reality called the Mind of God, where the "works were finished before the foundation of the world." It's up to us to enter in. To choose it every day and for every situation.

"We which have believed do enter into his rest."
Hebrews 4:3

DAY 261

In the secret place with God...

Stop. In quietness and silence, step back and know that all we think needs to be done right now, is already done. There is no progression, no progressive healing, no progressive coming forth in the Mind of God. It's done. By entering into that awareness we have peace, because we know and we believe and we are assured. We are not judging reality by what we see with our eyes, but by what we know is true about the nature of God, about the Presence of God, about the word. That is entering into the rest.

It is there that healing is automatically established. It is there where we understand the principles that we might be violating, where we might be clinging to something that is painful. It is there where our motives and intentions and the deep intricate workings of our own souls are exposed to us, so we can make the corrections that need to be made. It is there where pride is abased and true humility and meekness are exalted. It is there that those who have walked in obedience and humility, in the secret place with God, are exalted.

How are they exalted? Life comes forth in their experience, and they are blessed beyond their wildest imaginations. It is there where we come to know and to understand clearly what this Christ nature truly is and who we really are. It's there where "we" and "they" are blended into the Eternal Oneness of God. It's there where we finally see and acquiesce to the truth that "The earth is the Lord's and the fullness thereof and all that dwell therein." (Psalm 24:1) It's there where everything appears in our life on this earth in the state of Infinite Glory that already is in the Mind of God.

"His rest shall be glorious."   Isaiah 11:10

DAY 262

I'm not going to let it in.

Like it or not, we are subjected to world conscious-ness, what the world sees and believes. We must stand against the thoughts that we don't want to experience. Like diseases we hear about on TV, see in newspapers, magazines, on the radio, everybody's talking about it. It's a hypnotic obsession with health and with disease and even with weight. We walk through this *atmo-sphere of thought,* and without realizing it, we take on the thoughts contained in it as though they were a reliable image of truth. We accept it and before we know it, we're struggling with it just like everyone else.

We can stand at the door of our mind and say, "That thought is absurd. I don't want to have to experience it, so I'm not going to let it in." We can say no to a thought like that when we recognize what the truth really is. If we don't know what the truth is, it is impossible to stand against untruth.

The only way to overcome any thought or belief in the world consciousness, is to be elevated to a higher belief, a higher thought, a higher consciousness. The only higher consciousness that is available is the Mind of God, the Mind of the Creator. We go to that Mind and say, "What is the image held in the Divine Mind of God concerning this?" We go back to who formed us in his image and likeness. He did not create something to be perfect (for Deuteronomy 32:4 says the "works of his hands are perfect") only for it to fall into disrepair. If it can fall into disrepair, it's not perfect. The image held in the Mind of God has not changed. What has changed? You have. You've taken on an aberrent thought, contrary to the Divine Mind.

"I would rather be a doorkeeper in the house of my God than to dwell in the tents of wickedness."
                                                            Psalm 84:10

DAY 263
Challenge it at the level of thought.

We see something in a certain way because we first believed it. We define what we see by what we believe is true. We can choose to challenge it at the thought level and not on the material, physical level. We can lay the ax at the root of the tree, (Matthew 3:10), meaning we're going back to the thought or imagery or belief. We can challenge the right of disease to exist in the body, we can challenge the right of something to be out of control, such as our weight. We can challenge something governing us and destroying our peace. We have a right to live in a state of wholeness and health because we were created that way. We have a right to live in the form and beauty and order that God holds in his mind. No matter what we believe, no matter what we experience because of those beliefs, it does not change what God sees and knows.

We go to God and say, "God, please help me make this go away." The grace of God is always available and he always hears our prayers, but he doesn't recognize the same problem that we think we're seeing. He sees what he knows is true. His joy is that we would line up with what he sees and knows is true. So our prayer is, "Make me to see this as you see it."

We believe that if we don't fix it, it's not going to get done. We feel personally responsible. We hear, "God helps those who help themselves." That is a lie. The fact is, God helps those who trust in him. When we let go of the sense of needing to do it ourselves, we are able to realize God's Presence and help. When we yield to the fact that the Life that flows through us is God, we take on a sense of peace, knowing that Life is governing its own creations. And that includes you!

"Faithful is he that calls you, who also will do it."
1Thessalonians 5:24

DAY 264

The answer will come.

1Chronicles 28:9 says, if you seek me with your whole heart, in that day you shall be found of me. In the day you really want me to communicate with you, I will. You don't have to sit real still with your eyes closed. I personally can't sit still that long, and I've never had a problem hearing from God. I enlarge my heart, I open my mind to receive whatever God would speak to me that day, in whatever way he chooses to answer what I've asked. I know and believe that the Spirit of God will somehow communicate the answer that I need to hear. It doesn't make any difference if I'm running around doing what I have to do with my life, or if I'm sound asleep at night, I always get the answers and you will too. It will come in a way that will be unique for you and you will know that you know that you know, that you just got the answer. If you don't hear, you can ask again, not because God needs to hear again, but because you need to remind yourself that's what you're waiting to hear. It will come when you least expect it, so quit watching the boiling pot. It will come.

"Be merciful unto me, O God, be merciful unto me: for my soul trusts in thee. Yea, in the shadow of thy wings will I make my refuge, until these calamities be overpast. I will cry unto God most high, unto God that performs all things for me. He shall send from heaven and save me. God shall send forth his mercy and his truth."
"Be exalted, O God, let thy glory be above all the earth. I will sing and give praise. Awake up my glory."
Psalm 57

DAY 265
Take on a different image of yourself.

God meant for us to live in wholeness and harmony and perfection and order. God meant for us not to be worried about life ever falling apart on us. That was never intended for us. God wants us to live free of all that, above even the thought of disease, above the fear of disease, above the experience of disease, above this obsession with our bodies. He wants us just to receive what has been made, and understand what we are. Receive it and love it, give thanks for it, rejoice in it.

It says in Matthew 6:27 that no matter how hard you try, you can't add one cubit to your stature, you can't make yourself any taller. You can't change one hair on your head, you can't change the form of your body. When was the last time you told your liver how many enzymes to put out to break down some food you ate? When was the last time you told your bone marrow how many white blood cells to send out, and where to send them? When was the last time you directed any parts of the internals of your body to function properly? When was the last time you even knew about them? You take it for granted, because there's a Divine Intelligence that formed all things and that created all things to work in perfect order, under the guidance of the Eternal Mind of God. We trust that, we don't mess with it, we know it's true, it goes on all the time without our concern.

You are under one government, the government of the Mind of God. Go to the drawing board, to your true and Eternal Source, and ask what God's image is of you, and you will be delighted. You will take on a completely different image of yourself.

"In thy book all my members were written, which in continuance were fashioned, when as yet there were none of them."   Psalm 139:16

DAY 266

What if we had nothing to fear?

In the middle of the night I heard this sentence: *Nothing shall by any means hurt you.* I allowed myself to be lifted up and carried in my heart into such a place, allowed myself to feel what it feels like when you know there is nothing that will ever have the power or ability to hurt or to harm you in your entire life. I was so overwhelmed as I let myself go into that feeling. I thought, I wonder what life would be like if not just myself, but if everybody was able to feel and know the truth of that sentence, with no restrictions and no impediments? What would the world be like if we had nothing to fear?

The life we live as humans is lived in a defensive posture. How much of our life is based on protecting ourselves just in case something may happen? What would life be like if we knew beyond a shadow of a doubt that nothing shall by any means hurt us?

We wouldn't have to worry, we wouldn't think that someday we might not have enough. We'd have confidence and trust that the God that brought us here will care for us in every aspect of our experience. Why would God cease to care for us abundantly, exceedingly abundantly, for any reason?

I found the sentence in Psalms 119:165. "Great peace have they which love thy law, and nothing shall offend them." That's what I felt, incredible peace, more than I've ever felt in my life. What peace, if we allow ourselves to enter in to that thought. Just abandon ourselves with confidence and assurance and peace and quietness inside, knowing that nothing shall by any means ever hurt or offend us. That's quite a promise.

"Because you have made the Lord... your habitation, there shall no evil befall you, neither shall any plague come nigh your dwelling."   Psalm 91:9-10

DAY 267

You'll heal them.

"Great peace have they which love thy law." (Psalm 119:165) There is a law called the Spirit of Life. There is One Eternal Life out from which everything comes. If we knew that, we would look at ourselves in an entirely different way. We would cease to be victims, vulnerable to all kinds of hurt, either from within our own body or from without. We would realize there is only one life being lived, not only for ourselves, but for everyone else and everything else. We would stop seeing just people and things and start seeing that one harmonious, perfect Life. We would treat ourselves differently. We would treat others differently. We would treat our environment differently. We would see everything as an expression of that One Life.

2Corinthians 5:16 says, "Henceforth we shall know no man after the flesh." Not even Jesus are we to know after the flesh, it says. We're not to continually look back to someone who lived 2000 years ago, we are to realize that someone lives right now, as the law of the Spirit of Life. Everywhere we look, we see that Some-one appearing. That Being is expressed as you and me and everything else that's formed, if you have eyes to see it, a heart to believe it, and a desire to know it and embrace it.

Romans 8:2 says that if we live out from the law of the Spirit of Life, we are not under the law of sin and death. You can't come under both laws, you give up one to take on the other. Love the Law of the Spirit of Life, embrace it, know it, see it, accept it, believe it. See it in everyone else, see that Life in them, and you'll heal them.

"Peace be unto you: as my Father has sent me, even so send I you."   John 20:21

DAY 268
The Wisdom of God is our inheritance.

When Bill Gotherd was little, he couldn't pass a class, but they continued to pass him on. He never learned anything, because he couldn't read. He was up to seventh grade, but his mind still had not kicked in.

His mother prayed for wisdom. One summer she sat him down and they read the book of Proverbs. They read it again and again, and he started to commit some of it to memory. By the end of the summer, that river of the Spirit of Life was flowing freely through his mental body and his emotional body and it had unscrambled the congested energy there. He was thinking clearly, he was able to receive instruction, to understand. He began to pass in school, and eventually went on to get several doctoral degrees. He then started a world wide ministry, teaching how to resolve human conflict.

The book of Proverbs talks about Wisdom and understanding, perception and clarity of thought. It talks about how we possess the elevated thought and Wisdom of God. That is our inheritance. It talks about how to get to that place.

No matter what situation you may find yourself in, there is a way out of this, a sure way out. Start with the book of Proverbs. Read it out loud. You don't have to understand every word, just read it. You will be amazed that the words themselves have the power to open up that congested energy of human belief which is blocking the flow of intelligence and stability of thought and action. Pray to know and understand that the mind of God is stable, balanced, clear, full of intelligence. It lacks nothing that needs to be known. And it is freely revealed to you whenever you ask.

"Wisdom is a tree of life to them that lay hold upon her, and happy is every one that retains her."

Proverbs 3:18

DAY 269

*Give up ownership of your own mind
and possess the Mind of God.*

When we see people excel at something in life, we think, how did they do that? They didn't do that. They found a way to take their own limited thoughts, their limitations of capacity and ability, and set that aside to allow a higher mind, a higher intelligence, a higher ability, to flow through them. To the degree that you choose to give up ownership of your own mind and emotions, personal ownership of the responsibility to govern and control and direct them in order, and you turn to the Divine Mind and the ever present Spirit of that Mind to govern, to flow through your mind, you will also find yourself able to excel.

I used to tell my kids, every time they were going to take a major test, if you go in bearing your own limited mind, believing that the answers and the understanding must come from the limitations of the human mind, then you have every reason to be concerned. But if you go in knowing and declaring that you possess the mind of Christ, the clarity, the understanding, the intelligence and the Wisdom, and you insist on being at peace with that, not being terribly concerned, you will succeed. They learned to do that, and they did succeed beyond their wildest imaginations.

We don't live out from our own mortal energy, our own mortal strength, our own perception, our own education, our own understanding, our own knowledge, our own intelligence. We possess the mind of God, the mind of Christ. We're told to grab hold of that Mind as our own possession and inheritance. We are told to live out from that Mind.

"He wakens my ear to hear as the learned."

Isaiah 50:4

DAY 270
What is true in the Mind of God?

The eighth commandment given to Moses is "Thou shalt not bear false witness against your neighbor." (Exodus 20:16) In the Mind of God, to agree with anything about yourself or another that is less than the perfection of that which we are, is declaring and agreeing to a lie. It simply is not true in the Mind of God. Every time we declare a disorder about ourselves or someone else, that's what we're doing, we're bearing false witness.

With physical or mental disease, don't allow yourself to come under a diagnosis. Refuse it. You have the Mind of God. There is only one Mind, and it is God's Mind expressing itself as you, in visible form. You have access to that Mind. You are not living out from a human mind capable of disintegrating or degenerating.

A simple prayer is, *God, enable me to see myself as you see me, enable me to let go of my own personal idea of what's wrong with me, enable me to allow you to direct my thoughts, and to realize the truth of how you see me and how I am. Allow me to step aside in all my human efforts and all the confusion of my mind and my thoughts and my heart and my emotions. Allow me to step aside so that the pure energy, the pure Presence of the Spirit of God, that which formed me, that which breathed Life into me, that which animates me, which had purpose for me to come here, might have a free flow and a free expression of its Presence.*

All these things that appear, mental or physical, are only the result of an inaccurate image and understanding of ourselves, who we are, why we are here, and an inaccurate image of the God that formed us.

"Let every one speak truth to his neighbor."
Zechariah 8:16

DAY 271

No one can take anything from you.

Are you holding judgement against anyone? Go back to God in prayer. He is the source of that person's life. Say, *I am clearly not seeing that person the way that you see them. I am not seeing that person the way they have been truly made to be.* Your concern should not be how they're acting, what they've done or not done. Your concern is *how do you see them?* Will you "judge righteously" or will you judge after the "seeing of your eyes and the hearing of your ears?" (Isaiah 11:3) Will you choose to see them as they truly are? No matter what has been hurled at you, it can't hurt you, because you're under the government of God, who is good.

If somebody has hurt or offended you, don't let it be your problem. Stay at peace. Hold to the truth that everything you have comes from the Divine Source. No one can change the truth of who you are. You can't let another govern you. As soon as you let other people govern you, you shut down the flow of Divine Life.

Nobody can take anything from us or cause us to lack anything, though it may appear that way. It is not true. If you hold to that, it will turn itself around and you will be abundantly blessed. The only thing that can cause you to suffer in this type of situation is to believe that someone has the power to take something from you. Everything that's been given to you has been given to you by God, so nobody can really take from you what God has chosen to give. When you hold to that truth, that flow of faith starts again and your peace is abundant. Everything you are and everything you have is the result of the ever Presence of the fullness of God, the Divine Life that you are living.

"He that shuts his eyes from seeing evil shall dwell on high."   Isaiah 33:15-16

DAY 272
How do we change our consciousness?

We are a disease-ridden society. Why? Because we have a consciousness of disease. How do we change our consciousness from one of disease and the fear of disease, when this is all we've ever seen our whole life? To change our consciousness we've got to go back to the Source of Life, back to our first understanding of what Life is. If we examine that, find the flaw, correct it, then the conclusion will be different.

If we start out believing our lives are encased in our mortal body, passed down from our parents, our life is defined as that which has gone before us. We hold in consciousness an expectation that we are vulnerable to disease, as they were before us. If we start with that premise, we conclude that our body is what defines our life. If our body is feeling good today, then our life is going to be good today. If our body is very sick and weak, then our life is very sick and weak. If our body stops functioning altogether, our life has ended. We conclude that our body is the dominant voice and our life is subservient to that.

After a traumatic incident in my life, I realized I had to step back and take a different look at life. One night I awakened, sat straight up in bed, and said out loud, "I get it, there is only One Life. It is this one Divine Eternal Infinite Being, and out from that being comes everything that is formed. All that is formed has come forth as an expression of that Life, to teach us about that Life." I didn't just hear there is only One Life, I felt it and I saw it. In that moment there was a paradigm shift, and Life became a vast entity of its own, an Eternal energy, an Eternal Presence, an Eternal Being, filling all infinity.

"To be spiritually minded is life and peace."
Romans 8:6

DAY 273
Light will swallow up the darkness.

The purpose for everything being formed is to define and express the One Life. We look at the beauty and perfection and order of a rose, and we realize the beauty and the order of that One Life which formed the rose. We look at the innocence of a baby, and we realize the innocence and the purity of thought of that One Life which formed the baby. We look at the joy and happiness of people in love, and we know what that feels like inside, and we realize that love is the very substance of that Life. We look at the seasons changing, we look at the day coming in the morning, engulfing the night, and we realize the constancy and the Divine Order and the perfection of that Life. We realize that light--illumination, understanding--will swallow up the darkness of confusion, just as the morning sun swallows up the long night. We realize that no matter how long the winter is, new Life will always come forth out from the midst of it, and spring will always come. We learn to trust that no matter what the physical appearance, Life will still come forward.

We learn all these things about that One Life by looking at that which it has made, including us. We realize it is that Life that formed us and flows through us and lives out its existence as us. We realize the immutability, the constant, unchangeable nature of that Life. Life is not only what formed us, but what animates us, and as we allow its flow through our consciousness, our experience will take on the nature of this eternal One Life that flows throughout all of creation.

"Thus saith the Lord: If ye can break my covenant of the day and my covenant of the night, that there should not be day and night in their season, then may also my covenant be broken."   Jeremiah 33:20-21

DAY 274
Realize the absoluteness of Life.

Life is not contained within that which it has formed. It cannot be. That which is formed does not dominate that which formed it. Our body cannot dominate Life. Life governs our body and Life we find to be good. We find it to be completely and wholly perfect. We find it to be trustworthy, because it never changes its basic nature. We realize the absoluteness of it. That's the Law of Life. What we have been calling life is not law, but belief, an attitude in the human consciousness.

Life is an entity outside of us, a Being. It has no form, that's why it's called the Spirit of Life. Life is not contained within the visible, it's not contained within the human body, it's not contained within the animal, it's not contained within that which it has formed. Everything it has formed is an expression of its Soul, its Being. It flows throughout creation. The air all around us is filled with this nature of divinity, infinity, wholeness, perfection, beauty, order.

It is incumbent upon us to allow it to flow through us, because the more we allow it to flow, the greater is our expression and experience of Life. We see Life as something vast and eternal and infinite. It has no boundaries, no parameters, no beginning and end. As it flows and pulsates and fills all space, it creates out of its own thought, its own Being.

Now I see a much greater vision of Life. Now, instead of seeing a tree, I see strength, I see something constant, year after year, and something that gives out Life. I look at my dog and I see the faithfulness--it is a formation of loyalty and love and devotion. I see the Life that formed her, not just the form.

"God gives to all, life and breath and all things."
Acts 17:25

DAY 275
Love is the law.

Recently a friend had her purse taken, and was very distraught. I said to her, "Love is a law, a law of everyone's life. There is no being created to steal, to be greedy, to hurt or harm another, to gain at another's expense. That is not the Law of Love, that's human belief that says people can act that way. That is not the Law of Life. The Law of the Spirit of Life is Love. The Law of Love is not self serving, but self offering, for the good of the whole. It's not needing to take from another, but it's knowing that I already contain all things. I would not take from another, but would give of my own good that another might also experience goodness. That's the Law of Love. To believe that someone could steal something to hurt another, or to gain for their own self, is denying the Law of Life. We're not going to believe that, no matter what happens. We're going to hold to the truth that the Law of the Spirit of Life is Love. The Law is Love."

We held to that for three days, but she was beginning to despair of ever seeing that purse again. I said, "It doesn't make any difference whether you see it or not. To see it would be a real testimony to the truth, but it doesn't change the truth. The absolute truth is that the Law of the Spirit of Life is Love. No one has been created in such a manner that they could live a life contrary to that Law." The fifth day she got a call from a teenage girl who wanted to return the purse, intact. The truth won out, the Law of Love.

"Thou shalt love thy neighbor as thyself. Love works no ill to his neighbor: therefore love is the fulfilling of the law."   Romans 13:9-10

DAY 276

This is how healings happen.

The answer to suffering is to stop seeing Life the way we have been seeing it. I know a woman who was diagnosed with degenerative corneal disease and was rapidly going blind. She resisted having a corneal transplant because she knew in her heart and mind that any kind of degeneration was contrary to the law of Life. She knew she was formed by the Divine and Eternal and pure and perfect Life, and that did not include degeneration. She really wanted to see the truth be evidenced, be expressed.

She heard someone say, "God saw what he had made and he saw it was very good," from Genesis 1. All of a sudden she realized that the only person *seeing* is this One Life, and this Life sees everything that it has made. She realized that she was believing she was separate from that One Life, having her own individual human life and needing to see out from human eyes.

The moment someone said, "God sees everything that he has made," she began to realize that if she allowed that Life to flow through her, and allowed herself to see everything that has been made through the eyes of that One Life, then she would see clearly. She did that for days and days and days. Everything she looked at she said, "God sees everything that he has made." Very rapidly the vision began to clear and very rapidly the belief that she was a separate entity from that Life began to fade, and more and more she began to feel that sense of oneness with that One Life that knows no boundaries and no limitations and no loss and no lack.

This is how healings happen.

"Thou have made known to me the ways of life; thou shall make me full of joy with thy countenence."

Acts 2:28

DAY 277
Life removes the most stubborn human obstacles.

It says in Romans 8:2, "The law of the spirit of life has made me free from the law of sin and death." That means if we line up with the understanding of Life, the rhythm of Life, the flow of Life, the goodness of Life, we can avoid violating the law, and allow Life to flow unencumbered. When it flows freely we get to enjoy the experience of it, which is wholeness and health and supply and abundance and goodness, not only for ourselves but for everyone.

The law of death includes all the miserable experiences that we call life, but it's not life at all. And it's not a law at all, it's a belief. That is the law we have put ourselves under, but it is not a law. I know it is not a law because there is a law greater than that, which dismantles the power of it. If it can be broken, it can't be a law. It has to be a belief, an attitude we've accumulated in the human consciousness. What breaks its power is the law of the Spirit of Life, the ultimate and the absolute.

If we step back from our own thoughts and our own human effort, pause and let Life speak, let it reveal itself however it chooses to, it will remove the most stubborn human obstacles. It will demonstrate the nothingness, the weakness, of that which we have called law up until now, that which we have felt so afflicted by, so victimized by. It removes the worst of all human scenarios without effort. When the sun comes up in the morning, what happens to the darkness of the night? The rising sun dispels the darkness without effort. Once we grasp in our mind and heart the reality of this One Life and let it flow through us, just let it be, we find things changing with no effort.

"Upon whom does not his light arise?"　　　　Job 25:3

DAY 278

God is Love.

Human consciousness is in a transition right now. We're being elevated to a place where we are ready to say enough is enough. The epidemic of AIDS and the epidemic of cancer might finally cause us to lift our heads out of the ostrich position. How is it that we who are created by God in the image and likeness of God can refuse to question? We embrace a God that calls himself Love, goodness, who is omnipotent, a power that fills all space with this Love and goodness, so how can we acquiesce to such convoluted thought, not only about our bodies, not only about our life, not only about disease, but about God? When are we going to step back and say, if God is Love, then what is this nonsense that we are living in? There was a time when mankind realized that we come from pure goodness, that we serve goodness.

As we are good, as we are kind and generous and loving in our thought, in our judgments, in our opinions, in our actions, then we are able to feel the rhythm of this Eternal Life flowing through us. When we deny that law of Love, when we are harsh and bitter and angry and critical, we actually stop the flow of this Eternal Life and Love through us, and disease or accident or conflict, or poverty, or confusion is the result. Life is an absolute state of existence, it has laws that are associated with it. There is a law of Life and we can't swim upstream against the flow of that law and expect to fare well.

I long for the day that humanity lives this life in joy and peace and love and freedom. I don't just believe this can happen, I know that it's going to happen.

"Enter into the joy of thy Lord."　　　　Matthew 25:21

DAY 279

Live for the good of the whole.

The law of Life is that we love one another as we would have others love us. And that we love Life, which is God. How do you love that Life? You're careful to secure the flow of that Life. Romans 8:2 says, "The law of the spirit of life has made me free from the law of sin and death." If we line up with the understanding of Life and what it really is, the rhythm of it, the flow of it, the goodness of it, we allow Life to continue to flow unencumbered, freely, without effort, and we get to enjoy the experience of it, which is wholeness and health and abundance, not only for ourselves but for everyone.

How do we get with the flow? We recognize that the nature of this Life is Love. Love says, "What can I do to increase the good of the whole? I just open my eyes and look out away from me and notice the world around me, notice the need, how I can help, how I can make someone's way a little easier, a little gentler, a little freer, a little happier."

At the end of the day you find you spent the whole day not grasping, not grabbing for your own gain. You spent the whole day giving. Giving even if it costs you something. But at the end of the day you find you are richer, healthier, happier, and more whole, just because you flowed with the law of Love that day. You lived for the good of the whole.

That's going with the flow of the law of Life. That's the nature that created us, the nature that freely flows through us; that's our true nature. That's what God sees when he looks at his creation: Love, goodness, Life. That's all he sees, his Life, because there is only One Life, and it's his Life.

"Let us do good unto all."   Galatians 6:10

DAY 280

There is no death.

There is no such thing as death. The minute you leave the body, you continue to live. You continue to live because Life is God. And the only Life that is, the only Life that flows through and animates creation, is the Life and the Presence of the Spirit of God. That never dies. It looks to you like your independent, autonomous life, but it really is the Spirit of God calling itself you.

There is no death. We leave this body, we go on to higher consciousness. How can I know? I know there's no such thing as death in Life because I know that Life is God and I know it's Eternal. I know that we have always existed, that we've come into this little parenthesis of eternity we call humanity, and we will continue to exist after that. We all exist as that One Divine Life.

If we realize that, we will deny all the convoluted human belief, opinions and judgments that say that Life can fall into disrepair and die. Instead we say, what is the nature of this Life that we live and how can I go with the flow of it? You always win when you go with the flow of least resistance. If you're going to resist the flow of Life, if you're going to do it your way, if you're going to try to live on your own terms, it's going to be an uphill swim and a struggle. You actually block the flow, the easy, rhythmic flow of this Eternal Life through you, and end up shipwrecked.

Divine Life is goodness, pure goodness. It's not good and bad, it doesn't take you behind the woodshed if you're bad. It doesn't have to. The fact that we choose to go in an opposite way from the flow of Life will bring about its own destruction. Above all else, Life is Love.

"I have no pleasure in the death of him that dies, saith the Lord God: wherefore turn yourselves and live."
Ezekiel 18:32

DAY 281

The goodness of Life is ours.

Have you ever paused in your hurried experience of your definition of life and felt the Presence of the Divine and Eternal Life that flows throughout all of creation? We race around trying to accumulate as much as we can into our own little energy space, trying to make everything as good and comfortable and peaceful as we can. Allow yourself to pause and feel the Presence of Life as it fills all space with its own Being. Realize it flowing through you. Allow yourself to step back and gently go with the flow of it, feel the rhythm of it. If you're not resisting, not denying its Presence by trying to make life happen for your own self, then you get the benefit of everything contained within that Life. You get all the goodness, all the abundance, all the love, all the companionship, all the opportunities, every wonderful thing, including wholeness and health in your body.

Let a crack be opened in your understanding of what Life is. Let one tiny little ray of light shine through that one little crack in the armor. It's enough to heal anything and everything, so powerful is the Presence of that Life.

We have not come to serve ourselves, we've come to love others as we would like them to love us. We do not need to grasp and be self serving because we live in the realization that we contain all things. We are complete as we stand, because the true Life of us is this Divine Life and it is complete. We've come to be the Life, to let that flow out. The goodness of Life is ours to experience and enjoy just by being aware of its Presence.

"The people that walked in darkness have seen a great light. They that dwell in the land of the shadow of death, upon them has the light shined."   Isaiah 9:2

DAY 282

Divine Life is a law.

Why do I say Divine Life is a law? Because every single time we let it flow, it dissolves and absorbs whatever is on the human scene that's causing a problem. Whenever we let Love flow, it's like the dawning of a new day--as the sun comes up, the light begins to shine. What happens to the deep darkness of the night? It just goes away, just by virtue of the Presence of the Light.

That is exactly what happens on the human scene when we let just a particle of the Light of that Love flow in our thought, in our attitude, in our judgments, in our opinions. When we let it flow not for our own gain but for the gain of the whole, our own energy field is opened up. When that happens, that law of Divine Life flows into that space and whatever we have been encumbered by is absorbed, dissolved, healed.

A gentleman came to the clinic with a serious life-threatening health problem. He was harsh and intimidating, a ruthless businessman. We were not getting anywhere with him solely on a physical basis, so I talked to him about love and about letting love flow. I told him that the Life that formed him was within him and he was a result of the flow of that Life, and it was the Life of God. I said, if any of us choke down that flow of energy, we get ill, and the way to open up that flow is by forgiving, by turning the other way in our thoughts and reactions to people. He started crying and I could see that hard shell crumbling right before my eyes.

He became gentle, smiling, concerned about others. He got out of his shell and reached out with love. Within three months all the disease was gone, he was healed. He learned to love.

"The merciful one does good to his own soul."

Proverbs 11:17

DAY 283

He sees his own Life.

We have been taught that we are not worthy. That we are inferior to God and we need to spend our life trying to find a way to get back into his graces. No matter how hard we try we still carry around that sense of unworthiness. Worthiness is something that comes from deep down inside. Worthiness comes from the Presence of the Spirit of Love, from God in our hearts. Worthiness is not something we can ever earn, no matter how many prayers we make, no matter how many times we run up to the front of the altar, no matter how many times we try to imitate goodness, we still don't feel right inside, because it's not going to come from human effort.

In the eyes of God, we've always been worthy. We have never been inferior to his own Presence and his own goodness. How do I know? Because we were born and created "in the image and likeness of God." (Genesis 1:27) Because "It is he that hath made us and not we ourselves." (Psalm 100:3) Because "All the works of his hands are perfect." (Deuteronomy 32:4) Because "Of his fullness have we all received," (John 1:16), every one of us. Because "He is the true light that lighteth every man that cometh into the world." (John 1:9) I know that he formed and created us and all of creation after his own nature and out from his own nature. I know everything is good and whole and pure and perfect and wonderful, as he made it. I know that when God looks upon his creation, upon you and I, he sees the perfection, the beauty and the order, he sees what he's made, and he sees his own Life.

"I and my Father are one."   John 10:30

DAY 284
I'm not going to tolerate it!

God sees his own Life soaring and flowing through us, bringing newness of Life, every moment of every day, offering joy and peace and wholeness and health. Anything that does not come under that definition is manmade. It's something we have thought ourselves, allowed to come into our experience, because of the sense of unworthiness that comes from feeling separate from the Life of God. That's where tolerance of disease comes from. Look at the horror of disease, then look at the goodness of God. It doesn't make sense. The more we think of the goodness of God, the more we see life without disease, and the more we see healings.

Here at Living Beyond Disease, we see healings all the time. Why? Because we expect to see them. We expect to see them because we don't buy into the thought that disease is something we are supposed to experience. We don't tolerate it. We have zero tolerance for the whole concept of disease. and zero tolerance for the belief that we are unworthy. Choose to see Life as God sees it, through his eyes, through his heart.

I follow the teachings of Jesus. I believe this is what he's taught us, and what he secured for us. He opened our eyes to see it and I received it. I don't deny the wonders that we are. We've always been this way, but we were unable to get past the teachings and the concepts of fallen humanity. If you see yourself as unworthy, you will act out a life that is unworthy, an inferior existence. You will draw suffering into your experience because you feel it is needed to purge that unworthiness. Rise up, say, "I'm not going to tolerate it!"

"You have eaten of the fruit of lies: because you did trust in your way, in the multitude of mighty men."
Hosea 10:12

DAY 285

You are the righteousness of God.

Many years ago, when I was grappling with a sense of unworthiness, guilt and condemnation, I found a scripture that said, "You are the righteousness of God in Christ." (2Corinthians 5:21) We all read that, it wasn't a foreign thought to me, but I don't think I really believed it. I began to think about it and say it over and over. "You are the righteousness of God. You are the righteousness of God. That's the way he's created you, that's the way he sees you, that's the way you are. You are the righteousness of God." I spent six months rehearsing that over and over and over, and it helped me. It helped extricate me from the mess I was in, it helped me get my feet on the ground, it helped me get going on a different path, where I was not repeating the same offenses.

But it didn't make a change in me from within. Saying it doesn't make my heart really believe it. Saying it is a good thing to do. Knowing it is a good thing. But better to have it with no effort, effortlessly flowing out from within, so you're actually living life out from that feeling and experience of worthiness, feeling accepted and beloved and worthy of goodness. This is not an egocentric thing, not from pride, but on the contrary, it comes from a deep humility.

What actually made it flow out from within me came with the understanding of forgiveness. I was led to reconcile with my father, and by opening and expanding my heart and letting love flow out where before there was judgment and criticism, other areas spontaneously opened up. The only way we can open up our hearts to effortlessly feel that sense of worth is to see everyone else as worthy!

"Awake to righteousness."   1Corinthians 15:34

DAY 286
We have forgotten.

Our sense of unworthiness comes from taking on the human consciousness that is filled with judgment and criticism. We look out at a world that we don't like. We don't see it as worthy. We don't see it as beautiful. We don't see it as filled with the Spirit of Love and Life. We don't see it as full of joy and goodness.

We have not trained ourselves to look past the way people behave and to know that beyond that image they are acting out, there is the Christ, there is the Love, there is the Divine Life. They haven't seen it yet in their own selves and that's why they're acting like they're acting. But it resides within nevertheless, and it's up to us to see it in others, it's up to us to know it's there. It is up to us to look out at everyone and know it's there. Even people who have done awful things to us, even people in whom we can't find a reason to see something good.

Let me give you a reason. God sees it. God sees them worthy. God sees his own goodness and sees his own Life in them. The reason they are not acting out from their true Christ nature is they have not seen it. It's the same reason you and I don't always act out from that pure nature. We have forgotten. We don't see it within ourselves. The only way a sense of worthiness can be achieved within our own selves is when we choose to see it in others.

That's not to say we condone destructive behavior, we're just choosing to look past it, and to know that past it is the "true light that lights every one that comes into the world", and "of his fullness have we all received." (John 1:9,16)

"Peter asked, How often shall I forgive? Seven times? Jesus said, Seventy times seven." Matthew 18:22

DAY 287

He draws us.

A lady wrote to me about her employer who was a scam artist who ripped her off for $24,000. This was not the first time he had done this. The employees got together to file a lawsuit against him, to stop him from hurting others. When she got into the lawsuit, she got breast cancer and had surgery, though she had no insurance, due to her employer's theft. A lawsuit is the human way, but there is a divine way. We spoke of a "higher" way. She had a bigger responsibility than just not suing him. She needed to pray for herself, that God would open her eyes and her heart to be able to see him as God made him.

That's called the Christ, the visible expression of the invisible God. (Colossians 1:15) We need to come to a place where our heart is so enlarged that we see through the heart and eyes of God. We see what he has made, something beautiful. That's how he draws us. He sees the beauty of his own Life, and that draws us into a greater experience than the human experience.

When you do that, you are acknowledging other people's worth. You have chosen to see beyond the veil of human consciousness, and by doing so you release that Life from within them, which heals them of their behavior and restores them to a life of worthiness and honor. It also heals you, as it allows an internal sense of worthiness to flow out from you.

She dropped the lawsuit and immediately the hospital and the doctor forgave her of her debt for her surgery. Better than that, she felt a freedom when she thought of that man, she felt the Presence of the Christ Life within him. Because she felt it in him, she was able to feel it in herself. Best of all, she was healed.

"I drew them with bands of love."   Hosea 11:4

DAY 288
True forgiveness produces a healing.

   Whatever judgment we send out, that's what we're
going to feel about ourselves. You know why? Because
there's only One Life. It looks like there are a billion of
them, but there aren't. There is One Life out from
which all this activity on the human scene has been
formed to express that Life. When we do it to another,
we're doing it to ourselves. All judgment comes back to
the heart that sent it out, whether the judgment is unto
condemnation or unto mercy. How we see "out there" is
how we feel "in here." The heart of Mercy is the heart
that lies within each one, whether it's been allowed to
come forth or not.
   What is forgiveness? It's not just saying, you've done
this bad thing but I forgive you--that's arrogant, condescending. We don't acknowledge the offense and then
try to X it out. True forgiveness is not acknowledging it,
but getting past it. Not denying it, but just not reacting
to it and seeing what the reality is. Real forgiveness is
saying, "I see such a beautiful Life beyond what you are
seeing and feeling right now, and it's the real reality of
you. I see there is nothing to be forgiven because I'm
looking past the veil into this pure and holy existence
that we all really are." True forgiveness releases the
other. True forgiveness produces a healing in the person.
   When you do that it enhances your own sense of
personal worthiness. Then you will not accept, for your
own self, bad behavior or disease or anything that
comes from the human consciousness and the human
belief. You will only accept that which has been offered
to you by the Life that flows through you, the Divine
Life of God.

*"Son, be of good cheer, thy sins be forgiven thee...
Arise and walk."*   Matthew 9: 2,5

DAY 289

Agree with what is true about God.

The Life that we live is God flowing through us. He breathed his Life into us, therefore our life is his Life.

Once I prayed for a woman who appeared to be dying. The prayer was something like this: *In this very moment, I'm filled with such a rage and hatred of disease, and at the same time my heart is filled with the realization that God is Love. The Life that flows through her and flows through all of us is the One Divine Life of God. I don't know how to reconcile what I am seeing with what I am knowing. God help me to reconcile these. I choose to honor you by declaring that God is Love, and that this disease has no part of your nature or your purpose for your creation.*

She was healed. All I did was choose to agree with what is true about God and about our Life, right in the face of what was declaring itself to be the dominant factor. It made a shift in my mind and my heart that I will never forget. I saw that disease is not the enemy, but our belief in it, our acceptance of it, is the enemy. Because it denies the Presence of God. It denies that God is the Life of each one of us.

She was healed. Her entire appearance changed overnight. All tests were perfect. But she got involved in a lawsuit against the father of her child. I told her not to do it. "You've got such a Divine Life flowing through your Life. You have received so much Mercy from God, I don't think it would be wise for you not to show the same Mercy and Love as was shown you." Instead of embracing my counsel, she got mad and left. A few months later she began to manifest the same symptoms again and soon died. I saw what happens when we shut down the flow of forgiveness and mercy.

"Be ye merciful as your Father is also merciful."
Luke 6:36

DAY 290
Reclaim our true being.

The acceptance of disorder or confusion or dis-ease in any area of our life is a result of a human state of un-worthiness, which is part of the human consciousness. It's part of the human consciousness to feel inferior and unworthy, and therefore vulnerable to unhappiness and destruction. In order to have within us the intrinsic strength to be able to stand up and say, "No, I will not accept this experience," we have to deal with this issue of worthiness and unworthiness.

Some people react to a sense of unworthiness by becoming prideful and aggressive, to compensate for the feeling of vulnerability and victimization. Other people walk around with a sign on their back that says, "kick me," and when they get kicked, they say, "I expected it, I knew it was coming." Either thought comes from a sense of unworthiness. That's part of the package of the human consciousness.

To escape from that, we must escape from the human thought and belief and we must grab hold of the Mind of God. God doesn't see us as unworthy. He sees us as that which he has made in his image, quite worthy of love. He's created us to be creatures of Love, of wholeness, of goodness, of Mercy, of Wisdom, because that's what he is, and he's made us out from his own being. We don't see ourselves that way. We're told that we're born separate from God--they call that original sin. God has never seen us separate from that which he has made, nor separate from him. It's a matter of reclaiming that which has always been our true being. We need to come out of the human consciousness and step into a higher understanding.

"It is high time that we awake out of sleep."
                                                    Romans 13:11

DAY 291

Look beyond.

We look out upon a world we see as being unworthy, less than whole, less than perfect. We see others as being sick, although God doesn't see them as sick. We agree in our mind with what they are seeing and believing about themselves. We see criminals, people out of control, poor, angry, sick and defeated. When we see anything less than the whole perfect creature that comes forth from the consciousness of God, we are agreeing with what that person sees about himself. When we do that, we hold them in that state. And we end up with the exact same thought about ourselves.

There is no way to extricate yourself out of the sense of being separate from your own intrinsic goodness and holiness and wholeness, as long as you choose to see somebody else in a state of separateness. If you don't want to be bound by a sense of unworthiness, then do not look out upon a world with eyes and heart that judge others to be unworthy. You must look beyond the offense. You must look beyond the disease. You must look beyond that which the whole world sees, if you are going to experience your own life beyond that.

The key to forgiving oneself is to forgive others. The original Webster definition of forgiving is to send it away, to reject it, to not impute it to the offender, to remit the offense. You can't do that if you see them as an offender. You have to look past it and send it away. Send it away from the person. Cast it away that you might see that person in their intrinsic wholeness. By casting it away, it no longer belongs to them, nor does punishment belong to them. They're free. You have healed them. You have healed yourself.

"It is glory to pass over a transgression."

Proverbs 19:11

DAY 292

Send it away.

We have been sent here for one purpose, and that is to remove the human consciousness, the human belief, from those who are enslaved by it. We do that by this action called forgiving. What that means is no matter how that person is behaving, no matter what they have done, whether they are in the throes of disease or in the throes of a criminal personality, or in the throes of the typical human thought, no matter what we see, we are to send it away, knowing that it does not belong to their true nature.

It's like a barnacle on the bottom of a ship, it has attached itself to the ship, but it is not part of the ship. We send it away. We tell it to go. We send it away because we know what they don't know, that it does not belong to them. They have identified with it as though it's a part of them. The whole world has agreed with that identification.

Forget yourself for just a moment and reach out to another, someone who comes to your mind, and send away whatever offense you see, be it a physical disease, poverty, whatever. You will find you have the power to do that. You will find that's exactly what we are intended to do. That's why we're here, to do that for one another. You will find they are healed. You will find the simplicity of freeing another, from disease, from offense, from whatever has enveloped them. You are exercising the Mercy of God. You send it away as though it is a barnacle, as though it is moss growing on a tree. You will find it responds to your words, and it goes. It will happen because it's true.

"Through your mercy they also may obtain mercy."
Romans 11:31

DAY 293

Allow Love to flow freely.

When we send something away, does it stay away? Sometimes. Sometimes you have to tell the person, "That's not part of your nature." They can't make that separation between what they're experiencing and their true self. It's only when it's sent away that they get the feeling, the reality sweeps over them...that was not me. "This is not me, it is something that attached itself to me, and I've been acting out from it." Then when it tries to come back, they can rise up and say, "No, I'm going to send that away."

What blocks us from forgiving is the human thought that a person should suffer for what they've done. But by feeling that we ensnare ourselves in that same consciousness, leaving ourselves vulnerable to experience what that person has experienced. We have not fulfilled the reason for which we've come. We've choked down the flow of that true Spirit of Life that would flow through us to reach out to others. When we choke it down, we become the very thing we hated.

What if they're not repentant? Do it anyway, so that they can be free to see the difference, to feel the difference, to feel what it feels like to be free of that offense, so that they can choose to turn away from it. That is repentance, to turn away from the way you've been going and go in a different direction.

Sometimes we can't choose to do it for ourselves, and it takes another person to love enough, to allow Love to flow freely enough, to send it away. Then can we realize the contrast between what we have been experiencing and acting out, and what we really are.

"Who can understand his errors? Cleanse me from secret faults." Psalm 19:12

DAY 294

We're called to Mercy.

Disease is simply the result of a thought, a thought that needs to be dealt with. Sometimes people suffer from an infirmity that keeps coming back. Often the reason it's coming back is they are holding in consciousness that age-old consciousness of being unworthy. They're a victim and there's nothing they can do.

Mercy is always available, but you cannot receive Mercy until you can give it. Hardness of heart cannot reach out or forgive another, because it has never experienced Mercy. Mercy is to send away the offense and look upon another as though there were no offense. Until you can do it for another, how can you experience it for yourself? It is much easier to look at another person and know their suffering is not true. It is a thought, a belief, externalized on the body, not a part of their true nature.

As I habitually forgive and release others, then when a thought attempts to attach itself to me and manifest as suffering, I can realize that no matter what it feels like, it really is just a suggestion of thought from the human consciousness. I don't accept that as part of my own nature and so I send it away. And it goes.

As I habitually forgive the offense, the debt, let it go, and choose to see that person in their true Eternal Divine nature, free of all these barnacles of attitudes and actions, then if it happens to me it's easier to make that separation. That's what we're called to do.

"If one be overtaken in a fault, you who are spiritual, restore such a one in the spirit of meekness, considering yourself, lest you also be tempted. Bear one another's burdens, and so fulfill the law of Christ."
Galatians 6:1-2

DAY 295

*As you see worthiness in others
you will feel it in yourself.*

I met a woman diagnosed with a year to live. After a
few months she was so sick she could not continue
treatment. She decided to just give her life to God and
let him choose what to do or not to do. She read my
book, *Of Monkeys and Dragons,* and listened to every
one of the radio programs. She then realized a huge
contrast between the way she felt about herself now
and the way that she had been thinking about herself
prior to that. She realized she didn't like that person,
and chose to become a different person.

Listening to these truths and reading about them, and
hearing the testimonies of the people who have done
it, encouraged her to be able to make the separation in
her own life and to heal herself. Now she is willing to
do for others what she was given the grace and ability
to do for herself. She will never see that disease again,
and she likes herself better for looking out upon a world
with Mercy rather than with judgment.

As you see worthiness in others, you will feel it in
yourself. As you see wholeness and perfection and
beauty and order and completion in another, you will
feel it for yourself. As you see another created as Divine
Love, irrespective of what has attached itself to them
in thought, you will feel yourself as a part of that Divine
Love. It's a principle and it can't be denied. We are all
either suffering under the consequences of breaking that
principle, or we are prospering because we have found
it to be true and chosen to live out from it. That's how
Life is--you either go with the flow or you suffer the
consequences of trying to swim upstream.

*"As you would that others should do unto you, do also
to them likewise."*   Luke 6:31

DAY 296

"They shall not hurt in all my holy mountain."

Remember the scripture that says the lion will lay down with the lamb and the child will play with the adder? And in all my holy mountain, there will be no one to hurt or to destroy. (Isaiah 11:8) What is that? That's the kingdom of peace. That's the consciousness of God, that's the consciousness of the Christ, that's the consciousness of the spiritual being that you are and I am. That is available to us now. This is not a future event. This is a description of that realm of awareness that is entirely devoid of problems or suffering. When we get it, when our thought is elevated to live out from that, then all of nature and all of creation will come under the authority of that as well.

I believe the only reason the creatures in nature are in that survival mode is because we are. I believe that when the thought of man is corrected and when we are willing to acknowledge our Christ nature, when we are willing to yield up the old and understand and live out from the new, I believe we'll see nature change as well.

Creation and its experience is under the umbrella of man, of our experience. We need to get under the umbrella of the Mind of God and not the human mind. "All creation groans and travails in pain together ...waiting for the manifestation of the sons of God." (Romans 8:22,19) Peace on earth depends upon our choices. What mind are we going to come under, the human mind, or the Mind of God and the government of good?

God never created his creation to suffer, to struggle, to be so burdened. God formed all things out of his being to be perfect, and to be maintained and governed by the law of the Spirit of Life.

"The earth shall be full of the knowledge of the Lord, as the waters cover the sea."   Isaiah 11:9

DAY 297
Take a great big dose of the Mind of God.

The greatest principle is Love. The law of Love says that this energy, this Presence, fills all space, under all conditions, and is continually forming out from its own being. That which it forms is in the image of that which formed it. We need to know the nature of that energy. We need to know, what is the principle of Love?

We need to clear up the strange imagery that has caused us to dance to a tune that is not coming out from that Divine Mind at all. It is a strange and distorted sound. We're trying to find some rhythm in it. We're trying to dance to it, and it's not working for us. We need to know the Mind that is God and understand the thoughts of that Divine Mind. The antidote for the thought that surrounds us, the human consciousness, is a great big dose of the Mind of God. When that appears in our thought, it drives out the confused and erroneous thought process. When the thought changes, the human picture changes. Once the energy is opened up, Life comes. We don't have to tell it what to do. As a matter of fact, we cannot tell it what to do, that won't work. You simply desire the flow, the uninterrupted flow of Life. If necessary, send away the confused thought so that which is real can freely flow.

The person is not the problem. We impersonalize the problem and realize that we are seeing nothing more than confused energy, erroneous thought, part of the human consciousness. It has no real substance. The person within is still intact and whole and complete, because that's what was formed from this Divine Life.

"How precious are thy thoughts unto me, O God! Search me O God and know my heart: try me and know my thoughts: see if there be any wicked way in me and lead me in the way everlasting."   Psalm 139:17,23,24

DAY 298

Go straight to the heart.

A woman called to tell me of her brother's incredible healing. She and her family had not seen him for a couple of years. One day he showed up at his sister's, very ill and emaciated. She pressed him to go to the hospital, but he left and went to his parents' house. They called EMS to take him to the hospital, where he was diagnosed, not only with AIDS, but with an immanently terminal situation.

His sister hopped on a plane to her parents town, a Southern Baptist small town. The first thing the father said when he met her at the airport was, "Now they'll all know." She said, "That's right, Dad, everybody's going to know because we're going to tell them the absolute truth. We're going to ask them to rise up in the Spirit and the heart of Christ, and to pray for his healing and to love him."

She went to her church, she went to the newspaper, she made it community knowledge. She asked for 100% love and support, and this little community rose to the occasion. They were able to rise up in the Spirit of Divine Love, see the wholeness and the goodness of that person, envelop him in love. They withheld all judgment. They didn't condone or excuse, nor did they impute anything to him, but they ignored it and went straight to the heart of that person they loved.

That was six years ago and today he's healthy, happy, and HIV negative. The real healing here was of the thought of the people of that community. When the Love within us, the Christ Love within us, becomes one with the Christ nature of another, it always produces healing.

"When Christ, who is our life, shall appear, then shall ye also appear with him in glory.   Colossians 3:4

DAY 299

Let it pass on by.

We have one right: to love. We don't have the personal right to be treated with respect, to demand obedience, to be treated right. We have one right, and that's the right to look past any offense and to love.

One of the greatest examples is Jesus on the cross. The very people that he healed, poured out his Life for three years to give them the absolute truth of the heart of God, are yelling, "Crucify him." He doesn't take offense, rather he says, "Forgive them, they have no idea what they're doing." (Luke 23:24) Because it got forgiven, we are now able to know and understand and walk in this whole new consciousness of Divine Life.

I know a woman who was diagnosed with multiple sclerosis. I knew something had choked down the flow of energy, and as soon as we discovered what to do to open that up, the problem would go away. She talked to me about having a falling out with her only child. She was offended by what happened. She became defensive and angry. She felt her personal rights were violated. If we are going to insist on our own personal rights, we're going to be taking offense all the time, choking down the flow all the time.

It's not like you have to take it. You don't take it. You just step back and let it pass you on by. You know that's not you, that's not them. That's forgiving. That's sending it away. That's moving in the Divine Love. That's insisting on seeing the Christ in every situation. Go right past it into the heart that never changes. By connecting with that, the person is healed. This woman did that and opened up a channel of energy making a dramatic change in her health.

"What is that to thee?"   John 21:22

DAY 300

See the good.

If we fear something, we give energy to it, which empowers it. We become subservient to it, we dance the dance as it pipes its tune. We don't challenge it, we're too absorbed in the hypnotic trance of fear. We can come to a halt and say, "This isn't the direction I want to go. Do I need to dance this dance?"

In the Bible is the story of Daniel, who was thrown into the lions' den because he continued to worship The God of Israel. (Daniel 6) Symbolically, those lions can be anything in your life that you fear--poverty, accident, divorce, attack. When you fear something, it's as if you're experiencing it all the time, and you become a victim to it, whether you ever actually see it in your experience or not. The lions never did devour Daniel, and the king asked, "How did you ever survive these lions?" Daniel said, "My God has sent his angel and has shut the lions' mouths that they have not hurt me. For before him innocency was found in me."

What was it about innocency that protected him from the lions? Innocence is not ignorance, not helplessness, not dependence, not fear. There is a higher concept of innocence. It is one who has chosen harmlessness. One who has chosen to see through the mesmerism of evil, the hypnotic trance of fear, who has looked at it and chosen to see through it. One who has fully embraced forgiveness and Mercy and Infinite Love, one who shares these Divine attributes with others.

I used to walk with a friend who was terrified of dogs, so every dog would come out barking and showing their teeth. I would always stand still and think, "You've been created by the same Source as I, your nature must be good." I see the good in it, and it walks away.

"Refuse the evil and choose the good."   Isaiah 7:15

DAY 301
You are made from pure Divine Love.

Innocence is choosing to see through that which is believed about evil, choosing to see that it is merely a mask created by fear. Once you have done that, innocence feels like harmlessness. You realize you are harmless and so is everything else, because everything was created by Divine Love, and the very substance of all that has been created by God, who is Love, is Love. It's harmless. It's not weak, not vulnerable, just harmless. It's not to be feared, it's guiltless. To be innocent is to be worthy to live in a state of wholeness, free of fear.

To be innocent is to be unable to perceive, and therefore to fear, evil in anything or anyone. It is that state of harmlessness which says, "I cannot perceive evil in you, and I cannot fear you, because I refuse to perceive evil in you. I know who made you, I know why you are, who you are. I know what God sees, I know what really is. I know what never changes. If I choose to see what I know is true beyond the appearance, how can I fear you? I have to see that you are made out from pure Divine Love, and you are incapable of producing harm. I have to see you innocent, guiltless, worthy of every good thing."

How can I fear ever being in a situation where I am not safe? I don't expect hurt or harm, I don't see anyone as capable of harm. I choose to see through whatever they may be believing about themselves and to see instead what has truly been made that cannot be changed. True innocence is a sense of dignity, a sense of strength, and the expectancy of only good.

"Be not overcome of evil, but overcome evil
with good."   Romans 121:21

DAY 302

Why do I have to forgive?

We live looking out at what is appearing. Our focus is on correcting the predator, the disease, the weather, the employer. We must stop looking out at appearances and instead assume responsibility for the way we have viewed the world...with a fearful heart. We have viewed ourselves as potential victims, and we've lost our innocence. True innocence is a sense of self-worth, a feeling of being enveloped in goodness and in Love, with no expectation of harm...nor could we harm another in that sense of goodness and Love.

Can we live like that? Like Pollyanna? Everyone laughed at her fearless, carefree attitude, always choosing to see goodness, but she didn't get hurt or harmed. We want to look at the way we are looking at the world and what we are unconsciously expecting and fearing. We need to realize this is what we are drawing, by the fear that we project. The more energy we give to it, the more we experience the very thing we fear.

The burden of responsibility is upon the victim. I used to wonder why, when something harmful is done to me, is it my responsibility to forgive that person? It doesn't seem fair. Why does the burden fall upon me? In my sense of righteousness, the responsibility should be on the predator. If you're going to hurt me, why do I have to forgive?

I have to do it because nothing will go well in my life until I do. Not doing it stops the flow of Life, right then and there. The word forgive means to send away...to send away your belief, your thought, your fear, your expectation of an awful thing coming, and to send away the other person's belief about themselves as well.

"Whatever sins ye remit, they are remitted unto them, whose sins ye retain, they are retained."

John 20:23

DAY 303

Partake of Life.

Let's go back to the Garden of Eden and the symbolism of the tree of the knowledge of good and evil versus the tree of Life. (Genesis 2) We were told, "Do not partake of the tree of the knowledge of good and evil." A tree puts out fruit, you eat the fruit. The trees represent the two distinct atmospheres of thought we choose to live in. Within each atmosphere are thoughts, ideologies, beliefs, of which we partake. The fruit of your thought is your experience. If you partake of those thoughts, you will partake of the experiences associated with them. If you partake of the thoughts of the knowledge of evil, all you see is the potential evil. The serpent came to suggest evil. The Hebrew word for serpent means fear. Fear projects the possibility of evil. That's what it means to eat of the tree of good and evil.

Let's just partake of LIFE, of God, of goodness. If we are partaking of Life, we're talking about the Divine Life, the One Life of God. That's the Life out from which all of creation has all been formed, that Life we all share. That is what we are to partake of. It says, when you partake of the knowledge of evil, in that day you shall surely die, but when you partake of the knowledge of Life, you shall live in goodness forever.

An angel with a flaming sword stands at the gate of the Garden of Eden, that paradise, that sense of overwhelming goodness. How can we gain entrance? The angel means a messenger from God, the sword means cutting away, fire means purification. We need to let the words of truth cut and burn away, send away, that which we have held as reality which has drawn destruction into our lives. We are worthy to experience good. In the face of goodness, evil is nothing.

"To depart from evil is understanding."   Job 28:28

DAY 304
"I will pour my Spirit out upon you."

Justice in the Mind of God is not the same as justice in the mind of man. Justice in the Mind of God says, "You could not, by the belief system you possess right now, live the fullness of the commandments of God. Because you could not do it, I will pour my Spirit out upon you (Proverbs 1:23) and your sins and iniquities I will remember no more. (Hebrews 8:12) With that Spirit of mine, I'm going to take away that stony, hard, heart, and take away the human mind, and replace it with my heart, my Spirit, my Mind. (Ezekiel 36:26) That's going to cause you to be able to walk in a manner which produces Life for you and not death." God's justice is, "I'll do it for you. You can't do it, you've tried, you've failed." We can't do it ourselves with the human consciousness. We must be elevated to a higher consciousness, to the Mind of God. The justice of God is really the Mercy of God.

Our justice says an eye for an eye, you must be punished, you must pay the penalty. God's justice says, "If you live out from my nature, my Spirit, my Presence, it will so change your heart and so change your thought process that you won't want to do those things. The only reason people ever transgress is because they do not see themselves as God sees them. If a person sees themselves as God sees them, they see the holiness, they see the purity, they see the uprightness, they see their righteousness. They don't want to transgress.

How did Jesus heal the man with the withered hand? (Matthew 12:13) How did Jesus heal anybody? He never saw them in the same mode that they saw themselves. He saw and judged them through the Mind and heart of God, as God sees and judges, as he made us to be.

"The goodness of God leads one to repentance."

Romans 2:4

DAY 305
Healing comes by a change in our image of ourselves.

True healing comes by a change in our image of ourselves, or a change in how we see one another. I read a
story about a man who was an alcoholic, and his daughter went to someone representing the Christ. She said,
"Would you please pray for my father? My father drinks
and my mother works so hard, but he takes those wages
and uses them to buy more to drink. We go hungry
because there's no money for food." This person said, "I
will go with you to your house." He blesses the mother,
and says, "You have been so strong, so patient, it's time
for your family to take on the appearance of the wholeness of Christ. It's time for this to end." He blesses the
children, then he goes to the bed where the father is
passed out. He wakes him, takes his hand, and says,
"There has been a tragedy in the town, a terrible flood,
and I'm going to go and help the people who have lost
their homes. Would you come with me to help them?"
The man said sure, and got up and followed him.

He became engrossed in taking care of people with
this terrible need. It gave him such joy and purpose. It
changed his image of himself. Six months later he
looked at his own home, saw the disrepair it had fallen
into, and went on to rebuild it for his family. Then he
realized he hadn't had anything to drink in a year, while
he was working so hard to help others. He was healed
because his image of himself was changed. He began to
see himself as God saw him.

God never saw him as an alcoholic. God never sees
somebody sick, God never sees someone in poverty.
God does not see us in our selfish state of iniquity.
Healing comes when we are able to see ourselves, or
another, in the same light as God has always seen us.

"We are risen, and stand upright."   Psalm 20:8

DAY 306
I will never lack by giving.

We're told that the law of life is survival of the fit-test, self preservation. I realize now that is not the law of life, that is the law of death. That is what produces suffering, pain, disease, and every other negative human experience that has ever been imagined. When we live out from a nature that believes that it has the right to preserve its selfhood at the expense of anything and anyone else, when we we take on that kind of selfishness, we have begun to die. Life is experienced when we love, when we give.

I grew up in a very difficult home life. I grew up fighting and feeling I had to protect myself and my sister and brother. That was not really living. What saved my life was when I became a nurse and I could reach out to people who were scared, who were suffering. When I moved into the pediatric intensive care unit, I completely forgot about myself. All I saw were people I could help, people I could love. I found my life when I gave my life. I will never lack by giving.

As long as we continue to live out from whatever negative understanding or thought or imagery we have of ourselves, or of the world, or of our experience, then we are living out from death. The day that we can reach out and give, even when we feel like we have nothing to give, is the day that we begin to live.

Jesus said, if you would find your life you must lose it. (Matthew 16:25) He said the Kingdom of God is right here, right now, and if you want to enter into it, you must lay down that self preservation mentality, in order to get true Life. That's why he said, "The first will be last and the last will be first." (Matthew 19:30)

"What is a man profited if he shall gain the whole world and lose his own soul?"　　　　Matthew 16:26

DAY 307
Feel the swell of the current of Life.

To live, I must give. That's exactly how the human body functions. The human body functions by every system, every organ, every cell, giving of its substance for the good of the whole. It gives out of its own nature to give, without restraint, without looking to see what it's going to get, it just gives because that's its nature, to give.

That's the nature of Christ. The nature of Christ is the nature of Life. The nature of Life is the nature of God. It gives because it is its nature to give. That's when we find our healing and that's when we find our good. In order to do this you have to realize you don't lose by giving. You have to realize you live out from the abundance of the goodness of God. God will not allow you to lose by giving. You live in abundance.

I see it as a flow, a river of Life. I get this feeling of a current of Divine Life and all the attributes of the Spirit of God in this river of Life, and us caught up in it. See yourself living in this flow of the river of the Presence and Spirit of God, the abundance of every good thing.

King David said, in Psalm 23, "Surely goodness and mercy shall follow me all the days of my life." He felt the swelling of the current of Life overcoming him constantly. He lived in the presence of such goodness because he lived in the Presence of God.

I choose to let the Mind of God rule my Mind. To let the heart of God rule my heart. To let the Spirit of God rule my Life. Now surely goodness and mercy can follow me every day of my life.

"God is able to make all grace abound toward you, that you, always having sufficiency in all things, may abound to every good work."   2Corinthians 9:8

DAY 308
Identify with the Life within.

Do you wonder, "What am I going to do to get out of this mess?" That is called the human struggle, human effort, and that is our enemy. It always produces a sense of fear and failure because we, of ourselves, cannot find our way out of whatever situation stands before us. That causes us to go into the depths of despair. If it's something you're trying to pull off, it usually gets you in deeper. It's awful to feel personally responsible to figure out how to find your way out.

Surrender to the Life within. Don't surrender to the circumstances and allow them to rule over you. Identify with the hope that lies within, with the Eternal Life that lies within. As we identify with it, we strengthen it, we empower it, we literally raise it up in consciousness. We begin to focus more on that than on the problem. We find our days are filled with expectation and joy, even if the events do not appear to have changed. Why? Because we are not looking at the events as though they had the preeminence to govern our life.

When we look at the situation and see that as an enemy, we fear it, we resist it. This is empowering it. Let us stop resisting. Let's become vulnerable to the Life within that is seeking a higher mode of expression. That is what we must be vulnerable to. That's what we must trust. That's what we must surrender to. That's what we must behold. That will cause us to cease this constant struggle.

There is nothing you need to do. There is nothing to be gained by the human struggle, and a lot to be lost. Allow the dynamics of the Eternal Life of God that resides within you to build up and to burst out, and to manifest and define the glory of its Life.

"The battle is not yours, but God's." 2 Chronicles 20:15

DAY 309
Surrender to the Eternal Life within.

Jesus was not surrendering to the people that were hanging him on the cross, he wasn't surrendering to their hate and their confusion and their darkness. He was surrendering to the Eternal Life that dwelt within him, the Life of God, that pulsating Eternal Life. He knew that nothing could ever dominate that, hold it or restrict it. He did not struggle against the darkness, nor did he acquiesce to it. He didn't resist it, he didn't fear it, he didn't hate it, he didn't focus on it. He focused on the Life. On the Life that is within, that cannot be overcome by any darkness. He said, "Put up your sword." (Matthew 26:52) Stop resisting.

Be still inside and enter into the rest. What rest? It says, "He that has entered into God's rest, also has ceased from his own works." (Hebrews 4:10) Stop the human struggle that's going on inside, lay down your arms, put up your sword, stop resisting. Be still and submit and surrender and trust that Life within you. All of creation is able to do it and so are you. There isn't a creature created that does not know this principle. They do not struggle against the winter, they don't struggle against the night. They fold up and become quiet and serene, and they wait. All the while their focus is on this incredible Life that's within.

Focus on this Divine Life within, all of its goodness, all of its glory, its Mercy, its gentleness, its kindness, its compassion, its Wisdom, its understanding, its knowledge, its strength. Think about all of the attributes of this Life: it is Omnipresent, it is Omnipotent, it is absolutely unchangeable, it is your possession and your inheritance. It is what animates you. All that comes from the Presence of that Life within.

"Be filled with all the fullness of God." Ephesians 3:19

DAY 310
I come under the authority of the One Life.

The life we are living is the Divine Life of God and can't be subservient to the environment, the world, people, circumstances or events. God governs our life because it is God who is living his Life AS his creation. We can live out from the tranquility and the peace and the quiet confidence of knowing there is but One Life that is being lived. It is God himself living out that intact, immutable, uninterruptible Life of Eternal Divinity and holiness and goodness and beauty.

Once I get into that mode, I can sit back and let that Life take the preeminence. I can learn to see it everywhere, enjoy it everywhere, and I can learn to recognize it in myself as well. I'm going to live my life realizing that I live in beauty and order and goodness and harmony and peace. And I'm going to insist on that when something else comes knocking at the door saying, "I am confusion, I am chaos, I am darkness, I am disease, I am poverty, I am death, and I have a right to be here and to destroy your day, your week, your life."

I'm not going to open the door to that, because there is One Life and that Life is sovereign and it is good and pure and innocent and holy. It is the Life that is being lived out as my Life, and the Life of all creation. I come under the authority of that, and confusion has no place here.

You can do that when you have thought on the truth of where you've come from and who you really are, when you've thought of the truth of the goodness of God. We need to find what is absolute. We need to find truth. We can find out from the Spirit of Truth, from God himself.

"Commit thy way unto the Lord, trust also in him, and he shall bring it to pass."   Psalm 37:5

DAY 311
Judge according to the truth of God.

The promise and revelation is that we're going to be freed from the confusion of many voices. We're going to find the peace that comes from putting ourselves under the authority of the absolute truth of God. This One Life has formed all things as a description and a demonstration and a manifestation of its very own being. We will learn to respect ourselves more, to think more highly of ourselves and the bodies we wear, we will learn to repect one another. We will treat others with more dignity and honor and respect, even if they are not living the kind of life that we have judged to earn respect. It makes no difference, because we will say, "Behind that mask, behind that veil of confusion they're living out from, is the One Life of God. This is the son of God, the holy son of God. I'm going to deal with this person in the honor and respect due to the son of God, because that's really who I'm dealing with."

Be it known this day that everyone we deal with is that One Life, that one person, including ourselves. When we deal with another maliciously, we're cutting off our own life, the flow and the goodness and mercy of our own life, because there is only One Life.

Our job is to stop seeing "we" and "they". This is "judging righteous judgment." (John 7:24) That's saying everybody who is not like us is not part of this oneness. That is not judging according to the truth of God. Our job is to see that "The earth is the Lord's and the fullness thereof; the world, and all they that dwell therein." (Psalm 24:1) This is knowing the Mercy of God, this is understanding the heart and Mind of God.

"Holy Father, keep through thine own name those whom thou have given me, that they may be one, as we are."   John 17:11

DAY 312

It's all God.

Every single day we should be living out from the peace and the rest and the quietness and confidence of knowing and seeing and believing and feeling and expressing and declaring that it's all God. God, all in all. Omnipresence: the all and the only God Life that is. Once you start seeing that, it starts appearing everywhere. Once you insist on seeing it in a person, they start acting like it, even if you never say a word to them, even if they live on the other side of the world. Once you start insisting on seeing it, it pops up everywhere, because you're honoring it, you're strengthening it, you're empowering it. You're taking the scales off your own eyes and allowing yourself to see what has always been present.

There is One Life, there is one son of God, and we are all representatives of that one son. There's Jesus, the head, and there's us, the body--that makes one son of God. The whole world is viewed by the heart and Mind of God as his one, only begotten, precious, holy, son, bearing his name, his character, his attributes, his nature, and his Life, bearing all that he is.

"We have many members in one body... We, being many, are one body in Christ, and every one members one of another...Be kindly affectioned one to another with brotherly love; in honor preferring one another...Distributing to the necessity of saints, given to hospitality. Bless them which persecute you, bless and curse not...Be of the same mind one toward another."
Romans 12:4,5,10,13,14,16

DAY 313

We see the truth with our hearts.

Have you ever noticed, the human consciousness always perceives lack? We always perceive limitation. We always see everything as absent. In order for us to see what God sees, to see what God has made, to see what is real, there has to be a huge perception change. We have to be able to go from the human perception of life to the true perception of life. One day we finally realize that life is not as we have been defining it, Life is an expression of God himself. Everything, all of creation, has been formed to define the Life of God, to reveal, to unfold, the Life of God.

What about cancer? How does that define the Life of God? Cancer isn't real. In the Mind of God that's not real. In the Mind of God, there is no death. God is Life. In the Mind of God there is no destruction. God is beauty, God is order, God is harmony, God is peace, God is goodness, God is eternal. You say, "Then where does all the trouble come from?" It comes from the human perception of life.

The Bible calls it a veil, a veil cast over the faces of all peoples, and when that veil is removed, there will be no more sorrow, no more tears, no more destruction, no more death. (Isaiah 25:7) How does that veil go away? We have the capacity to see as God sees. We have within us the consciousness of God himself. It says we have the mind of Christ. (1Corinthians 2:16) We have the ability to see what the human perception is not seeing, just by yielding to the mind of Christ, the divine consciousness within. Do we see the truth with our eyes? No, we see it with our hearts.

"We all, with open face beholding as in a glass the glory of the Lord, are changed into the same image, from glory to glory."   2Corinthians 3:18

DAY 314
We are sent to bear witness to truth.

We behold the truth in our hearts and it becomes so real, it becomes greater than that which we see with our eyes. Life becomes more real to us than death, health becomes more real to us than sickness, the allness and the abundance of goodness becomes more real to us than lack and limitation--then we're healed. It may take time before that is evidenced, but it doesn't make a bit of difference, because we know that we know that we know, in consciousness and in the depths of our being, that the wholeness of God is intact and cannot be maligned or destroyed. Just because the human perception declares it to be so, that doesn't make it so.

Look at the springtime, even though you are in the dead of winter. Look at the harvest, don't be concerned about the seed that's still lying in the ground that appears so dead. Don't look at the midnight hour of darkness and fear and pain, but know the day is going to arise, the sun is going to come up. Everything in nature declares there is an appointed time to the end of the struggle.

Why do people suffer? One reason is the law of cause and effect. If we live out from the human perception, then we're going to sow back into our lives all that the human perception has to offer. For instance, if I judge and react, that's what I'm going to receive as well. That's one level of suffering.

On another level, we suffer because we don't know who we are, or where we've come from. We are sent by God to this human realm of darkness as bearers of the truth of God, as light. We've been sent to bear witness to the truth in the face of error.

"Of his own will begat he us with the word of truth."
James 1:18

DAY 315

Be filled with the knowledge of the truth of God.

We are not born, but sent. Rather than identifying with the human that's here by the will of the flesh, identify with the Christ that's within. That Christ has been sent, and we've been sent for the exact same purpose that Jesus was sent. "As my father sent me, so send I you." (John 20:21) We must take up the banner. We have the same Spirit. The same Spirit that raised Christ from the dead dwells within you, it will qucken your mortal body. (Romans 8:11) We have the same Spirit within us that motivated and animated Jesus and allowed him to do all that he did, and say and understand all he understood. That's what we possess, and we need to begin to act out from that perception.

We have been sent by God as Light, (James 1:17), Spirit beings, truth bearers, to undo the works of darkness. For this cause have I come, that I might undo the works of darkness. (Romans 13:12) We must undo the works of darkness by knowledge of the truth.

If we have been sent to dispel darkness, then you must understand that when these conditions and circumstances come up in your human experience, which are a denial of the absolute allness of God and the truth of all that we are, then this is part of the human consciousness. It is a thought, a suggestion that comes out from the human consciousness. You, as a light, are being placed right in front of that darkened unbelief, that error of perception, for the purpose of dispelling that darkness and letting the space be filled with the knowledge of the truth of God.

"Loose the bands of wickedness, undo the heavy burdens, let the oppressed go free, break every yoke... then shall your light break forth as the morning, and your health shall spring forth speedily."   Isaiah 58:6-8

DAY 316
I'm going to challenge it and I'm going to win.

We suffer when we take these experiences that come out from the human darkened perception, and we possess them. We say, "It's true, I have this disease." "It's true, I've lost my job and now I'm facing poverty." "It's true, my husband walked out the door and now I'm facing aloneness." That's the human scene that would come to declare its power. It says, "I am a power greater than the goodness of God. I am darkness, but I am greater than the light that you bear."

I say, "No, you're not. I'm not going to possess you as my own. I'm not going to suffer, I'm going to enjoy the process of dispelling this darkness and claiming my true being as the Light of Christ. I know that spring will always come, the light will always shine. Life is Life and nothing can ever interrupt it, because Life is God."

We are sent into this realm with a purpose and we know what it is. We know who we are. Then something comes up in our human experience, out from the darkness of human consciousness. What do we do?

I maintain a separateness and realize this is a suggestion, no more than a thought. I keep it away from me emotionally and deal with it "out there." I'm going to know that I am the light, that I have been sent by God, as the light, to dispel this darkness. I'm going to know the absolute truth of God that fills all space with glory and goodness and wholeness and perfection that can never be changed, in spite of what the picture looks like. I'm going to stand here, look right at it, and I'm going to deny it was created by God, therefore it has no substance, no source, no origin and no right to exist. I'm going to challenge it and I'm going to win.

"I can do all things through Christ which strengthens me."   Philippians 4:13

DAY 317

Grace is the answer to every human situation.

If I don't know what truth is necessary to dispel this darkness, then I'm going to calmly defer to the Mind of God. The Spirit of Truth was sent to lead me into all truth. I'm going to ask it for the wisdom and the understanding and the perception that is needed to cancel out this darkness. "You shall hear a word behind you saying, this is the way, walk ye in it." (Isaiah 30:21)

I'm not going to deny the truth by embracing this thing as though it is real. Poverty cannot be real in the allness of abundance. Lack of direction cannot be real when we know our direction comes from God. Disease cannot happen when the totality of all I see is the body of Christ. When God made us in his image and likeness, he said, "It is good." (Genesis 1:31)

The words of these truths, in and of themselves, will not change anything. We must, from our hearts, see Life everywhere. Behold the perfection, the order, the beauty, the harmony, right in the face of the evidence to the contrary. You can't make yourself see it when you have already acquiesced to the fear and suffering. When you've taken it into yourself, possessed the problem as though it's your own, you're coming out of human belief. As long as you are embracing the problem, you can't take the truth and make it go away.

Only the Spirit of Truth will change it. What causes that Spirit to flow? Grace. Grace is the activity of the Spirit of Truth on the human experience. You allow grace to take over and it will, as soon as you cease your human struggle. Grace is the answer to every human situation. It's always present, always flowing, it moves any mountain, reduces it to level ground for us to walk on with no struggle.

"My grace is sufficient for thee."   2Corinthians 12:9

DAY 318

I come to do the will of him who sent me.

Today I'm going to repent, go in a different direction and stop possessing this problem. I'm going to identify as that Christ light being and know this cannot affect me.

I am not subject to accidents. I am not subject to poverty. I am not subject to disease. I am not subject to limitation, to lack, or the absence of anything good. I am the expression of the fullness of God. "Of his fullness have we all received." (John 1:16) I stand as who I am. "As he is, so are we in this world." (1John 4:17)

Where there is light, the darkness flees, and the light takes over the space the darkness seemed to possess. When you walk into a dark room and turn a light on, where does the darkness go? Who knows? The light fills that space. The light is the truth, and I am the truth. I know who I am. This is the day I will behold Life and I will cease to behold out from the human perception.

When you have ceased from your own works, that's what Jesus called denying yourself. He said,"Take up your cross." (Matthew 16:24) What's the cross? It's the change of identity, where the old has died and the new is born. Now I live out from who I really am. Now I remember why I've been sent, and that I am the light, I bear the truth, and nothing can hurt or destroy this truth. I am not vulnerable, I am not perceiving myself as victim to anything. I come to do the will of him who sent me. I will allow the reason I've been sent to be fulfilled in this situation, right here, right now.

"You are the light of the world. A city that is set on a hill cannot be hid. Neither do men light a candle and put it under a bushel, but on a candlestick, and it gives light unto all that are in the house. Let your light so shine and glorify your Father, which is in heaven."
Matthew 5:14-16

DAY 319

Live in a sense of gratitude.

Gratitude is an exercise of our will that forces us to declare that all is well, right this very second. I'm breathing right now. There are people that love me right now. We have to pull ourselves back from the future of what may be and live out from the immediate now. Right now my body is fine, it's healthy, it's strong, it's fed. I want to stay in this *now* and enjoy this *now* and be grateful and thankful for the wonders of all my supply being met with such abundance, right here, right now.

We are always looking to the future. The same goodness that fills this space right now will be there to fill that space, right then. Where do you think it's going to go? You didn't secure all the wonders that you are experiencing right now--that was the very Presence of God, who is only good, who fills all space and place with goodness and is constantly revealing the presence of goodness, by all the good that we are experiencing.

The only time we can perceive a lack is when we're looking ahead. But right this moment you can find goodness if you pull *in* and think about what's good this very moment. This lets you live in the present and lets you experience a moment of peace, a moment of confidence. It also helps build security for the days ahead. If all my needs are met right now, why would the Presence of unchangeable goodness, the presence of Infinite Love, all that God is, change? Why wouldn't that be there when I get there? People who live that way live out of a sense of wonder, they are always seeing the fulfillment of this, wonderful things are in their path, enabling their way to expand and be blessed. They live in a sense of gratitude.

"Behold, now is the day of salvation." 2Corinthians 6:2

DAY 320
Be grateful for what you have right now.

Out from our own imagery, out from whatever energy we expend, is what comes back to us. Whatever we perceive to be true is what we're going to live out from. We can't perceive lack and limitation and live out from abundance. It doesn't work that way. We've got to pull back and exercise the discipline of our will and enter into a sense of gratitude for what is, right now. What if you don't believe that you're healthy right now? What if you don't believe that you have Life surging through you, and strength and wholeness? What if you believe something is really wrong?

We will remember the nature of God, who formed us, who breathed Life into us, who put us here and has a purpose for us being here and who said he would fulfill that purpose. "Take no thought for your life, (Matthew 7:25) because every day I'm going to make sure that everything you need is abundantly given to you." You can't see that or experience that if you are living out from the constant sense of lack. So you don't feel good, something doesn't work, why don't you think about the things that do work? Be grateful for the good you feel.

Try doing nothing more with your life, don't change the path you are on, except for being grateful for what you have right now. When you do that with your body, your body senses that, it starts letting that flow of Life churn again, that energy, that vibration, that frequency of Life begins to soar through you, through that sense of thanksgiving. Before you know it more and more of your body begins to feel stronger and stronger and then you can be grateful for that.

"Whatsoever things are true, whatsoever things are pure, whatsoever things are lovely, if there be any praise, think on these things." Philippians 4:8

DAY 321

*Deep within us is an eternal well
that cannot run dry.*

Do you feel like your opportunities are all dried up? That you've been set aside, not appreciated, passed over? Remember the man in the New Testament (John 5) who was crippled from birth? He thought if he got into the water when the waters were moving, he'd be healed. But he said, "Everybody always gets there before me, and my opportunity is gone. I always just miss my boat." He thought his source came from a physical well. But it comes from the well which is down deep within us, an eternal well that cannot run dry. We open it up, we unclog it, with gratitude.

Do you feel alone and isolated and abandoned? What we don't realize is that right this very moment we live and walk and talk and laugh and love in the Presence of all Love, all acceptance. We are cherished, we are beloved. There is a constant outpouring of good for us. The only way to recognize that, to receive it, to feel it, the only way to live out from it, is to take the little that we do perceive and be thankful for that. Get that river of Life starting to flow again.

Just for one moment, pretend, if you need to, that you have the abundance of every wonderful and good thing, with the security of knowing that you'll always have it and it will never leave you. Get into the feeling of that. What would that feel like to you? Being an absolute, complete being, you have everything and you have the joy to experience everything. Do not hesitate to live out from that knowledge and expectation of persistent good.

"Trust in the Lord...so shall you dwell in the land and you shall be fed. Delight yourself in the Lord and he shall give you the desires of your heart." Psalm 37:3-4

DAY 322

Love is huge!

In this very moment you live in the Presence of Divine Love. If you don't feel it, that doesn't change the truth of it. You don't feel it because you have been looking at what you don't have, so that's what you feel. What would it feel like to believe that God is Love? God is all in all, and fills all space, so Love is all in all and fills all space. It fills the space we live in, it's all around and about us, enveloping us with its Presence of goodness. Can you be grateful for that moment?

Can we experience the fullness and the completeness, right this moment, and be so grateful for it that we are not afraid to give love, or to give of our time, because we feel so abundantly full of time to give? Can we be so grateful that we're not afraid to give some effort, to use our talents, because we know that we always will have what we have this moment, and more and more as we focus on this moment.

What if you felt so much that way that you radiated completeness? A sense of joy? Perfect peace and contentment? *Life is good, Love is huge, my security goes deep, and my joy is difficult to contain. It's just bursting out! I'm so grateful for this moment.*

This is how we've been created. This is who we really are. This is the truth. This is the depth of us, this is the soul of us, this is reality. We must return to that knowing and we must learn to live out from it. It comes by gratitude for it, and by expressing it. You can't express it until you start being grateful for what you feel you have. Then the more you give, the more space you allow for more to return to you. The more gratitude you feel, the more your heart is expanded to realize more of your good.

"Rejoice with joy unspeakable."   1Peter 1:8

DAY 323

Use what you have.

Use what you have. If you have a sweet spirit to give a smile to somebody, use it. If you have the time and the ability to do something for someone and it comes in your path, do it. If you have enough in your pocket to give to someone that has less, give it. Don't be afraid. You're only afraid to do it for fear of what you may not have later. You're believing that your good comes from a horizontal supply. No wonder we live in fear.

If I thought that my financial gain came from the stock market, came from my job, or came from any of my own efforts, I would live in fear too, but I know it doesn't. If I thought my health came from my body, I would be in fear too, but I know my health does not come from my body. My life, my health and my strength are all attributes of the Presence of God that surrounds me and fills me and is the substance of me. I know that's not going to change. Even if I don't feel it this moment, it's still true. I can be grateful for that.

Does your freedom to live and to enjoy life depend on the circumstances that surround you? If so, and if you don't like your circumstances and they look very confining, you will perceive lack. Or you can perceive freedom of your own soul, freedom to think, freedom to understand, freedom to grow in wisdom, freedom to grow in knowledge, freedom to grow in that incredible feeling of the Presence of goodness all around. Freedom to know that all you need to know and understand is constantly being poured out to us by the Presence of God.

"Your Father knows that you have need of these things. Seek the Kingdom of God and all these things shall be added unto you. Fear not little flock, for it is your Father's good pleasure to give you the kingdom."
Luke 12:30-32

DAY 324

"I am your life."

You have the Mind of God. You have that sweet Spirit of Love and goodness. You have all the characteristics and Spirit of God. Be grateful that you have it, and it will begin to pour out from you.

You have the physical strength and sense of wholeness in your body, because it says, "I am your life and the length of your days." (Deuteronomy 30:20) The length of your days is not determined by somebody's diagnosis, nor by your age, nor by whether an accident happens, it doesn't come from your body. The length of your days is determined by He who sent you for a purpose to be fulfilled and He is going to fulfill it. (Philippians 1:6)

Your strength comes from the unchangeable, eternal, ever present, Life of the Creator of all things. That strength is never diminished, regardless of the human circumstances. Your Life does not come from your body, don't give your body that kind of power. Be with the Life that really does surround you right this moment and be grateful for it, and your body will begin to feel that energy and that Life.

If you feel you have no Life flow left to pour out, or to give, or even to let it flow, know it is not from your energy or your life, therefore it always is. You may not feel it, but you can give gratitude for what you know is always there. Be grateful for the Life that surrounds you, that Divine Life that brought you forth, formed you, breathed itself into you. It's the reason you exist.

"The everlasting God faints not, neither is weary...He gives power to the faint, and to them that have no might he increases strength...They that wait upon the Lord shall renew their strength, they shall mount up with wings as eagles, they shall run, and not be weary, and they shall walk and not faint."   Isaiah 40:28-31

DAY 325
Perceive the goodness all around.

Remember Jonah, in the Old Testament, who got swallowed by a whale? (Jonah 2) I don't know what whale you feel that you have been swallowed up by right now, but I know I've had some in my life. It got pretty slimy and dark and scary in there. But I got out the moment I realized that I was not there because of the events that looked like the reason I was there. I was there because of my perception, and my lack of gratitude for what I had, even though I was going through difficult times. Instead of being grateful, I was looking at the material picture, seeing it shutting down on me, feeling I didn't have what I needed. The more I thought I didn't have, the more I was afraid. The more I was afraid, the less I had, until my perception was in the belly of the whale. I got spit out on dry land, just like Jonah, the day I realized my Life came from God, who is the Source of my Life. All the good, did not come from anything I was reaching out for on a horizontal plane. I could not continue to blame this horizontal existence, the persons, places, or events.

I began to feel gratitude for that Presence, and I began to feel stronger and stronger, and more and more grateful, even though I was still in the belly of that whale. I offered, as it says, a sacrifice of thanksgiving. I always wondered why they call it a sacrifice, until I got in that whale, and then I realized how hard it is to lift one's self up from that and to perceive the goodness all around. Though I don't see it or feel it, I'm just going to know that it's here, and I'm going to give thanks for it.

"There shall be heard in this place...the voice of joy, and the voice of gladness...the voice of them that shall say, Praise the Lord...They shall bring the sacrifice of praise into the house of the Lord." Jeremiah 33:10-11

DAY 326

I need to get out of the way.

Your identity is the holiness of God, your identity is the righteousness of God. Not because you've earned it, not because you necessarily act like it, but because that which is born of God is holy, is righteous. We have to accept that is our identity, that is the new creature in Christ (2Corinthians 5:17).

It says, "Be ye perfect, even as your Father in heaven is perfect." (Matthw 5:48) And "Let us go on to perfection." (Hebrews 6:1) It's not just words. It really is causing us to make the transition out of the identity of the old, mortal man, full of fear and effort, and the struggle to gain something. Once we let go of that and we take on the new nature, we find what this new nature is, then we can learn to live out from it.

I start with the premise that my life is not my own. I was sent here by a Creator who created me with a purpose. It would be in my best interests to yield myself to that Mind, to that intelligence, to that will, so that I might gain the understanding of that purpose. And that I might also, step by step, find out how I am to walk. How am I to fulfill this?

When I was a brand new Christian, the prayer I prayed most was, "I'm so confused, I wish I had a roadmap or a blueprint." I finally realized there is a Spirit of Truth, a real viable being, God's gift to me. That Spirit of Truth has always been and will always be with me. It's always speaking, it's always declaring truth, always revealing the path I should be walking. I found that the best way for me to walk, the most peaceful, secure, and confident, that produced the best results, was when I remembered my life isn't my own. I belong to another. I need to let him do it. I need to get out of the way.

"My help comes from the Lord, which made heaven and earth."   Psalm 121:2

DAY 327
Build on a solid foundation.

I've found I need to pause in any given situation to see if this is the way I should go. I just ask, *What should I do? Where should I go? What should I know? What is the wisdom of God in this situation? What is the Mind of God? I need to know.*

If I was down in the dumps, I would ask for a song to come to my heart and fill my heart, so I could start singing and come out of the dumps, and it always worked. I'd ask for a teacher, and it would come, through a book, a lecture, a group. I stayed very faithful to where that Spirit of Truth led me. I wanted to be clear I didn't move without that. I wanted to be clear I got everything from that. I wasn't just accumulating knowledge, but I was actually learning how to apply it to every situation that came in my path.

Are you committing yourself to a relationship with the Spirit of Truth, and to obedience to it? The barometer of knowing what you're doing is, are you being a "doer of the word, or a hearer only?" (James 1:23)

In Matthew 7:26, we read about one who builds his house on the sand. When the winds blow, and the trials and tribulations of life come against you, if you've not built on the foundation of doing that which you have been hearing, then your house just kind of blows away. But I can build on the solid foundation of what I hear, that which I get a witness to in my spirit, that's true and feels right. That which I know God is speaking to me through the Spirit of Truth.

"The Father will give you another Comforter, that he may abide with you for ever, the Spirit of truth...You know him, for he dwells with you and shall be in you."
John 14:16-17

DAY 328

Everywhere I am, God is.

How do we apply these truths? Be grateful for them. Be grateful for the nature of God, which doesn't change. God could never be interrupted by anything that humans believe, anything we do. God's purpose can't change, his being can't change.

Be grateful that God is Omnipotent. If we can be grateful for just that one thing, that God is all powerful, then we won't be giving power to everything else under the sun. We'll be giving power to God only. Here's a truth we can start putting into practice. If God is all powerful, why are we giving power to all this other stuff, thinking that these things can rule over us?

Another truth is, God is only good. God's power is the power of good. We can begin to trust this one power, and become more confident, more secure. If we apply that one truth to all our situations, we have peace.

God is Omnipresent, all around and about us. If he's all power and all presence, and he's only good, then what is it that surrounds me? The power of goodness. It's everywhere I go. "If I make my bed in heaven, if I make my bed in hell, behold thou art there." (Psalm 139:8) Everywhere I am, God is. In him I live and move and walk and laugh and love and have my being. (Acts 17:28) I'm living out my life in the Presence of and in the atmosphere and in the being of the all powerful, every-where present, only Presence of Infinite goodness.

Are we grabbing hold of what we're hearing and using it? Are we applying it, making a little journal, writing it down, looking up the words, meditating on them? If so, truth begins to become part of our new nature and we begin to live out from that.

"Be steadfast, unmoveable, always abounding in the work of the Lord."   1Corinthians 15:58

DAY 329

The more I listen, the more I hear.

Truth is not just an accumulation of a bunch of under-standings. Truth is a viable Being. Truth is God. Truth is all around us and it's speaking to us all the time. We only have to tune in to it. Just pause. You say, "I can't hear it. I don't know how to differentiate the impulses of truth from the impulses that grip my heart all the time." None of us knew how to do that when we first started. Do with that what you do with anything, pray.

Here I am, wanting to hear from a conscious realm, from an intelligence, a Wisdom, a knowing, an understanding...from goodness, from someone that will direct and lead my life and walk me right out of whatever mess I'm in. I don't even know how to hear and I need to know how to hear. Help me to hear.

This is a valid prayer. Why wouldn't it be answered? The whole purpose of the Spirit of Truth is to lead and guide us into all truth. It came for that purpose. Don't think it's not going to have its purpose fulfilled. We're talking about God here. We only need to be quiet and it will speak. Once we have prayed to hear we can trust that God will direct us, often out from our own mind. It's really not until our mind is silenced, to some degree, that we can hear it. For me, I got to where I could understand, I got to where I expected it, I got to where it became very familiar. The more I listened for it, the more I heard, the more I obeyed, the more it hap-pened. That's how it will be for anybody. It's what's supposed to be. There's no road map, no magic prayer, no formula. It is a relationship with the Spirit of Truth. Every single thing you hear, that you know is true, you apply it.

"When you go to the house of God, be more ready to hear...Let thy words be few." Ecclesiastes 5:1

DAY 330
Truth promises an abundant life.

Remember the story about the loaves and the fishes and all the multitudes that needed to be fed? (John 6:5) There was a little boy there with a basket with two fish and some loaves. Jesus took those, gave thanks, and multiplied them and gave them to everybody. There was enough for everybody and plenty left over. The people were astounded at the miracle, and followed him. He said, "Are you following me only because of the miracles? What are you seeking?" (John 6:26) Are we seeking only for what we can gain, or do we really want to know what this is all about? Do we really want to commit our life to something greater than what we've committed it to so far?

When I was in Bible college, we used to say, "You're going to lay your life down on some altar or another, you might as well have it be the altar of truth." You can lay it down on the altar of materialism, the altar of personal love, the altar of fame, the altar of the American Medical Association, but to lay your life down on the altar of truth is to gain your life back. Truth is a *VIABLE BEING* to whom we owe a committed relationship of obedience and understanding. This is a good place for us to give our energy and our devotion, because what it promises is that we get an abundant life back.

If you seek for just the loaves and the fish and the miracles, you get your loaves, you get your fish, you get your miracles, and next week you need another miracle. But if you learn truth, then it's a well that springs up from within you that never, never runs dry, and you never again find yourself in these needy situations.

"Them that honor me I shall honor."   1Samuel 2:30

DAY 331
Healing is a byproduct of the awareness of Divine Life.

Healing is a byproduct of a relationship, of an awareness that you live in Divine Life. When my daughter was healed of mental retardation, it was not because a prayer was prayed, it wasn't because I did anything magical, it wasn't because anybody else did anything magical. It was a byproduct of the relationship that was being developed between me and God. It was a byproduct of an awareness, a constant awareness of this Divine Life all around me.

Whatever you might be struggling with, if you would get into a relationship, an awareness of the Presence of this absolute Eternal Life that is good...it's all powerful, it's all present...you'd realize the tremendous attributes of it. Nothing can stand up to it, interrupt it, block it, stop it. It might look like that's what's happening, but you have to look away from the evidence, whatever picture the darkness is painting. Look away and look into Divine Life as the Source of all that is.

That's what I'm grateful for. That's what I'm going to look at. That's what I'm going to practice. I'm going to insist on seeing Life everywhere. I'm going to see Life because I know Life is all around me, and I live and walk and move and talk and laugh and love and have my being in it. Nothing can interrupt that. The human belief can work its way in there and cause you not to be able to enjoy it, because you've lost your awareness of it, but you can go back to being aware of it at any time. Healing is a byproduct of the awareness of Divine Life. You don't ever want to forget that.

"Thus says the Lord that created you: Fear not, for I have called thee by thy name, thou art mine...
I am thy God."   Isaiah 43:1-2

DAY 332

"Arise up quickly."

In Acts 12 is the story of Peter in prison, bound with two chains. "Behold, the angel of the Lord came upon him and a light shined in the prison, and he smote Peter on the side and raised him up, saying, Arise up quickly. His chains fell off from his hands. The angel said to him, Gird thyself and bind on thy sandals...Cast thy garment about thee and follow me."

There are many types of chains and many types of prisons. You can be imprisoned by the fear of your own body, by your own thoughts, your own actions and reactions, your own sense of unworthiness, your own intolerance.

An angel means a messenger from truth. A light shined in the prison means that whenever truth comes, you've sensed the illumination in your soul. Right where there was darkness, now there's light. He said, "Arise up quickly." What we get from that is, use the truth right away, as soon as you're illuminated. Apply it to the circumstance.

To gird yourself is to be strong, to make a declaration that you are going to apply this truth, no matter what, until you see the fruit of it. To bind on your sandals means I'm going to walk it out. I'm going to declare the truth. I'm going to stand firm in what I am knowing.

To cast your garment about thee and follow means to throw off the old garment of unworthiness, victimhood, sickness, poverty, and follow the truth you just heard. You need to put on a whole new garment that says, I am a new identity. I am an expression of the one Divine Life. That's the garment we need to cling to as our true identity.

"Awake, awake, put on thy strength, put on thy beautiful garments."   Isaiah 52:1

DAY 333

Come into oneness.

What foundation do we build on? Our foundation is that we are made in the image and likeness of God, (Genesis 1:26), and he's never changed that. We are the light of the world, as Jesus said. (Matthew 5:14) "He is the true light that lights every man that comes into the world." (John 1:9) That light is the Life of God. "Of his fullness have we all received." (John 1:16)

We must start with the premise that we are worthy, we were created worthy, and we're beautiful to behold. In order to be able to live beyond any confusion that the human consciousness has perceived, the first thing we have to understand is who we really are. We've got to make that conscious change of perception. We have to agree to it based on truth. Once we agree to it, we will be able to perceive it.

When we entered this human consciousness, we didn't see ourselves separate from God, unholy and unworthy. We saw pureness and holiness and goodness and Life and Love. We have been educated to believe we are separate from pureness, from holiness, from our true identity. With that consciousness we can never come into a realized state of being one with God.

Jesus said, it's simple. All you've got to do is lay down your sense of selfhood, what you perceive yourself to be. He says one that would try to gain his life will lose it, but one that's willing to lose what he believes is his identity, will find it. (Matthew 16:25) He says you can't put new wine in old wineskins, but if you're willing to empty out the old, then the new can come in. (Matthew 9:17) It doesn't make you a different being, but it makes you realize what you have always have been.

"God has made man upright, but they have sought out many inventions."   Ecclesiastes 7:29

DAY 334

Correct the thought.

We humans are always reaching out for God to fix something. As soon as he fixes something, we need something else fixed. The Spirit of Truth comes right out of the heart of God to teach us, to show us who we are. It seeks to correct the thought that caused the problem to start with. We can keep going to God to have all these individual problems corrected, or we can put on the brakes and say, "What is the thought?"

The thought is that we have a sense of lack. Coming from the human consciousness, everything is lack: I lack health, I lack wealth, I lack love, I lack time, I lack, I lack. The confusion of this thought process, this kind of identity, is bound to show up as confusion on the body, in our relationships, in the workplace.

If we knew who we were, we would never have a sense of lack, we would have a sense of abundance. Because I am one with this Eternal Life that is God, I can't ever lack anything. We really only need one prayer: *God, open my eyes to see who I am, what I am, and why I am.*

The Spirit of Truth will lead and guide you into all truth. (John 16:13) It will show you who you are. It will reduce all this mass confusion to a simple understanding of identity. You begin to see, *I am Light. I am Life. I am Love. I am Mercy, I am kindness, I am truth.* How can dis-ease or confusion or lack have any place? Reduce the whole thing to one word, darkness. I am the Light and that is darkness that comes from all that confused thinking. "God who commanded the light to shine in the darkness, has shined in our hearts." (2Corinthians 4:6) You are the Light.

"And the light shined in darkness, and the darkness comprehended it not."   John 1:5

DAY 335

Make the separation.

When confusion is in our thinking and in our consciousness and when the whole world's running around all
confused, then you can expect that confusion will appear on the body, or in the mind. It comes from darkened, convoluted thinking, from not seeing things
clearly. Have you ever wondered why so many people
were blind that Jesus healed? All those blind people
were getting healings because it was telling us that we
have been blinded by the human educated belief of why
we're here, and who we are. That's what needs to be
healed, not the effect, but the root cause.

We are part of the one and only Life. In Colorado they
say there is only one aspen tree. If you follow the root
system underneath the soil, you find there's only one
aspen tree and all those trees are just offshoots from
that one root. One Life. It takes individual drops of
water to make the ocean, but they're all of the same
exact property, they're all water. Look how many mol-
ecules of air there are, but it's all the same atmosphere.
There is only One Life and it's the Eternal Life of the
Creator.

"He's the Father of lights." (James 1:17) I am light.
I'm part of the One Life. I have come to dispel darkness. I take all evil, all sorrow, all sickness, all hate,
everything unclean, and reduce it to darkness. And I'm
going to impersonalize it. That was darkness, not that
person. As long as you perceive that a certain person
hurt you, you will never be healed. You've got to separate darkness from the person. That person, too, is the
One Life, the Light. Darkness has to go once you make
that separation.

*"When I sit in darkness, the Lord shall be a light
unto me."*   Micah 7:8

DAY 336
Dynamic strength comes from knowing who I am.

Am I seeing myself as the light, or am I seeing myself as experiencing this darkness? Can I say, "This is a just a suggestion, a temptation to take this unto myself and believe this is part of my existence or part of my nature?" Or am I buying into that suggestion, saying, "This is part of me, this is coming out from me?" Can I say, "I am the Life, I am the Light, and this is darkness. I'm not going to allow it to find expression through me, not through my body, not through my mouth, not through my thoughts, not through my mind?"

We have a choice when we come up against anything out from the realm of darkness. Do we forget who we are and believe the darkness to be a part of ourselves? If I believe this is part of me, and I take that identity and I embrace it, I'm going to feel unworthy to be that One Life. I'm going to feel separate from that One Life, and I'm going to feel guilty, or I'm going to feel fear, or sadness. I'm not going to have that dynamic strength of being that comes from knowing who I am, which enables me to say "No!" to this.

Are we able to retain our identity and declare the darkness is not part of us, in spite of the fact it may be showing up on our body, in spite of the fact it may just have come out of our mouth, in spite of the fact we've been entertaining these thoughts all day long? Can we stop and say, "Wait a minute, I've been listening to darkness, this is not me. This is not me thinking this, this is not part of my nature. I'm not accepting this. I am the Light, I am the Life. In that Life can dis-ease ever manifest itself? No.

"God gives them light, and they shall reign for ever and ever."   Revelation 22:5

DAY 337

"Innocence was found in me."

Daniel said he was not devoured by the lions because "Innocence was found in me." (Daniel 6:22) That was his understanding of himself and why evil could not touch him. It's only a sense of unworthiness, self-condemnation, feeling separate from our Source, feeling separate from the holiness that we are, that makes us accept things into our experience and not challenge them.

If I see myself as an innocent being, is it because I've never done anything wrong? No. I have allowed darkness to use my mouth and my heart and my mind, but it was never me. Once I realize that, I say, "This is how God made me, this is who I am, why would I allow darkness to use me to manifest something I don't even believe?"

We've got to start seeing darkness outside of ourselves and separate from us. Even though things seem to come from our body, or we seem to be entertaining them in our heart. We've got to see them as intruders, something that is not part of our being, and therefore does not need to be part of our experience. I don't want it, I'm not interested in it, I have no reason to let it come. I'm going to stand and challenge it.

If somebody does not challenge this, we're going to be like a herd of sheep and we're going to go flying off the edge of the cliff together. We've got to be willing to hear the voice of the Shepherd that says, "This is not the way it needs to be, there is another way."

"Behold, the Lord passed by, and a great and strong wind rent the mountains, and brake in pieces the rocks before the Lord, but the Lord was not in the wind, and after the wind an earthquake; but the Lord was not in the earthquake: and after the earthquake, a fire, but the Lord was not in the fire: and after the fire, a still small voice."   1Kings 19:11-12

DAY 338
Start with an EXPECTATION OF GOODNESS.

All bad behavior comes from acting out of an image of ourselves that is contrary to our true identity. All acceptance of disease or pain or suffering or poverty is a result of us accepting something that is an intruder into this realm of goodness that we have been created into, because we don't yet know our true identity. How can you challenge something if you think it's you? How can you challenge something if you think you're so unworthy that you deserve it? How can you challenge it in someone else if you haven't impersonalized it, if you still think it really does come from that person?

When you start to suffer, the reason you're suffering is that you took it unto yourself, you gave it a cause, you personalized it, you thought it was coming from you, you thought it was part of your experience. If you knew who you were, you wouldn't allow it to manifest itself through you, you wouldn't let it use you.

Darkness knows when it's up against the light, and it can't overcome it. But if you don't know you are the light, it has no problem overcoming it, because your light's so dim. You don't know who you are. What you are living out from, what you are expecting, be it light or darkness, is what is going to meet you around every turn. You can make a change.

Let's do it together. Let's stand up and challenge this thing, let's send it away, and let's start living out from the Life of light and goodness and hope and gladness and laughter. Let's start with an expecation of goodness and joy and health and abundance, and I promise it will meet you at every turn. One day we will all make that change, and there really will be a new heaven and a new earth. (Revelation 21)

"He is strong in power; not one fails."   Isaiah 40:26

DAY 339

We are made in the image and likeness of Love.

By the grace of God, after many trials and tribulations, I discovered that God is Love, and that Love is Mercy. Being made in the image and likeness of God, we are made in the image and likeness of Love. The Eternal substance of our being is the Presence of Eternal Love. We don't have to gain something that we don't have, it is the true substance of our life, and it's always there in every life. It's always there because that's who we are.

When we allow that Love to flow, with no concern for how we're going to gain by allowing it, with no concern for ourselves whatsoever, our life is blessed beyond anything we can ever imagine. We allow it to flow, not because the object of our love has earned it, not because the object of our love is worthy, not because we will ever get anything back from giving, but simply because it is our true nature to feel that way and to behave that way.

When we do not look upon another with mercy, because they haven't earned it, or when we do not look upon another with gentleness and tenderness and grace, because they don't act well, then we shut down our own Life flow, because the true essence of our being is Love. We choose to love in spite of what another has done. When someone does something horrible, we want to get the Mind and heart of God on the matter. The Mind and heart of God is Love, and it doesn't change. It does not change because the object of its Love is unworthy of it. Religion has taught us that we're going to get the eternal ax if we don't do what's right. There is nothing about the nature of God that upholds that image of him. God is Love and God is Mercy.

If we love one another, God dwells in us, and his love is perfected in us."   John 4:12

DAY 340
We are sent not to condemn, but to show mercy.

Long ago, my heart was filled with rage and sadness as I remembered the pain and the anguish of my childhood. There was nothing I could draw on from my heart to visit my parents, and actually, it never would have occurred to me to do so. Then I realized it was no accident that I was in that family. I was deliberately sent from God, with the heart of God, not to condemn, but to show mercy. As Mercy began to soften and then dominate my heart, healing was the obvious conclusion.

God is Mercy, above all else. Mercy is Love expressed when the object of that Love has not earned it. What good is mercy if we have to earn it? The nature of God is Love, and that Love is merciful. It looks upon the object of its Love with the exact same tender, gentle, judgment, whether we have walked upright or whether we have failed, whether we have been miserably self-serving or whether we've been a Mother Teresa. Love is constant, it doesn't change.

Once we know the nature of God, then we look to the substance of our own being, because that's what we're made from. We say, "That's what I am, down inside of me. That is the substance of my soul." The exact same performance is necessary from us as we see coming from God. We must look upon the world with the same tenderness, the same compassion, the same goodness. If we don't, that same judgment that we feel another deserves falls upon our own lives. We treat others the way we think God is, even if we don't even know God. It isn't until our image of God is corrected that we begin to understand how we sabotage our own happiness.

"Put on mercy, kindness...forbearing one another, forgiving one another...and above all put on charity, which is the bond of perfectness." Colossians 3:12-14

DAY 341
Come out of yourself for a moment.

In every life there are many opportunities to give and to serve for another's good. Every life has those in it who have a need. You may have somebody in prison, or somebody in the prison of the kind of life they have chosen. Maybe they have brought much misery into your life. But the day comes when you stop being concerned about you, and how this is affecting you, and you begin to see that person as the pure Love of God. It's down deep inside, and it's trapped in there. They don't know it, they can't feel it. If you think their life has made you miserable, think for one minute how miserable they have been. Come out of yourself for a moment.

Down deep inside all that human appearance is the Glory of God. People show up in our lives as opportunities for us to reach out in love, whether we reach out physically, or whether we just close our eyes and realize, "In spite of what I see, there is the fullness of God, the Life of God, the Glory of God. I'm going to call it forth, I'm going to strengthen it, I'm going to honor it, I'm going to declare it, I'm going to pray for it to arise. I'm going to give that person the opportunity to experience that in his life." It would heal him, it would restore him, it would change his whole life.

Every life has those in it who have a need, and they're usually the most difficult, the ones that have caused everybody the most problems. Are these just tests for us? I don't think God tests people. I think they are opportunities for us, opportunities to let that love that's within us be released, to let it flow, thereby healing us and healing the person to whom it's flowing.

"Love your enemies, bless them that curse you, do good to them that hate you, and pray for them which despitefully use you." Matthew 5:44

DAY 342
Allow goodness to flow out from us.

We all have our own agenda for our lives, some image of the life that we wish to achieve. God has his agenda for our life too. "It is he that has made us and not we ourselves." (Psalm 100:3) It is his intention and purpose that sent us here. If we allow that intention and purpose to be fulfilled, we will find peace and happiness and comfort and completion and health. But if we don't, if we set out to go our own way--the most comfortable, peaceful, self-serving way that we can find--then we shouldn't be wondering why we didn't get what we wanted. We have not yielded to the higher way.

The higher way that has been purposed for us to live is to let that love, that true substance of our being, which is love and mercy, flow out. This way will appear to be a road that seems to steer straight up a mountainside. This way will be for us to sacrifice all of our self preservation, all of our self concerns, all of our self interests, all of our self, self, self. Sacrifice our time, our love. Sacrifice immediate good, immediate gain, for the good of someone else. "Greater love has no man than this, that a man lay down his life for his friends." (John 15:13)

To give is ultimately to get even though it looks like when you are giving you are losing everything. Don't pay attention to what it looks like, just keep giving from your heart, because the Wisdom of God knows that happiness is elusive if sought by serving one's self. True and eternal good can only come from the Spirit of Good-ness, which is God. Eternal good can only come from the Spirit of Goodness flowing out from us. As we allow it to flow out, we experience it.

"Love bears all things, believes all things, hopes all things, endures all things."   1Corinthians 13:7-8

DAY 343

"Joy will come in the morning."

The way up is down. The way to live is to die, die to your own self interests. The way to gain is to go through periods of self-sacrifice and apparent loss. That's the Wisdom of God. What is in your life right now causing you grief and anguish? It's not there by accident. It is your opportunity to give, so that healing and restoration can happen. You have been sent as a restorer of paths to dwell in, as the repairer of the breach. (Isaiah 58:12) You have been sent to see and know the truth in these people even though they don't see and know it themselves. You have been sent to love, to have mercy, to pray to know what to do, what to see, what to pray, to fulfill that offering of love, so that they may live, and you also may live. This is a deliberate activity of the Wisdom of God, come as a cloak of confusion and devastation. It's your opportunity to reach out, no matter how long it takes, no matter what it costs you, no matter if anyone is looking or appreciating.

"Let not the left hand know what the right hand is doing." (Matthew 6:3) Jesus said, those that tell all that they are doing, they already have their reward. Be quiet about what you are doing, don't let people know, don't talk about how difficult it is. We don't want to be telling everybody the goodness that we've done. We want to do it from our hearts, willingly and joyfully. If it causes you suffering, that's between you and God in the middle of the night. By the next day, joy will come in the morning. (Psalm 30:5) You will be restored, you will be blessed.

"If you draw out your soul to the hungry, (those starving for Truth and Love) and satisfy the afflicted soul; then shall your light rise in obscurity and your darkness be as the noon day."   Isaiah 58:10

DAY 344

I want to be a blessing.

I had a dream one night, during the time I was caring for a friend with cancer in my home. Before I dreamed this, I had spiritual aspirations and ambitions. I wanted to be able to heal people. I wanted to be a blessing to people, but for three years the entire focus had to be Margaret, so I could not be out there doing all that I was doing prior to that. It felt like I wasn't moving in the direction I wanted to be moving. Not that I would have done anything different at the time. It wasn't much of a sacrifice because I wanted to care for her so much.

In the dream, there were multitudes of us, all dressed in white sweat suits, running down a roadway. It was a race and I was out in front, along with many others. I knew I was running the race well and I felt good about it. Then up in front of me I noticed there was confusion, and when I got there I saw a runner lying unconscious in the road. People were jumping over or going around, but I knew I couldn't do that. I stopped racing and I dragged this person off into the tall weeds on the side of the road. The person was Margaret. I sat with her head on my lap, watching all the runners go by.

I was sad because I knew I could never win this race now. I was ashamed of myself for being selfish, but those were my feelings. Pretty soon all the runners had gone and night had fallen. I looked up at the stars and all of a sudden this person whose head was in my lap became Jesus. He said, "Michele, you have not ceased to run this race and you have not lost anything. You must remember that the battle is not to the strong, nor is the race to the swift, but to those who show mercy, and they have already won the race."

"Blessed are the merciful, for they shall obtain mercy."
Matthew 5:7

DAY 345
Images impressed upon our mind rule us.

There is power in words and power in thought and power in the images we hold in thought. If they conjure up thoughts of destruction, confusion, discord, the Bible calls them graven images. Moses came down from Mount Sinai with his Ten Commandments, and the second commandment was, "Thou shalt not make unto thee any graven image." (Exodus 20:4) The word graven means impressed. A graven image is anything that is impressed upon our mind, our consciousness, that conjures up a picture that produces discord or confusion, that breaks apart the harmony and rhythm of Life, that has the power to govern and control us to our destruction.

Why are we told not to embrace these graven images? Because once we embrace them, they rule over us. Recently at the clinic we had a woman diagnosed with lung cancer. As soon as the MRI came back and told her that the tumor was wrapped around her trachea, she began to sit up at night gasping for air. She was not gasping for air before that The words that produce these images in thought are contagious and they're malignant. The words are much more malignant than any runaway cell that has ever been spoken about.

Graven images can be concerned with any number of fearful images. We believe if we experienced them, they would cause destruction in our lives. The words are more destructive than the actual experience. The experiences can be overcome, except for the power that the images we hold in thought give to those conditions. We're told not to accept graven images so that we will not experience these kinds of experiences in life.

"You shall not raise a false report: put not your hand with the wicked to be an unrighteous witness."
                                            Exodus 23:1

DAY 346

Choose harmony of mind.

Choose harmony of mind, harmony of thought. Once we take control of that, our body will respond in like manner. No disease will be able to overcome us at that point, because greater is the Life within us than the disruption of the Life. The disruption is temporary, but the rhythm and the harmony are eternal. Of far more significant strength and energy and power and influence are good thoughts than evil.

Most of our minds are worse than a trash compactor, with the stuff that we have inadvertantly allowed to settle in. We never threw up our hand and said, "No. I refuse to entertain such evil thought." We must come up with a solution to all this that we have embraced in thought. There's a scripture that says, "I would rather be a doorkeeper in the house of God than to sit and eat at a banquet table with fools." (Psalm 84:10) The house of God is the Mind of God, that which we desire to enter into and to hold that ground. To be a doorkeeper in the Mind of God which resides within every person created, is to stand and determine what thought we will allow to enter, and what thought we will keep out.

We have power over this, but we've never been told that. We thought our bodies governed our Life. We thought our minds were weak and just accepted whatever voices and whatever words were out there. There is within us this Eternal Being that we are one with. We are able to stand back from the whole scenario, the whole performance of our life and determine what we will allow and how it's going to play out. We are not victims of whatever comes up.

"Let the words of my mouth and the meditation of my heart be acceptable in thy sight, O Lord, my strength and my redeemer."   Psalm 19:14

DAY 347

Take hold of the course of your life.

We have the ability to take hold of the course that our life is taking. We are not victims of whatever comes up. You can govern what you say, what you think, what emotions you allow to rise up and rule you, because you are not your emotions, you are not your mind, you are not your body. The "you" that you really are is eternal. It's one with God. It's that part of you that existed before you came and that will exist long after you leave this physical sphere. You are an eternal being. The real you is very powerful, because it's one with God, one with that which created everything. You just have to get in touch with it...this is what true spirituality is.

True spirituality is coming in contact with that eternal "I" down deep within you. I call it the Christ, because the Bible calls it the Christ. The book of Hebrews defines the word Christ as the visible expression of the invisible God. It is that part of you that is one with God, that part of you that knows the Mind of God, that knows reality, that knows eternal harmony, that is cognizant of the flow, the rhythm of Life that is good and pure and strong and healthy and whole. It has the capacity to govern, and as a matter of fact, you're supposed to be governing. You are not supposed to be a victim.

We've given away the divine government that was entrusted to us, to first rule our own city, and then reach out to help another. Your first and foremost responsibility is to get control of the evidence of this life: your mind and your body, first, then your relationships, your finances, your fulfillment of social responsibilities, to your children, to your parents. Take hold of the course of your life.

"Draw nigh to God and he will draw nigh to you."

James 4:8

DAY 348

"It is very good."

I step back from what I'm thinking, the thoughts that are circulating around, the words other people are saying, even the words I've allowed myself to say. I step back from whatever my body is declaring right now. I get in touch with that Eternal Being that does not change. That uninterrupted, absolute, Eternal being that's one with God, that can't change, can't be interrupted, can't be disordered, can't be confused. It never changes. It is absolutely perfect, absolutely uninterruptible, incorruptible, undamageable, and perfect in all of its ways.

After creation was formed, God looked out and he saw it and he said, "Behold, it is very good." (Genesis 1:31) We looked up the word good in the original Hebrew and it said, that which is perfect, uninterrupted, incorruptible, undamaged. So the creation that God formed is not what you and I are seeing right now, with all this suffering and wars and poverty and anger and fear. God didn't create and form all that.

What he created and formed is that eternal you that is so quiet, so still, so confident, so assured, so powerful, that can rise up within you at your command. It can say to your mind, "Be still, you don't need to be thinking those thoughts." It can say to your mouth, "Shut up, you don't need to be saying those words." It can say to your body, "Get back in order. Be peaceful, get into the rhythm of Life, get into the strength of Life, get back into order." You can experience something on your body, but that does not mean that you have to let it govern your life. *You* control your life.

"We speak not the wisdom of this world...but we speak the wisdom of God...which God ordained before the world unto our glory."　　　　1Corinthians 2:6-7

DAY 349

Rise up!

You control your life. *You* say to your mind, I know what I choose to think and what I don't choose to think. I know what I choose to allow to dwell in my mind and what I'm not going to let in there. I know what is destructive and what is constructive. I won't listen to nonsense, not to bad mouthing, drama, gossip. I don't want to hear it. I don't want that kind of discord and confusion in my mind, so I'm not going to listen to it. No more than I'd watch a destructive or violent or lewd movie. Why? Because I'm protecting my land, I'm protecting this Life, because I want to see that which God created expressed more and more. I stand as a door-keeper, determining what I will allow in thought.

There is that within which is one with the Eternal God, that has all the characteristics and attributes of God. It is the authority of my life. I need to rise up and govern the mind, the emotions, the will, the body. We can accept that you can govern your mind, your will, your emotions, but the body, no. We think this body has a mind of its own, does what it wants to do. Nonetheless it's true, you can deal with an image of thought and it will correct the appearance on the body.

When you are in that place within, and you know you are, the words you speak become the power of God to this human experience. We need to know how to rise up, how to know what direction to take that authority, how to be sensitive to the impressions of the Mind of God, or the Spirit of God, how to know how to hear and respond, so that we can walk in this authority, demonstrating the fullness of Life and the harmony of Life that God is, and that God has formed us to live in.

"Can these bones live?...O ye dry bones, hear the word of the Lord."
                                        Ezekiel 37:3-4

DAY 350

Reprogram your mind.

We live in an environment of thought. The seasons that come and go would not negatively affect us, except we have first accepted that thought as a reality. There are plenty of us who get through the seasons and are not affected by them. We think certain diseases happen to women, to elderly, to children, but if we had not been preprogrammed to accept that in the universal human consciousness, we would not be experiencing it.

First comes the acceptance that we can be governed by disorder and confusion, that something can come to interrupt the harmony of our lives, and we're stuck with it. This is a universal belief. We live as victims. We believe we are victims to circumstances, situations and events. As long as we hold that thought, we experience that in our lives. We have to acknowledge that every one of us is holding in our thought multitudes of negative images engraven and impressed in our minds, that have the capacity to produce disorder in our lives.

How do we get rid of them? We need to reprogram our minds. We need to put in truth, we need to put in goodness, we need to put in thoughts that we want to experience, and crowd out those images of thought that we do not want to experience. "Be ye transformed by the renewing of your mind." (Romans 12:2)

Hebrews 9:14 says that the blood of Jesus Christ has purged our consciousness from dead works, meaning graven images, to serve the living God, meaning to serve the truth. We want our consciousness purged, we want our minds purified, we want to learn to examine the thoughts that come to our minds.

"Turn me and I shall be turned, for thou art my God. Surely after I was turned I repented. And after that I was instructed."   Jeremiah 31:18-19

DAY 351
"Before they call I will answer."

"Man shall not live by bread alone, but by every word that proceeds out of the mouth of God." This is spoken to us, not only by Jesus (Matthew 4:4) but earlier in Deuteronomy 8:3. It is the absolute foundation of relationship with our Creator. It's where we derive the true understanding of Life. Then we're not just led along in this herd mentality unto our own destruction, believing everything that comes out of the mouth of man. The only true and absolute authority is that which proceeds out of the mouth of God.

We are told that the foundation of a life of harmony and wholeness and perfection and peace and order, the foundation of a sense of oneness with your Creator, comes from hearing the voice of God. That has to be a true and valid experience, it has to be something that God expects. It is for every living being to be governed and directed by the wisdom, the understanding, and the truth of God, in every detailed aspect of our lives.

We were blessed with the greatest gift of all, the Spirit of Truth. We were promised that it would never leave us, never forsake us, that it would lead us and guide us into all truth and all understanding. (John 16:13) "Your ears shall hear a word behind you saying, this is the way, walk ye in it." (Isaiah 30:21)

"Before they call, I will answer; and while they are yet speaking, I will hear." (Isaiah 65:24) Before you called the answer was coming. That's the eternal "I", that spiritual being of us, that intact *you*. That is not your mind, not your emotions, not your body. All you need to do is inquire for a higher truth.

"One thing have I desired of the Lord, that will I seek after; to behold the beauty of the Lord, and to inquire in his temple."   Psalm 27:4

DAY 352

I am the Divine creation of God.

There is that within you that is the real you. It is not your mind, it is not your emotions, it is not your body. You have a body, you have a mind, you have emotions, but you are not those things. I have clothes and I'm not my clothes, I have a house, and I am not my house. I do not live in those things. I live separate and apart from those things. I am not those things, I am me, that eternal me, the Divine creation of God.

Years ago I learned that I can govern and control the thoughts I choose to think. I'm not going to mill around in past hurts, I'm not going to rehearse past injury, I'm not going to accept that my body or anything negative that appears in my body is more powerful than God, who alone governs the body. It's the same with emotions, they can be governed and are supposed to be governed by us. Our emotions are a gift of God so that we can relate to one another, but we were never intended to allow them to rule. Our emotions were not intended to rule, nor was our mind. *I* was intended to rule my mind.

That's how I quit smoking. I just rose up one day and said, "*I* don't want this anymore. *I* am not governed by this. I have believed in the past that I was governed by it, but I am taking that graven image of thought and I'm removing it from my mind. I'm putting in its place the truth that *I* govern my mind. I choose to believe that *I* am far more powerful and have far more authority than that silly little cigarette." We have to govern and control our minds or they become like a runaway train, and then we have to suffer the effects in our lives.

"Through wisdom is a house built, and by understanding it is established, and by knowledge shall the chambers be filled with all precious and pleasant riches."
                                                                    Proverbs 24:3-4

DAY 353
Determine what you will accept in your life.

We have the exact same authority and government
and control over our bodies that we do over our minds.
The origin of what appears on the body begins as a
thought, a word, an image of thought, and is accepted
as reality, and then it appears on the body. The only true
environment we live in is the environment of thought. If
you believe that you live on a toxic waste dump and it
can destroy your body, then it can destroy your body.

But you had to first believe that your body was that
vulnerable and that you didn't have the ability to rise up
and govern in authority and determine what you would
accept into your life and what you would not accept
into your life. If you have accepted destruction, you
must come to a place where you believe you can change
the course of your experience by changing your mind,
by yielding to a higher truth.

Our environment isn't what we see when we look out.
What we see was created from thought, from graven
images, from expectations, from that which we've
been educated to believe. I suppose if we were educated to believe that trees were purple, they'd all be
purple. We see out from that which has been programmed in. Our real environment then is our "sense of
reality," our thought.

The words we speak continue to reimpress the negative graven image in our mind. We can become our own
worst enemy by reprogramming the mind by the words
that we speak, and by the words we allow others to
speak around us. Or we can reverse that and reprogram
our expectation. We can be impressed by the truth.

*"He that will love life and see good days, let him
refrain his tongue from evil and his lips that they
speak no guile...Let him seek peace."* 1Peter 3:10-11

DAY 354

We are renewing our minds.

We are renewing our minds. We're singing songs, we're lifting up our hearts, we're reading our Bibles out loud. That blocks out all the destructive elements of thought and apprehension, so we can be caught up in a higher consciousness. So we can hear what the truth is that we need to know that will correct our images of thought. "The truth shall make you free." (John 8:32) In the quietness of your heart, when your mouth is quiet, when your thoughts are quiet, truth is revealed.

A true healing is not when something is altered on the body, but when there's been a renewing of the mind, so there's no fear, there's only confidence and assurance and quietness. That's called faith. Intense human struggle is proof that there is not faith. Wherever there's human struggle there is not confidence, quietness and assurance. How does that come? Faith comes by hearing the word of God. "Faith comes by hearing and hearing by the word of God." (Romans 10:17)

In order to get it, to achieve quietness, confidence and assurance, you want to find out what is in the Mind of God. What is the truth here that will supplant, change, and correct the disordered belief, that sense of vulnerability and mortality that's subject to all the destructive influences of this world? When you hear, and when you know, what is the Mind of God concerning any given situation, as that comes forward in your awareness, it immediately removes the destructive thought. Immediately. When it removes the destructive thought, and the image impressed upon your mind, with all of its emotions, you're healed.

"Let us hold fast the profession of our faith without wavering, for he is faithful that promised."
Hebrews 10:23

DAY 355
You contain all that you need to know.

The only way you can derive truth is by appealing to a higher consciousness, the Mind of God, the Spirit of Truth. This is going to be your best friend. This influence, this thing that you are truly one with, the real you, already knows all truth, is already cognizant of everything that you will ever need to know in this lifetime to walk in authority and dominion. To walk in wholeness and health and harmony in all of your affairs. This truth, this higher, holy, consciousness and awareness, is already one with that true being that you are.

How do we hear from God? One thing that stops us is that we don't know that we're supposed to. We don't know how natural that is. We ought to expect that that which formed and created us, that sent us here for a purpose, is going to divinely direct that purpose, is going to teach us.

You are an eternal being, one with the Divine Consciousness, the Mind of God, the heart of God, the Spirit of Truth. You are one with that already. Already you contain all that you need to know. But you must silence all these images of thought that are babbling out there, silence it to go within to find out what is the word of truth, or the voice of God, or the impression of Divine Mind.

When that understanding dawns, it is like the dawning of a new day. All of a sudden it's like the sun appearing. You weren't even aware of the intensity of the darkness until it began to vanish. You know you have just heard, or been impressed by truth, because the quietness, the confidence, and the assurance accompany that word and that truth. You now are moving in faith.

Healing is now inevitable.

"Great is thy faith. Be it unto you as you will."
Matthew 15:28

DAY 356

Jesus knew the power of words.

People come to me because they are suffering from something and they think the first thing they have to do is tell me the name of it, and then they have to describe it. Do they want to get rid of it, or do they want to build a shrine to it? They don't understand that every time they speak that word, they are driving the thought that has produced and allowed that experience in their mind, deeper into their consciousness. We do not have a clue about the power of our words.

Jesus had a clue, he said, "I only speak those words that I hear my Father say to me." (John 14:24) The words he spoke raised the dead, healed the sick, fed the multitudes, did all manner of things we don't even conceive of now. Those words were able to do that because he knew the power of words. We continue to use that power unto our own destruction, or to the destruction of others, by reiterating, and by agreeing. Don't we see that "By your words you are justified or by your words you are condemned"? (Matthew 12:37) "Death and life are in the power of the tongue." (Proverbs 18:2)

We need to start listening to the words flying around our heads. We need to start listening to what we agree with and what we say. We need to become accountable and responsible for our words, understanding that we have the power to hurt or to help, to heal or to destroy, both our own lives and the lives of others.

We were sent to heal. We were sent to learn these truths, to rise up in this thought, and to use our words constructively to heal, to restore, to repair, to redeem, to reclaim.

"Set a watch, O Lord, before my mouth, keep the door of my lips."   Psalm 141:3

DAY 357

You are one with the Mind of God.

You are one with the Mind of God. You inherited it,
you possess it, and that is what makes up the true you.
You already know the answer. Don't fear that the answer
will not come, you already possess it. All you have to do
is silence your mouth. I'm doing that now about something. I realize that I have "bought into" something, and
in my mind it's bigger than God, and I feel helpless in
the face of it. I have a graven image about this situation
and that's idolatry. I'm going back, down deep into the
"I" of me that is one with God, one with the truth, one
with the Divine Consciousness, one with the Eternal
Mind that knows the truth. I'm going for the truth.

Only the truth can remove the false. You can't just
scream, "Get out, get out." It may get out, but it's going
to come back. Only the truth can take the place of the
false. Understand that you contain the truth and there is
nothing that has the power to block you from hearing it
once you decide and request to know it, once you
inquire of the Mind of God.

*What is the truth, what is contained within the Mind
of God about this situation that I need to know? What
is the truth that will make me free from feeling vulnerable and victimized by this belief? What is the
truth that will reveal the Omnipotence of God in this
situation? What is it that I need to hear, that when I
hear it, will produce instant confidence and assurance?*

That truth produces an instant quietness where there
was conflict and confusion. When that comes, I am
instantly healed, because I no longer fear that image
appearing anymore. I know the truth that overcomes it.

*"Behold, thou desire truth in the inward parts, and in
the hidden part thou shall make me to know wisdom."*
Psalm 51:6

DAY 358
Allow the truth to come forward.

It's no news to God that you have no idea which direction to walk in, that you don't know up from down, in from out, right from wrong. We didn't come with a formula and a blueprint for life. That was deliberate. It's deliberate that we are put into this strange experience called humanity without the awareness of how to pull it off. Nobody really knows. Why? How come we don't know in any and every situation, "This is the way you should act, this is what you should think, this is what you should say, and this is what you should do?"

Because if we knew it, we'd have a relationship with the formula and the blueprint, not with God. We have to live out from a sense of oneness with God, that closeness. The only way that can happen is to be dependent upon it. The formula is, "Hear my voice and live." (Isaiah 55:3)

It causes us to draw in close to that which formed, created, and sent us for a purpose. It causes us to stop these feelings of being autonomous and alone and separate from God. It makes us realize we are receiving, not just strength, not just comfort, not just intelligence, wisdom, direction, but we are receiving truths that are above and beyond what man believes and is experiencing. Those truths are intended to lift us out of those experiences and out of that consciousness, and to enable others to be lifted out. That's the reason we're here.

Be still and allow the truth to come forward. Know that you are one with it, and it's your Father's good pleasure to continually pour out wisdom and truth and direction and understanding and awareness.

"God answers us in the joy of our hearts."
Ecclesiastes 5:20

DAY 359

You are one with the knower.

Stop looking for a cause for your problem. The only cause is that you have believed something to be true. You are holding in thought an image, engraven in your mind, which you believe is true. You have not yet challenged it and it's ruling over you. For good or bad, it's ruling you, like all images of thought rule us.

The first thing you've got to do is silence all that. For instance, "You're blind because of diabetes." You want to silence the blind, you want to silence the diabetes, you want to silence the vulnerability to disease, you want to silence that you are a body, you want to silence that you are a mind or an emotion.

You want to draw back and realize, I'm a created being, one with God, and nothing has ever changed that. There is no place where he leaves off and I begin, or I leave off and he begins. We're one, and in that state of oneness, I can draw on all the eternal truths and understandings. I can at any time draw on wisdom and direction and counsel and advice. I will know what to do, because I will pause and wait until I know. I'm going to hold still, and in a moment, or an hour, or a day, I'm going to know how to feel about this and how to respond to it. I'm going to know what direction to take. I'm going to know what to reject, what to accept. I'm going to know what truth is going to counterbalance and counteract this graven image of thought that has allowed me to experience this dis-ease.

You have to know that not only is the truth not withheld from you, but you have the ability to hear and to know, because you are one with the knower. You are one with the truth, one with the eternal realities.

"There is but one God, of whom are all things, and we in him." 1Corinthians 8:6

DAY 360

"Get understanding."

Proverbs 4:7 says, "With all your getting, get under-standing." In all your getting, get wisdom, knowledge and understanding. Why? because the understanding that comes from the heart and Mind of God will free you from all the convoluted beliefs of man that have caused so much suffering and pain. In all your getting, get Divinely inspired understanding.

The understanding, when it comes, produces quiet-ness, assurance, and confidence. That's faith. But under-standing has to come first in order for faith to kick in. As soon as it does, the picture begins to change. The expe-rience begins to dissolve and take on the appearance of that which you now understand to be true. The second thing is, you must silence all the words and all the thoughts and all the beliefs and all the fears. The pure truth is going to come, because it's speaking constantly. There is no time that God is not communicating the truth, is not communicating with your soul, with the real you.

"Before you called I answered," it says in Isaiah 65:24. Before you called the answer was there. "I knew what you were going to need and the answer was already there." Just ask. *Please silence all these voices in my head, all that's going on in my emotions. Please silence my mind, I don't want to feel this way, I don't want to keep thinking this. I want to walk away from it, so that I'm clear, so that I can hear what I need to hear.*

Just ask. It's not up to you. This is not your responsi-bility. This is the responsibility of the Spirit of Truth, to reveal truth to you. It will silence all the other voices, all your fears. It will also silence all the other words that are being spoken negatively around you. Ask it to help.

"The Father that dwells in me, he does the work."
John 14:10

DAY 361
God continually holds harmony and balance.

Ask to hear. Ask to know. Ask to understand. Don't be shy, it's your life. "Hear my voice and live."(Isaiah 55:3) It's the continuity and harmony of your entire existence that's at stake. The more you ask, the more you're going to receive. The more you depend on this Divine Being as the Source of your Life, and the strength of your Life, the more it comes forward and fulfills that. The less you depend on it, the more you depend on your own self, the less you get to see the effect of it as a Presence in your life.

What if you're afraid you'll hear something you don't want to hear? That comes down to understanding the heart of God, understanding we were formed by the Love of God. We're dealing with pure goodness. We are not dealing with a God that we have misunderstood for so many centuries, that will rain harm on us. We're dealing with a God of Mercy and grace and goodness. We're dealing with a God that, when we go the wrong way, and we cry out to understand, gently turns us to the right way. God is good. You don't have to fear what you're going to hear. It will always produce harmony, order, goodness, peace. It will always produce completion. It will always be good. That's the nature of God.

When God formed us, and formed the world, he formed it in Divine Order. He formed it in harmony and peace and goodness. It is the purpose of the Spirit of God to continually hold harmony and balance. Where there is an inharmonious situation, it is the purpose of the Spirit of God to reproduce harmony. That's grace, that's Mercy, that's the true heart of God.

"...to give unto them beauty for ashes, the oil of joy for mourning, the garment of praise for the spirit of heaviness...   Isaiah 61:3

DAY 362

I watch with awe.

Today, I look out at the sun as it ascends into its place of authority, as it rules and orders the day. I watch as it effortlessly drives away the thick darkness of the night. It occurs to me that I have absolutely nothing to do with this very predictable activity of Divine Life. It does not need my consent or my encouragement.

Today, I watch as the sleepy flowers turn to welcome the light of the sun. I watch as they freely open their petals to absorb the energy of the light. They trust, without thought, that the light will always be there. It is their nature to trust, to depend upon the light for their life. It occurs to me that I have absolutely nothing to do with this very predictable activity of Divine Life. It does not need my consent or my encouragement.

Today, I watch as the cold, dark and barren winter gives way to the bursting Life of spring. I am not afraid, I know that spring will effortlessly gain the ascendancy. Life will be reborn. Every year I watch this enormous declaration of the preeminence of Life. Every year I watch with awe and confidence. It occurs to me that I have absolutely nothing to do with this very predictable activity of Divine Life. It does not need my consent, nor my encouragement.

Today, I watch the birds as they migrate toward the north. They stop here every year and build their nests, lay their eggs, and hatch and feed their young. I have absolutely nothing to do with this very predictable activity of Divine Life. It does not need my consent, nor my encouragement. So it is with my life. Predictably governed by Eternal Order and harmony.

"While the earth remains, seedtime and harvest, cold and heat, summer and winter, day and night, shall not cease." Genesis 8:22

DAY 363

The law of Life never changes.

The squirrels scamper about as they prepare for their new families, caterpillars stretch as they find their way free of their protective cocoons. All of nature comes alive with expression of their specific demonstrations of the Divine Intelligence that formed and governs each one. They effortlessly yield to the gentle and faithful prodding of Intelligence, as it directs each activity of each day in the Life of each of its formations.

I notice how perfectly ordered each movement is as it responds to the invisible Presence that flows around it all. Never does nature question the Source of its Life, never does it doubt the intelligence that motivates it, never does it feel a personal sense of responsibility to self-govern, to break out of Divine Order and try to find its own personal direction. With unswerving trust and confidence, all of nature flows to the rhythm of Life which animates it. There is peace, and there is uninterrupted, changeless, eternal, predictable, order all about. I notice I have nothing to offer this scenario. It never asked nor wanted nor needed my help.

Tonight I look up at the stars and constellations that are particular to this month, and I reflect that people throughout the ages have beheld the same formations, generation upon generation. The stars will always be exactly where they are, and they never needed me to do anything. It is a law of Life. It never changes and it never will. We can know this, we can depend upon this, and we can rest in this law. We can trust it. And so it is with my life as it daily unfolds to express all beauty, order and harmony.

"Behold the fowls of the air: for they sow not, neither do they reap, nor gather into barns; yet your heavenly Father feeds them."   Matthew 6:26

DAY 364

Rest in the eternal law of Life.

I thank God that I could rest in the eternal law of Life and find security and safety and peace and the predictability of the Divine Order, the Divine Intelligence, the law of Life. I thank God, the Spirit of Truth, that it gave me eyes to see, and a heart to know and understand.

I was filled with the realization of the Presence all around me. I knew that I was one with this Presence, that I was formed and brought forth by it, that it flowed around and within me, that it was the intelligence of every atom, every cell, every system, and every structure that collectively was called my body. I knew that I was not consulted nor needed for the intelligence that flowed and expressed itself as the body, through the body. It was doing fine as the law of Life that it is. It did not need me to direct it, to order it, to fix it.

Could I trust it? Could I effortlessly depend upon it? Could I abandon myself to it, behold its wonders, as it unfolded Life as my body? What made me feel different than the rest of the creations of that Divine Life, that suddenly it needed me to step in, to direct, to be personally responsible for it? Why would I be different than all of creation, which yielded with such grace and such confidence? Was Jesus serious when he said that we should "take no thought for our life"? (Matthew 6:25) Was I ready to let go? To realize that the same Life that formed and flows and orders all of its creation also formed and flows and orders my body and actually is the Life of my body?

So it is. My body, my life, my relationships, my family, my finances, my home, all effortlessly and continually expressing Divine control.

"The beloved of the Lord shall dwell in safety by him and the Lord shall cover him all the day long, and he shall dwell between his shoulders." Deuteronomy 33:12

DAY 365

Behold the flow of Divine Love.

Can I now choose to turn away from the words, thoughts, beliefs and madness that govern the human consciousness? Can I choose the Divine Life to manifest itself as my Life?

Does the caterpillar feel personally responsible for its life? Do the stars feel personally responsible to maintain their path of orbit? Does the spring feel personally responsible to push back the winter? Is it not the same Life of it all?

Today, I am grateful to see and know and understand these things. Today, I humbly bow my head and repent for such foolishness. Today I behold as the darkness of the ignorance of "world thought" easily gives way to the brightness of the Light of truth and reality.

I need not feel unduly concerned about this, truth is not asking for my efforts, nor for my consent, nor for me to fix anything at all. Today I choose to be a **beholder** of the law of Life, the flow of Divine Intelligence, the warmth of Divine Love, as it unveils itself, pushing back the darkness of the human night.

"The Lord is my shepherd, I shall not want. He maketh me to lie down in green pastures, he leadeth me beside the still waters. He restoreth my soul, he leadeth me in the paths of righteousness for his name's sake.

Yea, though I walk through the valley of the shadow of death, I will fear no evil, for thou art with me; thy rod and thy staff they comfort me. Thou preparest a table before me in the presence of my enemies; thou anointest my head with oil; my cup runneth over.

Surely goodness and mercy shall follow me all the days of my life, and I will dwell in the house of the Lord for ever."   Psalm 23

SOURCES

Michele's Daily Inspirations have been drawn from her radio programs. You can hear Michele on the radio in many areas of the country, as well as on the website, www.livingbeyonddisease.com

Programs may be ordered in several formats: CD, MP3, tape or transcription, through the website or by calling 830-755-8767.

Days 27-33 are from *Of Monkeys and Dragons*

Day 1	Program 101	Day 27	Principle 1
Day 2	Program 103,	Day 28	Principle 2
	105, 106, 107	Day 29	Principle 3
Day 3	Program 101	Day 30	Principle 4
Day 4	Program 101	Day 31	Principle 5
Day 5	Program 102	Day 32	Principle 6
Day 6	Program 102	Day 33	Principle 7
Day 7	Program 103	Day 34	Program 109
Day 8	Program 104	Day 35	Program 109
Day 9	Program 105,	Day 36	Program 109
	106	Day 37	Program 109
Day 10	Program 105	Day 38	Program 109
Day 11	Program 105	Day 39	Program 109
Day 12	Program 106	Day 40	Program 109
Day 13	Program 106	Day 41	Program 110
Day 14	Program 107	Day 42	Program 110
Day 15	Program 107	Day 43	Program 110
Day 16	Program 107	Day 44	Program 110
Day 17	Program 108	Day 45	Program 110
Day 18	Program 107	Day 46	Program 110,
Day 19	Program 107		111
Day 20	Program 107	Day 47	Program 111
Day 21	Program 108	Day 48	Program 111
Day 22	Program 108	Day 49	Program 111
Day 23	Program 108	Day 50	Program 112
Day 24	Program 108	Day 51	Program 112
Day 25	Program 108	Day 52	Program 112
Day 26	Program 108	Day 53	Program 112

Day 54	Program 112	Day 91	Program 121
Day 55	Program 112	Day 92	Program 122
Day 56	Program 112	Day 93	Program 122
Day 57	Program 112	Day 94	Program 122
Day 58	Program 113	Day 95	Program 123
Day 59	Program 113	Day 96	Program 123
Day 60	Program 113	Day 97	Program 123
Day 61	Program 113	Day 98	Program 123
Day 62	Program 113, 114	Day 99	Program 123
		Day 100	Program 123
Day 63	Program 114	Day 101	Program 124
Day 64	Program 114	Day 102	Program 124
Day 65	Program 114	Day 103	Program 124
Day 66	Program 114	Day 104	Program 124
Day 67	Program 114	Day 105	Program 125
Day 68	Program 115	Day 106	Program 125
Day 69	Program 115	Day 107	Program 125
Day 70	Program 115	Day 108	Program 126
Day 71	Program 116	Day 109	Program 126
Day 72	Program 117	Day 110	Program 126
Day 73	Program 117	Day 111	Program 126
Day 74	Program 118	Day 112	Program 126
Day 75	Program 118	Day 113	Program 127
Day 76	Program 119	Day 114	Program 127
Day 77	Program 119	Day 115	Program 127
Day 78	Program 119	Day 116	Program 127
Day 79	Program 119	Day 117	Program 128
Day 80	Program 119	Day 118	Program 128
Day 81	Program 119	Day 119	Program 128
Day 82	Program 120	Day 120	Program 128
Day 83	Program 120	Day 121	Program 128
Day 84	Program 120	Day 122	Program 129
Day 85	Program 120	Day 123	Program 129
Day 86	Program 120	Day 124	Program 129
Day 87	Program 120	Day 125	Program 129
Day 88	Program 121	Day 126	Program 129
Day 89	Program 121	Day 127	Program 130
Day 90	Program 121	Day 128	Program 130

Day 129	Program 131	Day 166	Program 139
Day 130	Program 131	Day 167	Program 139
Day 131	Program 131	Day 168	Program 140
Day 132	Program 131	Day 169	Program 140
Day 133	Program 131	Day 170	Program 140
Day 134	Program 131	Day 171	Program 140
Day 135	Program 132	Day 172	Program 140
Day 136	Program 132	Day 173	Program 140
Day 137	Program 132	Day 174	Program 140
Day 138	Program 133	Day 175	Program 141
Day 139	Program 133	Day 176	Program 141
Day 140	Program 133	Day 177	Program 141
Day 141	Program 134	Day 178	Program 141
Day 142	Program 134	Day 179	Program 141
Day 143	Program 134	Day 180	Program 142
Day 144	Program 134, 135a	Day 181	Program 142
		Day 182	Program 142
Day 145	Program 134	Day 183	Program 143
Day 146	Program 135a	Day 184	Program 222
Day 147	Program 135a	Day 185	Program 222
Day 148	Program 135a	Day 186	Program 222
Day 149	Program 135a	Day 187	Program 222
Day 150	Program 135b	Day 188	Program 145
Day 151	Program 135b	Day 189	Program 145
Day 152	Program 135b	Day 190	Program 145
Day 153	Program 135b	Day 191	Program 145
Day 154	Program 135b	Day 192	Program 145
Day 155	Program 135b	Day 193	Program 145
Day 156	Program 137	Day 194	Program 145
Day 157	Program 137	Day 195	Program 146
Day 158	Program 137	Day 196	Program 146
Day 159	Program 137	Day 197	Program 146
Day 160	Program 138	Day 198	Program 146
Day 161	Program 138	Day 199	Program 146
Day 162	Program 138	Day 200	Program 146
Day 163	Program 138	Day 201	Program 146
Day 164	Program 138	Day 202	Program 146
Day 165	Program 139	Day 203	Program 147

Day 204	Program 147	Day 242	Program 207
Day 205	Program 147	Day 243	Program 207
Day 206	Program 147	Day 244	Program 208
Day 207	Program 147	Day 245	Program 208
Day 208	Program 147	Day 246	Program 208
Day 209	Program 147	Day 247	Program 208
Day 210	Program 147	Day 248	Program 208
Day 211	Program 148	Day 249	Program 208
Day 212	Program 149	Day 250	Program 208
Day 213	Program 149	Day 251	Program 208
Day 214	Program 149	Day 252	Program 209
Day 215	Program 149	Day 253	Program 209
Day 216	Program 201	Day 254	Program 209
Day 217	Program 201	Day 255	Program 209
Day 218	Program 202	Day 256	Program 209
Day 219	Program 202	Day 257	Program 209
Day 220	Program 202	Day 258	Program 210
Day 221	Program 202	Day 259	Program 210
Day 222	Program 202	Day 260	Program 210
Day 223	Program 202	Day 261	Program 210
Day 224	Program 203	Day 262	Program 211
Day 225	Program 203	Day 263	Program 211
Day 226	Program 204	Day 264	Program 211
Day 227	Program 204	Day 265	Program 211
Day 228	Program 204	Day 266	Program 235
Day 229	Program 204	Day 267	Program 235
Day 230	Program 204	Day 268	Program 212
Day 231	Program 205	Day 269	Program 212
Day 232	Program 205	Day 270	Program 212
Day 233	Program 205	Day 271	Program 212
Day 234	Program 205	Day 272	Program 213
Day 235	Program 206	Day 273	Program 213
Day 236	Program 206	Day 274	Program 213
Day 237	Program 206	Day 275	Program 213
Day 238	Program 207	Day 276	Program 213
Day 239	Program 207	Day 277	Program 213, 214
Day 240	Program 207		
Day 241	Program 207	Day 278	Program 214

Day 279	Program 214	Day 316	Program 223
Day 280	Program 214	Day 317	Program 223
Day 281	Program 214	Day 318	Program 223
Day 282	Program 214	Day 319	Program 224
Day 283	Program 216	Day 320	Program 224
Day 284	Program 216	Day 321	Program 224
Day 285	Program 216	Day 322	Program 224
Day 286	Program 216	Day 323	Program 224
Day 287	Program 216	Day 324	Program 224
Day 288	Program 216	Day 325	Program 224
Day 289	Program 216	Day 326	Program 225
Day 290	Program 217	Day 327	Program 225
Day 291	Program 217	Day 328	Program 225
Day 292	Program 217	Day 329	Program 225
Day 293	Program 217	Day 330	Program 225
Day 294	Program 217	Day 331	Program 225
Day 295	Program 217	Day 332	Program 225
Day 296	Program 236	Day 333	Program 227
Day 297	Program 218	Day 334	Program 227
Day 298	Program 218	Day 335	Program 228
Day 299	Program 218	Day 336	Program 228
Day 300	Program 219	Day 337	Program 228
Day 301	Program 219, 220	Day 338	Program 228
		Day 339	Program 229
Day 302	Program 220	Day 340	Program 229
Day 303	Program 220	Day 341	Program 229
Day 304	Program 221	Day 342	Program 229
Day 305	Program 221	Day 343	Program 229
Day 306	Program 221	Day 344	Program 229
Day 307	Program 221	Day 345	Program 230
Day 308	Program 222	Day 346	Program 230
Day 309	Program 222	Day 347	Program 230
Day 310	Program 226	Day 348	Program 230
Day 311	Program 226	Day 349	Program 230
Day 312	Program 226	Day 350	Program 231
Day 313	Program 223	Day 351	Program 231
Day 314	Program 223	Day 352	Program 231
Day 315	Program 223	Day 353	Program 231

To order books, go to *livingbeyonddisease.com*
or fill out the form below and fax or mail it in.

La Vida Press
107 Scenic Loop Rd. • Boerne, TX 78006
830-755-8767 (Ofc) • 830-755-6421 (Fax)

Of Monkeys and Dragons: Freedom from the Tyranny of Disease
(Book #1)

QUANTITY			SUBTOTAL
_____	Soft Back—English	$12.95	_____
_____	Soft Back—Spanish	$12.95	_____
_____	Hard Back—English	$21.95	_____
_____	Audio book—	$12.95	_____

The God That We've Created: The Basic Cause of All Disease
(Book #2)

_____	Soft Back—English	$14.95	_____
_____	Hard Back—English	$24.95	_____
_____	Audio book—	$14.95	_____

When the Wolf is at the Door: The Simplicity of Healing
(Book #3)

_____	Soft Back—English	$15.95	_____
_____	Hard Back—English	$25.95	_____
_____	Audio book—	$15.95	_____

Only Receive: No Barriers, No Boundaries
(Book #4)

_____	Soft Back—English	$14.95	_____
_____	Audio book—	$14.95	_____

Arise, Shine: For Your Time Has Come
(Daily Inspirations, Book One)

_____	Soft Back—English	$19.95	_____

SUBTOTAL _____

SHIPPING $2.95 PER ITEM _____

TOTAL _____

Name: _____

Address: _____

_____

Phone: _____ Email: _____